THE WORLD'S EASIEST COMPUTER BOOK

How to Use Computers, Cellphones, and Other Electronics the Simple and Low-Cost Way

Publisher's Note

The editors of FC&A have taken careful measures to ensure the accuracy and usefulness of the information in this book. While every attempt was made to assure accuracy, some websites, addresses, and telephone numbers may have changed since printing.

This book is intended for general information only. It does not constitute medical, legal, or financial advice or practice. We cannot guarantee the safety or effectiveness of any advice or treatment mentioned. Readers are urged to consult with their personal financial advisors, lawyers, technical and health care professionals. The publisher and editors disclaim all liability (including any injuries, damages, or losses) resulting from the use of the information in this book.

"Go and make disciples of all nations, baptizing them in the name of the Father and of the Son and of the Holy Spirit, and teaching them to obey everything I have commanded you. And surely I am with you always, to the very end of the age."

— Matthew 28:19-20

TABLE OF CONTENTS

Technology toolkit

how to choose, use, and improve your hardware

The rundown on desktop computers

Discover the desktop advantage

In a confusing world of smartphones, tablet computers, and laptops, the desktop personal computer (PC) may seem old-fashioned — but buying one may also give you advantages that newer technology does not.

- Desktops feature more ports for connecting peripherals like printers, backup drives, keyboards, and all those gadgets that need USB ports to recharge.

- A desktop usually comes with a bigger screen than laptops or tablets, and that makes everything easier to see and read.

- When you use a desktop, you can easily sit in a position that is not likely to cause aches and pains later. For example, with only a little effort, you can type with your wrists in a low-strain position at just below elbow level. At the same time, you can also position the monitor so you can clearly see it without hunching your back or neck. But a laptop or tablet may force you to sit or type in positions that contribute to neck, back, and shoulder pain.

- Portable laptops, tablets, and smartphones are regularly in far more danger of being bumped, scratched, or dropped than desktops, so a desktop may last longer.

- Desktops that have both a monitor and a separate box or tower may give you more bang for the buck. Compare the combined cost of a tower-and-monitor setup to a laptop that has similar speed, memory, and hard-drive space. You may discover that the combined cost of the tower and monitor is cheaper than the laptop.

- The tower-and-monitor setup may be easier and cheaper to repair or upgrade than a laptop, particularly if you or someone you know has experience with replacing RAM memory or other parts inside a computer tower.

A CLOSER LOOK

Desktops don't just come in the old monitor-and-tower form anymore. In recent years, the all-in-one (AIO) PC has become all the rage. This space-saving design eliminates the tower and builds the entire PC inside the monitor. In other words, the monitor is the PC. That means fewer cables, a neater appearance, and easier setup. But AIOs can be more expensive than the monitor-and-tower desktop and are difficult to repair or upgrade.

4 keys to picking the perfect computer

You probably don't want to buy the most expensive computer in the store, but you also don't want to wait forever for each Web page to load or documents to open. To uncover a reasonably priced computer with enough speed and storage to suit you, get expert help to figure out your minimum requirements.

Visit the free annual computer buying guide at *www.consumerreports.org* or the latest computer buying guide at *www.cnet.com* for details that can help you find the right CPU chip, minimum amount of RAM, and the minimum size and speed for your new hard drive.

To help set the minimum requirements, remember these facts about the key parts of your computer.

Central processing unit (CPU) chip. At the very least, you need to know the CPU's clock speed in gigahertz (GHz) and its number of cores. Each extra core is like opening an extra checkout lane at the grocery store — it moves things along faster. When comparing computers, more cores and more GHz of clock speed often means more overall speed. But several other factors can turn a slow chip into a faster one, so it still pays to seek the expert help available from CNET and *Consumer Reports*.

Random-access memory (RAM). The more RAM your computer has, the faster it can get things done. If you only use your computer for light tasks like surfing the Web, emailing, and creating documents, the minimum amount of RAM recommended by CNET or *Consumer Reports* may be enough. If you do video or photo editing or use a bunch of programs at once, you need more RAM than the minimum. You should also consider getting more RAM if you buy an all-in-one (AIO) computer, because you may not be able to add RAM later.

Hard drive. For most people, the minimum hard drive size recommended by *Consumer Reports* or CNET may be large enough to hold all their files, programs, and the Windows operating system, but you may need one or more terabytes (TB) if you keep a lot of videos, photographs, and other multimedia files on the drive, or if you buy an AIO. A terabyte is twice the size of a 500-gigabyte drive.

Ports and extras. The buying guides at CNET and *Consumer Reports* can also help you determine which ports and extras you need and which ones you can skip. For example, if you play high-powered video games, edit video or photographs, or do other advanced multimedia tasks, you need a high-end, dedicated, or discrete (separate) graphics card in your PC. Otherwise, you may only need the integrated graphics already built into your computer — and that may cost less.

BRIGHT IDEA

Need a better way to transfer pictures from your digital camera or smartphone to your PC? Get ready for good news. Some desktops may feature a flash or memory card reader that can help you move your photos or files more easily. Just make sure the reader is compatible with the specific memory card and card size (in gigabytes) needed for your digital camera or smartphone.

Choose the right PC for your needs

You don't just buy a PC for its looks. You buy it for all the cool things it can do for you. So make sure your new PC will have all the equipment, connections, and software it needs to tackle your list of cool things.

For example, if you want to use Skype to video chat with a friend or relative, visit *www.skype.com* to see what hardware requirements — and other requirements — your new computer must meet. You may discover you need:

- Windows 7 or higher.

- a web camera (webcam).

- a microphone and speakers.

- a broadband Internet connection of at least 100 kilobytes per second (kps).

In that case, you would want to choose a PC that could fulfill those requirements. Just keep in mind that your new PC may not provide everything. For example, it may come with a network port or adapter to handle a broadband connection. But you'll need to get an Internet Service Provider (ISP) and a modem to use that broadband connection.

If you plan to use other web services or software, visit their websites to check the minimum requirements needed for each one. Use that information to help determine what else you need in a new PC.

> **CAUTION**
>
> Before buying a PC, check whether the mouse, keyboard, monitor, and DVD or Blu-ray drive are included in the price. Some computers are sold separately from their monitors, and some PCs no longer come with a DVD or Blu-ray drive.

Pros and cons of touch-screen monitors

Like the touch-screen displays in tablets and some laptops, touch-screen monitor screens are supposed to be touched. Instead of using your mouse to click an option on-screen, you reach out to the screen and touch the option directly with your fingers. The screen responds as if you had used the mouse. You can also type on a keyboard that pops up on the screen instead of using a regular keyboard. Here are some other advantages.

- Touch screens are faster than mouses and keyboards, so you may get things done more quickly.

- They require less hand-eye coordination than a mouse or keyboard.

- People who find using a mouse difficult may find touch screens easier to use.

Touch-screen monitors also have disadvantages. You'll have to decide whether they outweigh the benefits.

- They are bigger, heavier, and cost more than other monitors.

- Constantly reaching out to touch the screen may make your arm ache or grow tired, a problem nicknamed "gorilla arm." Placing the touch-screen monitor at a lower height than a normal monitor and tilting the screen back like a laptop screen may help.

- You may still need your mouse or keyboard for some programs or tasks.

- Touching your monitor may leave fingerprints on the screen, but you can select a monitor with anti-smudge technology to limit fingerprints and cleaning.

- A few touch screens that work fine in Windows 7 may not work in Windows 8 if you eventually decide to upgrade.

- You'll need to learn several ways to touch the screen, such as tapping, swiping, or pinching, and when to use each one.

- These screens may dim a little over time.

The quality of touch-screen monitors and ease of using them may vary widely. Read reviews on the Web for any monitor you think you might buy. You can find expert reviews at sites like *www.cnet.com*, *www.toptenreviews.com*, and *www.pcmag.com*. Check for user reviews at *www.Amazon.com* and *www.newegg.com*. If possible, also try to test-drive a monitor before you buy.

Both Windows 7 and Windows 8 can be used with touch screens, but they can also be used with a mouse and keyboard alone. So it's up to you to decide whether a touch-screen monitor is worthwhile.

MONEY-SAVER

Touch-screen monitors out of your price range? You can get all the benefits of a touch screen by using your current monitor with a Logitech Wireless Rechargeable T650 Touchpad.

This hand-sized touchpad is large enough to support the touch-screen gestures for Windows 7 and Windows 8, and you won't get sore arms from constantly reaching out to the screen.

At around $80, this helpful accessory is less than half the cost of a touch-screen monitor. With a little practice, you'll enjoy all the benefits of a standard touch screen right at your fingertips.

Set your screen to avoid strain

Choose a monitor with features that help prevent eyestrain, neck aches, and sore backs. The monitor should offer tilt, swivel, and height adjustment options so you can lean the screen back, tilt it forward, rotate it, and raise or lower it.

Also, consider screen size as measured diagonally from one corner of the screen to the opposite corner. If your eyesight isn't what it used to be, a screen of 20 inches or more can help you see more easily — but only if it has the right resolution.

Native resolution, sometimes called recommended resolution, is the resolution the monitor was built to use. A higher native resolution such as 1920 x 1080 can make things seem more crisp and clear for many people. But if text seems harder to read on a particular size of monitor with a 1920 x 1080 resolution, try the same-size monitor with a lower resolution, such as 1440 x 900. If that doesn't work, consider a larger monitor at 1920 x 1080 resolution.

Of course, you can always use the built-in Windows options to either magnify part of the screen or enlarge fonts throughout the screen. For more information about enlarging fonts, see *Enlarge fonts and icons for squint-free reading* in the *Easy access: fine-tune Windows settings chapter*.

HIGH-TECH HEALTH

Using the computer can cause eyestrain, making your eyes feel achy and dry. Help prevent this by making your monitor easy on the eyes.

- Position the monitor so any source of light or sunlight is off to the side and won't create glare on the screen.

- Turn off overhead lights, and use a desk lamp or nearby lamp instead. Position the lamp so it never causes glare.

- Adjust screen brightness and contrast to see if changes make your eyes feel better.

- Use the 20-20 rule. Every 20 minutes, stare at an object 20 feet away for 20 seconds.

Protect your files with a digital security blanket

You can back up 750,000 photos, 230 movies, or more Word documents than you can shake a stick at if you attach just one thing to your desktop PC — a 1-terabyte external hard drive. This kind of drive may offer several advantages.

- Hard drives are readily available in two sizes — 2.5-inch and 3.5-inch. The 2.5-inch drive only needs one cable to attach to your computer and is easy to carry around. The 3.5-inch drive costs less per gigabyte of storage than a 2.5-inch drive, but it's not as portable. It requires a power cord as well as a cable to connect to your computer. On the other hand, if you need more storage space than most drives have, a 3.5-inch drive may be your best — and only — option.

- Use one of these drives as a backup drive, and you won't need to worry about losing your files forever. What's more, connect a 2.5-inch USB drive to another computer, and your files are instantly available.

- If the hard drive in your PC is smaller than a terabyte, and you run out of room, the external terabyte drive may have leftover space you can use.

- USB-connected drives often require no formatting before use. Once you follow the instructions for connecting the drive, it may automatically appear in the list of drives, and you can start backing up files to it almost immediately.

Just keep a few things in mind. For backups, choose an external drive with at least as many gigabytes of space as the hard drive inside your PC. Check what kind of ports you have on the back or front of your computer, such as USB 2.0, USB 3.0, eSata, Thunderbolt, or Firewire ports. Before buying an external hard drive, make certain the kind of port it requires matches one of the unused ports on your PC. And make sure your new drive comes with a free warranty before you buy it.

MONEY-SAVER

Check the documents that came with your computer to learn whether your PC has USB 2.0 or USB 3.0 ports. If you have USB 2.0, don't pay extra for any USB external hard drive that transfers files at USB 3.0 speeds of 625 megabytes (5 gigabits) per second or higher. Your data can only travel as fast as the slower USB 2.0 port allows.

But if you expect to get a computer with USB 3.0 ports before long, the faster USB drive may be worthwhile. The drive can work with your USB 2.0 port now, but will transfer files faster when you switch to a USB 3.0 port.

Stop a catastrophe and save big bucks

The electronics stores won't tell you, but dust can ruin your machine and cost you hundreds of dollars. In fact, dust has two ways it can cost money and harm your computer.

If you're lucky, dust only clogs the vents on your computer or slows down its moving parts. This can turn your computer sluggish and make the parts inside wear out months or years before they should.

If luck isn't with you, dust may creep into your rapidly spinning hard disk and cause far worse damage. Your files are stored on the surface of your hard disk, and that disk may spin at speeds ranging from 67 to 170 miles per hour.

The read/write head that accesses your files hovers above that disk but doesn't touch it. If one speck of dust causes that read-write head to crash into your hard disk, the impact is like a high-speed car wreck. It may destroy files, damage your system, or batter your hard drive so badly that it must be replaced.

To prevent this, clean up the dust about every three months. Turn off your computer, unplug it, and let it sit for 30 minutes. Dampen a lint-free cloth with distilled water or rubbing alcohol, and wipe down your computer tower. Use a hand vacuum to vacuum the vents on the back of the tower, but avoid causing the fans inside those vents to spin the wrong way.

If the computer is so dirty you must open it up to clean inside, check your documentation first to make sure opening your tower will not void your PC's warranty. Don't use a dust rag, vacuum cleaner, or any water inside the computer. Instead, buy a can of compressed air labeled for cleaning computers, and follow the instructions. Compressed air is also useful for cleaning your keyboard.

Beware this common shutdown mistake

You could be damaging your computer every time you turn it off. The only guaranteed safe way to turn off the PC is to click on the **Start** button on the screen, and click on **Shutdown**. But if you press the power button on your computer's exterior, and the PC abruptly shuts off, you're asking for trouble. Here's why.

As long as your PC is on, it stays busy, even when you aren't actively using it. For example, it may be saving the settings Windows must have to complete critical tasks, saving changes to your document, downloading a software update, or performing other vital functions. If you abruptly shut off the PC by pressing the power button or pulling the plug, Windows may:

- save only half the settings it needs, which may prevent Windows from booting up the next time you turn on the computer.

- save only part of your document, which may corrupt the file so you cannot open it.

- fail to safely shut down your hard drive, which may cause hard drive problems.

- seem to work normally until days or weeks later when mysterious problems crop up.

The shutdown process prevents all these errors because it makes sure all the necessary saving and other tasks complete before the computer can turn off. So unless your computer is frozen or experiencing some other emergency, don't just turn it off. Shut down your computer with the **Start** button on the screen, and save yourself a heap of trouble.

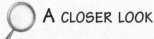

A CLOSER LOOK

Some PCs are set up so the power button on the computer's exterior is the same as the **Start** button on the screen. If you press the power button, and the PC obviously goes through the shutdown process before turning off, the computer is still safe. If you aren't sure whether your computer is shutting down properly, stick with using the **Start** button on the screen.

Easy way to multiply your USB ports

You know you need more USB ports when you have to unplug a printer or some other device just to use your USB flash drive. Fortunately, you can add a group of USB ports for less than $35, sometimes much less. Just use a hub.

When you plug the USB hub into a USB port, the hub splits the input from the port so you can use all the hub's USB ports instead. Some hubs have as many as eight ports, so you get more ports than you give up. But don't go hog wild and attach hubs to all your computer's USB ports. A few USB devices will not work with a hub and must use one of the ports on your computer.

4 ways to help your computer last

You can't afford a new PC yet, but your old computer is outdated and painfully slow. Try tips like these to help speed up your computer and keep it alive for longer.

Become a power updater. Check weekly or monthly for the latest software updates, drivers, and patches for Windows and for each of your most crucial programs. If you can't set up automatic updating for a program, visit the support section of the manufacturer's website to get updates.

Create a Windows Restore Point before installing each update just in case anything goes wrong. To learn how to create a restore point, see the story *Plan 'B' guards against disasters* in the *Windows 7 tools: update, maintain & protect* chapter.

Defend your digital turf. Use security software to regularly scan for viruses, spyware, and other malware, and keep that security software up to date. To get free protection against viruses and spyware, see the *Safe & secure surfing* chapter.

Offload files. Move the documents, pictures, video, and other files you've created from your internal hard drive to an external hard drive. This may ease the load on your computer.

Keep it simple. Your PC can only stand so many extra toolbars, gadgets, and other unwanted programs, so restrict the ability to install them. You can do this with tools like security software and parental controls.

Meanwhile, play it safe. Start thinking about how to get the best deal on a new computer, and be sure to back up your important files regularly on an external hard drive — just in case your computer suddenly gives out.

Fix a faulty wireless keyboard

Whether your keyboard refuses to respond at all or just fails to type some letters, these steps can help. After each step, check to see if your keyboard has begun working.

- Move the keyboard closer to the computer.

- Turn the keyboard off. Change its batteries before turning it on again.

- Many wireless keyboards can't work unless they can communicate with the receiver that came with them. If the receiver plugs into a port on your computer, check that it has remained firmly plugged into that port.

- Your keyboard's receiver may require a clear line of sight to the keyboard. Remove any objects that block that path, or reposition the keyboard so it's within sight of the receiver.

- If the receiver connects to a USB port, turn off the computer, and try moving the receiver's connection to another USB port on the back of the computer.

BRIGHT IDEA

The colors on some low-vision keyboards may remind you of a yield sign, but these gaudy keyboards may be perfect for someone with macular degeneration or another vision problem. These keyboards feature contrasting colors such as black letters — in boldface and large print — against a bright yellow background.

If you want a cheaper option, buy a sheet of boldface key stickers with similar coloring. Place each sticker atop its matching key to create a high-contrast keyboard that is significantly easier to see. You can buy the stickers or the keyboard from sellers at *www.amazon.com*.

Rescue your flash drive when it can't eject

Just when you thought it was safe to disconnect your flash drive from the PC, the computer won't let go of it. All you get is a message like this one.

Removable disk is currently in use. Save any open files on this disk, and then close the files or programs using the files before trying again. If you choose to continue, the files will be closed which might cause data to be lost.

Use the process below to solve this problem. After each step, try to eject the drive by right-clicking the **Safely Remove Hardware And Eject Media** icon in the **Windows System Tray** at the bottom right corner of your screen. Then click on the **Eject** option. If you see a message that promises the drive can be removed safely, pull the drive out of its port. Otherwise, move on to the next step.

- Wait one minute, and try to eject the drive again.

- If the warning message appears, a program is still using the drive. Check whether any files or folders on the drive are displayed in a program such as Microsoft Word, **Windows Explorer**, or a program you use to view pictures. Save and close the file or folder if you find it.

- Close each open program one by one. Sometimes a program creates temporary files or other harmless files on your flash drive, but closing the program ends that. Don't forget to close your Web browser, too. In at least one case, a browser-related program has caused a drive to refuse to eject.

- Check whether your antivirus program is currently scanning the flash drive. Wait until the scan finishes before trying to eject the drive.

- Make sure all programs are closed, and shut down the computer. When it has completely shut down, no software needs to write to the flash drive any longer, so you can safely remove the flash drive from its port without endangering any files.

Find the real reason your PC won't start

You turned on your PC but it wouldn't boot up. You even tried checking all the connections on the computer to be sure they were firmly plugged in, but the PC still won't boot. Here's what to try next.

Check the back switch. If your PC has a power switch on the back side, make sure it hasn't accidentally been flipped to the OFF position.

Test the connections. Check that everything is firmly plugged into the surge protector, including the power cords for both your PC and monitor. Confirm that the surge protector is firmly plugged into the wall. Also, make sure all the connections leading to your monitor are firmly fixed.

Set the surger. Be sure your surge protector is turned on. If not, turn it on and try to turn on the PC.

Perform the lamp test. If the computer still won't boot, unplug the surge protector from the wall, and test the outlet. Plug in a lamp and try to turn it on. If you can't, the outlet may be faulty.

Find the guilty party. Disconnect the mouse, keyboard, printer, and everything else from the back and front of the computer, but leave the monitor connection and power cord plugged in. Make sure no flash drives or USB hubs are still attached. If the PC boots up, one of your peripherals is causing the problem.

In that case, reconnect the mouse and keyboard and reboot. If the computer boots successfully, add back each peripheral one at a time, and try to reboot after each peripheral is reconnected. When the computer refuses to boot again, you've found the peripheral causing the problem. Visit its manufacturer's website, and check their support links for advice that may help.

LAPTOPS
Computing on the go

Take the confusion out of buying a new laptop

Finding the right laptop doesn't have to be hard. Just follow these 11 easy steps to help you make the right choice.

Set your budget. Decide how much you can spend, but leave room in your budget for software and accessories — such as a backup drive or extra battery.

Learn what the pros know. Four gigabytes of RAM may have been enough once, but technology changes so rapidly you may need more today. For expert advice on the minimum requirements for a CPU, RAM, and hard drive that fit your needs, consult the latest "Laptop buying guide" at *www.cnet.com* and "Computer buying guide" available free at *www.consumerreports.org*. You can also visit *www.pcmag.com* and *www.laptopmag.com* for laptop reviews and buying advice.

Take the power user test. If you play 3D games, edit video or photos, keep a large music library, or regularly run many programs at once, you need extra RAM and a CPU with more processing speed and power than the typical minimum requirements. You may also need a larger-capacity hard disk if you keep a big music, photo, or video library.

Select your size. A bigger screen often means more computing power, weight, and extras. Most laptops with the largest screens frequently make good desktop replacements. A smaller screen makes the laptop lighter and easier to carry. Thin, light laptops with large screens are available, but these may have fewer ports, no DVD drive, or other limitations.

Check the ports. Look for at least two USB 3.0 ports. Other recommended ports include:

- HDMI for connecting to an HDTV or monitor.

- SD card slot compatible with your smartphone or digital camera card.

Determine your Internet and printer connection. Be sure you know how your computer will connect to your printer and the Internet. Although many laptops have a Wi-Fi adapter, some have no Ethernet port. If you need a wired Ethernet network to connect to your printer or Internet service, insist on an Ethernet port, or investigate whether buying a USB-to-Ethernet adapter would deliver a fast enough Ethernet connection.

Consider battery life. Visit the laptop review section of *www.pcmag.com* to see battery life test results.

Choose DVD, Blu-ray, or nothing. Some laptops come without a DVD or Blu-ray drive. Make sure your laptop has one of these drives if you:

- watch movies or listen to music from a disc playing on your laptop rather than from streaming, downloading, or hard drive files.

- install software from disc rather than from downloads or a flash drive.

Pick the best graphics controller. The graphics controller draws the images on your screen. An "integrated graphics" controller built in to the CPU is all most people need. But you may need a separate, more powerful "discrete graphics" card if you edit video, play complex games like Skyrim, or watch Blu-ray movies.

Test usability. Before you buy, try the laptop's keyboard and track pad, play some of its music or video files, and test how comfortable it is to use and how it compares to other laptops. Buy the laptop online if the price is cheaper there.

Go easy on the eyes. If you want to watch Blu-ray or high-definition video, aim for HD resolution of at least 1920 x 1080. Otherwise, look for a screen with as close to HD resolution as possible.

A CLOSER LOOK

Some laptops come with a solid-state drive (SSD), a hard drive that replaces a spinning disk with unmoving memory chips similar to flash drive memory. This can make your laptop boot up and perform much faster than a regular hard disk drive (HDD).

The SSD also runs more quietly, uses less battery power, and is harder to damage. But be aware that SSDs cost significantly more per gigabyte than HDDs, and the average laptop SSD has only about half or quarter the capacity of an average laptop HDD.

Prevent identity theft when you part with a laptop

Before you sell, donate, or recycle an ancient laptop, make sure no one can find any credit card numbers, tax records, or other personal information on its hard drive. Back up all your files on another disk, and clean out the drive.

You might think deleting all programs and files gets rid of all personal information, but deleting only removes the pointers that tell where to find a file or program on the disk. A deleted file's or program's contents remain on the disk untouched, but they are labeled as "free" space. That data can be recovered, even from a drive that has been reformatted.

To solve this, many experts suggest running software that overwrites all the free space on your disk with ones and zeroes. Another expert points out that Windows sometimes puts copies of data from files and programs in places you may not know about, so he recommends overwriting your entire hard disk. Software is available for just wiping free space or for wiping the full disk. Here are some of the programs recommended by experts.

- Active@ KillDisk free from *www.killdisk.com*

- Darik's Boot and Nuke free from *www.dban.org*

- Disk Wipe free from *www.diskwipe.org*

- Eraser free from *eraser.heidi.ie*

- Shredit for Windows from *www.mireth.com*

- WipeDrive 7 from *www.whitecanyon.com*

These programs vary widely in what they do and the technical skills required. Research them carefully before you try one, and keep these thoughts in mind.

- If you're selling your old laptop to an online consignment site, they may consider a laptop with a fully-wiped hard drive as not working and may drastically reduce their offer to you.

- Before using drive-wiping software, make sure the laptop is fully charged and plugged into a wall outlet. Wiping the drive may take several hours, and running out of charge would be a disaster.

> **CAUTION**
>
> Don't try to wipe a solid-state disk (SSD) by writing ones and zeroes over the existing data. Software that does that can only wipe data on regular spinning hard drives.
>
> Why? To keep previously used parts of the drive from wearing out too early, SSDs have special protection that prevents over-writing and forces data to be written to an unused or less-used area of the disk.
>
> Research now suggests your SSD probably won't be properly wiped unless it is first encrypted and then cleared with special software designed to wipe SSDs.

Where to get cash for your used electronic devices

You just got a new laptop for Christmas, but you hate for your old laptop to just gather dust. You could place an ad in the newspaper or eBay, but why do all that work when someone else will do it for you.

Visit *www.wireflytradeins.com* to see what your old gadget is worth. They take laptops, monitors, e-readers, mice, tablets, HDTVs, cameras, camcorders, MP3 players, cellphones, and more — and they even take damaged or not working items. Search for your product by clicking on the photo. Next, choose the manufacturer. If you don't see your model number, click on the **Show All Models** button.

Click on your gadget when you find it, answer any questions you're asked, and you'll get a cash offer. If you accept the offer, click on **Accept** and print their shipping label. Wireflytradeins covers the cost of shipping your gadget to them. After they receive your gadget and appraise it, they'll send a confirmation email. You can expect payment two to four weeks later. Choose to be paid cash, receive payment through PayPal, or donate the money to charity.

Another site that pays for gadgets is NextWorth. NextWorth offers an online option for cash, or you can visit one of their 1,500 retail partners and get a gift certificate for the store where you trade in your gadget. Visit *www.nextworth.com* to find participating stores.

You can also try *www.amazon.com* where you can get an Amazon gift certificate in exchange for a wide array of gadgets, including a few desktops. Other good sites to check include *www.radioshacktrade andsave.com*, *www.gazelle.com*, and *www.gamestop.com*. Just be sure to read each site's explanations and Frequently Asked Questions carefully to make sure you get what you expect.

Safe rescue tactics after a spill

The faster you respond when something spills on your laptop, the better your odds of saving your computer from a watery grave. Follow these safe and easy steps.

- Check the AC adapter that plugs into the wall outlet. If it is connected to the laptop and its cord or end connections are damp, race to the circuit breaker panel, and cut power from there. Otherwise, rush to turn off the laptop.

- Quickly disconnect the AC adapter, remove the battery, and disconnect all cables, flash drives, and other attachments.

- Open your laptop wide, and turn the keyboard and screen face downward to help liquid drip out. Grab a towel, a clean cotton handkerchief, or the most lint-free blotter available, and blot liquid off the keyboard, screen, and any wet surfaces. Keep blotting until all liquid is gone, and no more drips out. Do not turn the laptop on.

From this point, your chances of saving the laptop depend on what you spilled. Water may not leave a harmful residue when it dries, but many other liquids are more likely to leave a damaging residue inside your laptop — especially those that are sweetened, milk-based, acidic like coffee or tea, or alcoholic.

If you only spilled a little clean water, drying the laptop may be your next step. If you spilled something that leaves a residue or you spilled more than a little water, contact a repair shop, tell them what you spilled, and ask whether you should bring the laptop in for cleaning now or let it dry for a day or so first.

To dry your laptop, prop it open, keyboard side down, in a warm, dry place where it won't be disturbed. Leave it for two days or longer.

After the laptop has dried, put the battery in, and try to turn it on. If it boots up successfully, do an immediate backup just in case the recovery is temporary.

If the laptop didn't boot up, remove the battery, plug in the AC adapter, and try to boot up again. If the computer powers up normally, the battery may need replacing. If it doesn't boot up or behaves strangely, take the laptop to the repair shop.

BRIGHT IDEA

Consider buying a transparent, protective keyboard cover that fits over the keys like a second skin and stays on while you type. It prevents liquid from seeping between keys and into your computer.

Also, when possible, attach a mouse and keyboard to your laptop, and set the laptop on a stack of phone books or reams of paper. Position the screen at eye level while your keyboard, mouse, and drink remain at elbow level. This protects your laptop from spills and helps prevent pain in your neck, shoulders, arms, and wrists.

5 surprising ways to boost battery life

Get more mileage out of your laptop before you need to charge it. Here's how.

Stop a power thief. Keep your DVD, CD, or Blu-ray drive empty when you're not using it. A disc spinning in the drive steals battery power every minute.

Do less multitasking. Using several programs at once drains your battery faster, especially if a program features lots of pictures, video, or other graphics. Programs running in the background — like iTunes — count, too.

Ditch the freeloaders. Find out which programs Windows automatically loads at startup, and stop loading the ones you rarely or never use. To learn how, see *Turn off programs for faster start* in the *Windows 7 tools: update, maintain & protect* chapter.

Turn off your keyboard light. If your keyboard is backlit, check the help files or the manual that came with your laptop to discover how to turn the keyboard off when you're in well-lit places.

Try these quick tips and tricks. They are simple to do.

- reduce screen brightness

- use **Sleep**, **Standby**, or **Hibernate**

- unplug USB-attached peripherals when you aren't using them

- keep your laptop out of the heat

- delay your anti-virus scan, large downloads, music and video streaming, and system and program updates until you can plug in

Conserve battery life automatically

In addition to all the steps you take to save battery power, your laptop can automatically save extra power for you. Here's how it works.

Your laptop manages its power usage and performance through a group of settings called a power plan. But more than one plan is available. For example, one "power saver" plan conserves power, while another may use more power to improve laptop performance.

A third "balanced" plan may offer you a compromise between the other two plans. Find out which plan your laptop is using to see if switching plans can conserve battery power.

- Click on the battery icon in the Windows system tray at the lower right corner of your screen.

- Click on **Power options** or **More power options**.

- One plan is already selected, but it's not the only plan available. Click on the **Show additional plans** arrow to see any other plans.

- Look for the **Extended battery life (Max run-time)** option, and click on the circle to select it. If you don't find this plan, click on the **Power saver** option.

High-tech health

When you can't use a separate mouse and keyboard, sit in a chair that allows you to lean back a little to minimize the strain on your neck. To help, tilt the screen upward slightly so it's easier to see.

If your knees are not at hip-level, prop them up on a box or footrest. Fold up a towel, and tuck it between the small of your back and the chair back to support your lower back. And don't forget to take regular stretching breaks every half hour.

Stop your laptop from randomly shutting down

Most laptop shutdowns happen for one reason — overheating. When your laptop overheats enough to put its delicate parts in danger of permanent damage, it triggers an emergency shutdown to save itself. Take these steps to prevent overheating, and end the problem.

"Cool it" for a few hours. If the laptop won't reboot right away, let it cool for a couple of hours. While you wait, buy a can of compressed air labeled for computers, and use it to clean dust and buildup from the vents.

Watch where you put it. A laptop that spends time on a blanket, quilt, or pillow cannot get the ventilation it needs, so it may overheat. Avoid thick, soft surfaces that block your laptop's ventilation. Keep your laptop on flat, hard surfaces, and you may solve your overheating problem for good.

Get creative to improve ventilation. Try a laptop cooling pad. If that is too expensive, try improving the laptop's ventilation when you use it. Set it on a hard, flat surface, and place a 2-inch rectangular pencil eraser, a triangular rubber door stop, or a tipped-over wine cork under each of the back corners.

Expert ways to print & scan

New ways to save on ink cartridges

Ounce for ounce, printer ink is more expensive than gasoline, vodka, or Chanel No. 5 perfume, according to recent information from Nuesion.com and Ninemsn.com. Fortunately, you can start using even less ink with these tips.

Remove Web ads and more. When you print a Web page, you don't want to print the ads, banners, and other ink-wasters. To fix this, add an item called a bookmarklet to your **Bookmarks** toolbar. A bookmarklet is a tiny program in a bookmark that performs tasks that help you when surfing and searching the Web.

For example, a free bookmarklet called Readability sweeps away ads and other unwanted items so you're only left with what you want to print. You can even choose to delete all pictures or automatically create footnotes showing the URL for each link. Visit *www.read ability.com* for this bookmarklet.

Other bookmarklets or programs let you choose specifically what to remove or may offer options that help squeeze more words into a page than Readability can. Check out these options.

- PrintWhatYouLike at *www.printwhatyoulike.com*
- PrintFriendly at *www.printfriendly.com*
- Printliminator at *www.css-tricks.com/examples/ThePrintliminator*

Change your settings. Many inkjet printers use more than just black ink to print black text and graphics. They print color ink underneath to make a darker black. When you print a document in black and white, set your printer to grayscale. That tells the printer to use only black ink to print in black, which can save a surprising amount of ink.

To change the setting to grayscale, click on the **Start** button > **Control Panel** > **Hardware and Sound** > **Devices and Printers**.

Double-click your printer's icon, and then double-click **Adjust print options**. Click on the **Color** tab. Select the grayscale option, and click on **OK**. If the grayscale option is not under the **Color** tab, check your printer manual or help files.

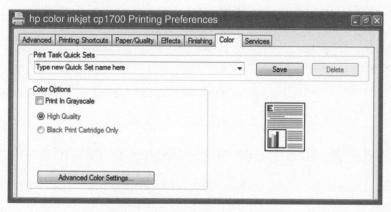

Select the Grayscale option

Make a digital copy. Instead of sending the document to your printer to convert to hard copy, make a PDF (portable document format) instead. A "Print to PDF" program sends a copy of the document to a digital file. The PDF looks like the printed file would, but it stays on your computer. Save the PDF to a folder in **My Documents**, and you can read the document whenever you want and print out a hard copy if you need it.

Because a PDF can be read on any computer that has the free Acrobat Reader program installed, you can also take the document with you on a flash drive or send it as an email attachment. Free PDF-creation programs include CutePDF available from *www.cutepdf.com* and doPDF at *www.dopdf.com*. Adobe Reader is available from *www.acrobat.com*.

BRIGHT IDEA

You can save a bundle on printer ink if you own a tablet computer, e-reader, or smartphone. Instead of printing a document or picture, copy it to one of these gadgets, and take it with you.

For example, use the free **Send to Kindle** browser add-on to send Web articles to your Kindle, or use Dropbox's free online service to transfer recipes, photos, and more to your tablet or smartphone.

For more about **Send to Kindle**, see *Send Web stories to Kindle for easy access* in *E-readers and tablets: hot tech at your fingertips*. For more about Dropbox, see *Maximize your storage protection* in *The Cloud: don't leave home without it*.

Solve the problem of streaky printouts

Streaks, missing colors, or faintness on your printouts may mean your printer is the victim of an ink clog. These ink clogs cause problems when they block the print head nozzle your print cartridge uses to dispense ink.

To fix the problem, check your printer's manual to find out how to perform a head cleaning to clear the nozzles. You can usually program the cleaning from the printer's front control panel. But be aware that you may have to clean the print heads two to five times to clear a clog. Make sure you print a test page after each cleaning.

If several cleanings don't clear the clog, check your printer manual, or visit the support section of the printer manufacturer's website for additional help. To help prevent future clogs, use your printer at least once a week, even if it's just to print a test page.

4 quick fixes for a troublesome printer

You click on the **Print** command, but your printer just sits there like a brick, doing nothing. If it doesn't start printing after a minute or two, follow these steps to put it back in action.

Check the display. The LCD display on your printer may show a message such as "load media." Load media usually means you need to refill the paper tray. If you see a more confusing message, check your printer manual or the manufacturer's website for an explanation.

Look for surprises. Check to be sure your printer hasn't somehow been turned off. If the printer is on, and it doesn't connect by wireless network, check the connections between the printer and your PC to make certain nothing has jiggled loose.

Reset the network connection. If a wired Ethernet network connects your computer to your printer, try this. Turn off your printer. Reboot your network router to reset the network connection.

To do this, pull the router's power cable connector out of its port, count to 10, and then plug the cable connector in again. Wait a few minutes until the router has fully rebooted, and then turn the printer back on. This may be enough to make your document print immediately.

View the queue. Each time you click on **Print**, Windows submits a request to the printer. That request is called a print job. The Windows print queue displays information about each print job until that job is completed. If your document does not print, you can check the print queue to see what's happening.

To do this, click on **Start** > **Control Panel** > **Hardware and Sound** > **Devices and Printers**. Double-click the icon for your printer, and then double-click **See what's printing**.

The print queue window appears and shows any jobs that are printing or waiting to print. If no jobs appear, check the printer to confirm nothing has printed. If no printouts are waiting for you, try to print again. If jobs display in the queue, the print queue may look like this.

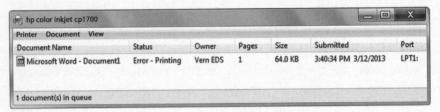

Print Queue displaying a print job

Closing all programs and rebooting your computer is one way to remove those jobs. But if you prefer not to reboot, click on **Printer > Cancel All Documents**.

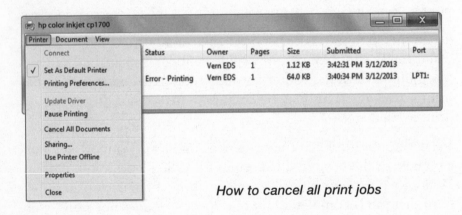

How to cancel all print jobs

When the jobs vanish, try to print again. If the jobs won't leave the print queue, close all programs, and reboot, before trying to print again.

5 simple steps to stop paper jams

Saying sayonara to frequent printer jams may be easier than you think. Just try these tips.

- To avoid jams caused when your printer grabs two pieces of paper, fan your pile of paper once in each direction before putting it in the tray. This helps keep sheets from sticking together.

- Fill the tray. Your printer may pick up some kinds of paper improperly unless the sheets are perched at the top of a full or nearly full tray.

- If paper is getting low, remove all of it before adding more to prevent an edge or corner from catching and causing a jam. Tap your stack of paper against a hard, flat surface to line up the edges before placing the stack in the tray.

- Check your paper guides regularly. If they're too loose, your paper may enter the printer at a jam-causing angle. If they're too tight, they may cause the paper to arch upwards in the middle and snag on the printer's inner workings.

- Cleaning helps remove ink, toner, or paper particle buildup that gums up the works. Check your printer manual or printer manufacturer's website for information on whether you need to clean by hand or by triggering an automatic cleaning system.

A CLOSER LOOK

To fix a jam, check your printer for a button to eject the paper. If it's there, use it. Otherwise, turn off your printer, unplug it, and consult your printer manual for instructions on how to remove jams. If you can't find your manual, try to download a copy from the support section of your printer manufacturer's website.

If you must remove the jammed paper by hand, use both hands to pull the paper in the same direction it moves while printing. After removing the jam, plug in the printer, turn it on, and try to print again.

Use a scanner to simplify your life

Turn your paper documents into digital files with a scanner. If you really want to get rid of the paper piles in your life, this is the way to go. You can also use two other electronic tools to cut down on paperwork and make your life easier. Just follow these instructions.

Scan your documents. You can use a standalone scanner or one that's part of an all-in-one printer. But before you start scanning, take steps to set yourself up for success.

- Make sure your computer is secure. You don't want identity thieves, hackers, or scammers to see financial or personal documents after you scan them. Find out how to access the Windows Action Center in *Decode cryptic security warnings* in *Windows security essentials*. Then correct any problems you find there. Also, keep your security software up to date, and read the rest of *Windows security essentials* to make sure you haven't missed anything.

- Create a system to organize the documents you scan so you can easily find what you need when you want it.

- Choose a scanner or software with an option to create PDF versions of scans. This can be particularly useful for scanning documents. If your scanner can't make PDFs, you can download free PDF software such as PrimoPDF from *www.primopdf.com*.

Use your cellphone. Receipts can be a pain to scan, so digitize them with your cellphone camera instead. Decide what categories you want to use to organize your receipts, and write the appropriate category at the top of each receipt.

Snap a picture of the receipt with your phone's camera, and transfer the picture to your computer using Bluetooth, a USB cable, or email. For an even better option for on-the-go scanning, see *10 surprising ways to use your phone's camera* in *Tap into the power of today's cellphones*.

Computerize your statements. You can also use your PC or laptop to put an end to piles of bills and statements. Visit the websites of your bank, utility companies, credit card company, and any other organization that regularly sends you statements and bills. Find out if they can send electronic bills or statements, and learn how to arrange that.

Also, see if you can pay bills online or set up automatic payments. Some companies let you make payments at their websites, or your bank may offer online banking to help you pay bills.

For safety's sake, only set up automated payments for bills that are consistently the same amount every month. And make sure you check your account each month to verify that the correct amount has been paid by the deadline.

CAUTION

Keep all your scans on just one hard drive or flash drive, and you could lose them if the drive is damaged or lost. Back up your scans regularly to an external hard drive or second flash drive, and make sure you always have at least two copies of your scans in case one becomes unavailable.

Keep sensitive financial documents and documents with personal information on a separate self-encrypting or password-protected drive. In addition, disaster recovery experts suggest keeping a third copy at a place outside your home, such as the home of a trusted family member.

Do's and don'ts for superior scanning

Create better scans, recover from mistakes, and finish your scanning faster with these handy tips. Some things you'll definitely want to do:

- Check your scanner's software for the timesaving batch or divide setting if you're scanning photos. With this setting, you fit several photos into the scannable area as if they were part of a jigsaw puzzle. The batch mode software then separates each photo into its own file after scanning.

- Decide how you will organize and sort your scans into folders. Create and name each folder before you begin scanning.

- Use your scanner's preview function. This can help you catch problems, straighten crooked documents, and avoid scanning a document more than once.

- Brighten a faded document or picture by placing one or two sheets of white paper on top of it after you put it on the scanner bed. This can make details more visible in your scan.

- Clean your scanner glass before you start scanning.

On the other hand, don't:

- edit or crop your original scan. Save the original, and make a copy. Do all editing or cropping on the copy. If you make a mistake you can't fix, all is not lost. You can simply make another copy from the original.

- scan paper clips or staples or anything else that can scratch scanner glass. Check every document for paper clips, miniature binder clips, or staples, and remove them before setting the page on the scanner glass.

- assign vague file names to your scans. "Picture 91, 2012" will be hard to remember and even harder to find. Locating "Group picture at JFK airport" will take less time.

Make your scans picture perfect

Don't wait until you discover smudges, streaks, or specks in the same spots on every scan. That's a sign of dirt on your scanner glass, and it may mean you have to redo all those scans. To make sure this doesn't happen to you, clean your scanner glass like a professional. Here's how.

- Mix a little vinegar into water, and pour into a spray bottle. Don't use window or glass cleaner or isopropyl alcohol. They can cause streaks.

- Find a soft lint-free cloth such as a microfiber cloth.

- Turn off your scanner and unplug it. Lift the lid completely away from the glass.

- Spray your homemade cleanser on the lint-free cloth. Never spray the scanner directly. Liquid may seep under the glass and cause damage.

- Wipe the cloth over the scanner glass. Wipe the underside of the lid.

- Wait a few minutes to be sure it's dry.

- Plug in the scanner, turn it on, and resume work.

E-READERS & TABLETS
Hot tech at your fingertips

What can e-readers do for you?

Using an e-reader is even better than reading a physical book, many people say. These tablet-sized gadgets allow you to read electronic versions of books, magazines, and newspapers comfortably and conveniently. The leaders in this technology are Amazon Kindle and Barnes & Noble Nook, with Sony Reader, Kobo Glo, and others offering their versions. So why would you want one?

Simplify and save. E-readers can make your life easier and more economical.

- Many libraries now loan books to your e-reader, and hundreds of free books are available online. To learn more about this, see *Read unlimited e-books for free* in *The Internet for fun, health & learning* chapter.

- You wouldn't carry a heavy stack of books everywhere, but you can take dozens of books with you on your e-reader. It's easier to carry than a laptop, and may be small enough to fit in a purse or briefcase.

- While others must go out to get a book, you can simply download one from almost anywhere, saving gasoline, money, and time.

Enjoy health benefits. A standard e-reader with features for disabilities may help you manage the usual problems of aging, even if you don't have a disability.

- Many e-readers support audio books or offer a text-to-speech feature that reads the book aloud — a real plus for commuters and those with vision problems.

- Increase the size of text, put away those reading glasses, and stop paying for large-print books. Adjusting the font size turns everything you read into a large-print version.

- Tweak the contrast between page and text through your e-reader's settings. Try changing the page background to gray or tan. Combined with black text, this seems to reduce eyestrain the most.

- Backlit tablets create even more of a contrast between text and background, while shining light directly into your eyes. This seems to help people with macular degeneration.

- For even less eyestrain, change the line spacing and words per line.

- Turning pages is easy. Just press a button, or swipe a finger across the screen.

- At less than one pound, an e-reader is lighter than some books, making reading easier if you have arthritis. Even better, you won't have to hold a book open.

Top questions to ask before buying an e-reader

Do you want apps, email, and Internet surfing, along with your reading? In that case, a tablet computer may suit you better than an e-reader. Just be sure to compare what you get for the price.

What's more, if you already have a desktop, laptop, smartphone, or tablet, you can read e-books with a free reading app instead of buying a separate e-reader. For an example, visit *www.amazon.com* to learn about Amazon's Kindle app.

But if the portability, price, and benefits of an e-reader are still best for you, consider these questions before buying.

- Do you want a glowing, backlit screen like your PC, or an easy-on-the-eyes e-ink screen? In a dark environment, you'll need an extra light to read e-ink screens, but they have a much longer battery life — as long as the battery doesn't power an add-on sidelight or overhead light for the screen.

- Do you want touchscreen controls or physical buttons?

- What size and weight is comfortable? Try holding a few e-readers to find out.

- Can you check out e-books from your library and what formats do they offer? Amazon's Kindle needs MOBI format while other readers require ePub. Your e-reader won't support all formats.

- How many books are available in the format your e-reader supports?

- How good is the battery life?

- Will you want to download e-books through your home Wi-Fi network, a 3G/4G cellular network, or through a PC's USB connection?

HIGH-TECH HEALTH

That pain or stiffness in your neck, back, or shoulders may come from using your tablet in your lap or in bed for long periods. Those habits can even lead to strains or injury. To prevent pain caused by looking down or hunching over a tablet, use a stand that props the tablet at a steep angle, and place the stand on a table — except when doing a lot of typing or screen input. Avoid using the tablet in bed, but if you must, tuck pillows behind your lower back and under your knees, and keep the tablet screen at eye level.

Send Web stories to Kindle for easy access

Read articles from the Web or documents from your computer on your Kindle using Amazon's Send to Kindle.

Amazon offers free browser extensions for Firefox and Chrome to help you instantly send text from the Web to your Kindle. And they provide free apps for PCs, Macs, and Android devices to push documents to your Kindle.

Send to Kindle is free if you are using Wi-Fi to shoot content to your Kindle. If you use Whispernet, sometimes referred to as 3G, charges may apply. If your Kindle can use both Wi-Fi and Whispernet, you'll need to navigate to your Kindle Settings and select Wi-Fi to avoid these charges.

To learn how to download and use these browser extensions and apps, visit *www.amazon.com/sendtokindle*, and choose the version of Send to Kindle you want. Click on the **Getting Started** link at the bottom of the page where you'll find lots of help, including a troubleshooting link. After installation, you'll be asked to register by signing in with your Amazon.com account email address and password.

Web developers can also add a Send to Kindle button to their Web pages, which makes installing the browser extension unnecessary. For those websites already using this feature, like *www.the washington post.com* and *www.time.com*, you'll see a small orange "k" inside a box near the specific article. The first time you click on it, you'll be asked to sign into your Amazon account and select your Kindle device.

7 super reasons to own a tablet

A tablet computer may be right for you if you want something lighter and more portable than a laptop, but more versatile than an e-reader. These battery-powered computers are sometimes called slates because the entire tablet is a touchscreen about the size of a stenographer's tablet.

Tablets typically measure around seven to 10 inches from one corner to the opposite corner, diagonally. They come with an onscreen keyboard instead of a physical keyboard, and you tap the screen or swipe it with a finger instead of using a mouse. Best of all, you may be surprised at how many uses there are for these take-along devices.

Watch movies or television. Buy and download an episode of your favorite show to watch during your lunch hour, or stream a movie to your tablet through your home Wi-Fi network and watch it on the back porch. If this is important to you, make sure your tablet has a high-resolution screen for sharp, clear images. Check out the chapter *TV & movies: cutting-edge ways to watch* for more information.

Read books or a newspaper. Download free reading apps and library apps for checking out e-books. Take advantage of free e-books available on the Internet, or buy a book, a single newspaper or magazine, or a magazine or newspaper subscription.

Amazon at *www.amazon.com* makes this easy. Once you've down-loaded your reading material, enjoy it anywhere. Read while waiting in the doctor's office, or download a travel guidebook to use while sightseeing. Get a tablet with enough memory to hold your new portable library, or make sure you're buying one with a storage expansion option, like a micro SD card.

Surf the Web and check email. Depending on your tablet and your preferences, you can connect your tablet to your wireless Wi-Fi net-work, a 3G/4G cellular network, or a public Wi-Fi network. Then do fun things like check email from the couch during a commercial break or find great recipes on the Web while grocery shopping.

Enjoy apps. An app — short for application — is a piece of software that generally does one thing, unlike multipurpose software such as Microsoft Word. Apps are usually free or cheap, and can do anything from compare in-store and online prices, to magnify the text on a paper restaurant menu, to help you manage medications. You can only use the apps written for your tablet's operating system, such as Android, Windows 8, or Apple's iOS.

Listen to music. Download MP3 files of your favorite songs, and enjoy music everywhere you go.

View photos. Load photos on your tablet, and take it along to show your pictures to relatives or friends.

Video chat. If your tablet includes a camera — preferably a front-facing web cam — you can use apps like Skype or FaceTime to video chat with anyone who also has a Skype or FaceTime account. For more information on setting up a video chat see *Simple tools get you video chatting* in the *Video chats bring you closer* chapter.

Best ways to boost your tablet's battery life

Little changes in your tablet's settings could make a big difference in how long your battery lasts before you need to charge it again. Experiment with these changes, and find out how much extra battery life you can get.

Dim the beacon. A bright screen drains your battery faster. Check your brightness settings, and learn how to adjust them.

Some tablets will automatically adjust the brightness based on the current lighting around you. Turn on that feature if you have it. Otherwise, adjust it manually — turning down the brightness while you're in bright lighting and turning it back up when you need it.

Stop the seekers. If your tablet has Wi-Fi, Bluetooth, GPS service, or 3G or 4G cellular service, turn them off when you're not using them. Otherwise, they constantly drain battery power by searching for a signal.

Even if you've turned off a Bluetooth device, your tablet's Bluetooth will continue to search for it. Go to your tablet's settings and turn off each service individually. To turn them all off at once, switch your tablet to airplane mode.

Secure your tablet in 8 easy steps

Malware, hackers, and identity thieves don't just target desktops and laptops. Use these tips to protect your tablet.

Be picky about apps. Only download apps from trusted marketplaces like Apple's iTunes, Google Play, or Amazon's Appstore. To lower your odds of accidentally downloading harmful or virus-infected apps, look for apps that:

- have been reviewed by a major publication, website, or blogger.

- are at least one year old.

- have a hefty number of positive user reviews written in understandable English.

- have large numbers of users.

- feature a link to the developer's website.

Know your permissions. When you first use an app store or download an app, you may be asked for permission to let them access information or functions on your tablet. Some apps limit themselves to the information and functions they need to operate, while others may also collect extra data for advertising or other purposes.

Check what information is collected by reading the permissions information usually provided with Android apps. Think twice about installing an app that asks for permission to do things or view information that is clearly not related to the app.

Avoid tinkering. Don't jailbreak your iPad or root your Android tablet. Jailbreaking and rooting mean you override the manufacturer's settings so you can use apps and other features that aren't normally available.

Unfortunately, jailbreaking and rooting also break the security settings protecting your tablet and compromise your ability to receive future software updates.

Defend your perimeter. Download third-party mobile security software that can protect against malware and malicious apps. You can get free spyware and virus protection from Lookout, an app available for both iPads and Android tablets.

Grab those updates. Install operating system and app updates as soon as they become available. They may include fixes for security problems.

Beware these links. Never click on a link in an email that appears to be from a financial institution.

Prepare for the worst. In case your tablet is ever stolen or lost, lock it with a password, passcode, or pin code. Also, back up your data regularly, and either enable the remote wiping feature on your iPad, or download an Android app that can provide this feature for your Android tablet.

Remote wiping removes all data from your tablet, so you definitely want to back up regularly in case you need it. The free avast! Mobile Security app can provide remote backup along with remote locking, anti-virus protection, and other security features.

Defend against hotspot hackers. If you use the public Wi-Fi networks available in libraries, coffee shops, and the like, be aware that others can electronically detect everything you see and do on your tablet. Don't view or do anything you wouldn't want strangers to examine, and follow the tips in *10 steps to stronger hotspot security* in the *Safe & secure surfing* chapter.

BRIGHT IDEA

You walk off the plane, leaving your tablet or e-reader tucked in the seat-back pocket. Unfortunately, without some kind of identifying feature, you may never see it again.

If your device isn't engraved with your information, you can write a contact phone number on a label in permanent ink, and securely fix the label to the back of your tablet or e-reader. Then check to see if your device has a Find function — like Apple's Find My iPad — which will help you locate it if it goes missing or gets stolen.

Get connected — tune into a Wi-Fi network

Your relatives encourage you to use their home Wi-Fi network while you visit them. To do this with a tablet, go to your **Settings**, locate the Wi-Fi network, and select it. Here is how you do it if you own an iPad.

- On your Home screen, tap the icon for **Settings**.

- On the left side of the screen, tap **Wi-Fi**.

iPad Settings icon

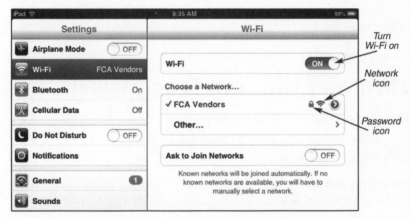

iPad settings to turn on Wi-Fi and log in to a network

- On the right side of screen, check whether **Wi-Fi** is **ON** or **OFF**. If it is **OFF**, drag the circle next to the word **OFF** to turn it on. Wait for a few moments while the iPad locates the available networks.

- Under **Choose a Network**, find the name of the network you want to join. If you see a padlock icon, you must have a password to access this network. Tap the name of the network, and enter the password, if needed.

When you are connected, the icon for that network turns blue.

A CLOSER LOOK

If you don't immediately see the **Settings** icon on your iPad, it may be on another screen. Below the icons, but above the dock, you may find a bright white dot with dimmer dots to the left and right of it. Each of the dimmer dots represents another available screen.

To see a screen to the left, swipe or quickly drag your finger from the left edge of the screen toward the center. To see a screen to the right, swipe from the right edge toward the center. Keep swiping through screens until you find the **Settings** icon.

Save money with a Wi-Fi only tablet

Almost 90 percent of tablet owners connect to the Internet through Wi-Fi instead of a cellular service, one survey found. This may be a smart, budget-friendly decision.

Save when you buy. You can connect a tablet to the Internet in two ways, through a Wi-Fi connection or through a 3G or 4G cellular connection. Tablets that only feature Wi-Fi capability may cost up to $130 less than tablets that also offer a 3G/4G connection. Wi-Fi only tablets also tend to have a longer battery life, which will save replacement costs.

Don't pay to connect. Your Wi-Fi connection may come from a private home Wi-Fi network or a publicly available network, sometimes called a hotspot. You'll get Wi-Fi service only when you are within the range of one of these and connected to it.

At home, you probably already pay a monthly fee to your Internet Service Provider (ISP) for an Internet connection. If you also have a home Wi-Fi network, adding your tablet to that network won't cost anything. If you don't have a home Wi-Fi network, you can learn more about them in the *Network necessities: how to set up, fix & secure* chapter. Many public Wi-Fi networks are free. To access others, you'll have to pay a fee — hourly, daily, weekly, or even monthly.

Connecting through a 3G/4G cellular service is different. A cell-phone carrier — like Sprint, AT&T, or Verizon — provides your connection to the Internet, so it doesn't matter if you're in an area where Wi-Fi is available. But you will depend on a cellular signal, which can be spotty in some areas.

You'll pay a monthly fee for having your tablet on a cellular plan plus a flat rate for the amount of data you use while connected. Depending on your carrier and your choice of plans, a cellular connection can cost a little or a lot. Check all the options your carrier offers for your particular tablet.

To learn about using your smartphone to connect your tablet to a wireless hotspot, read *Tethering: share your phone's Internet connection* in the *Tap into the power of today's cellphones* chapter.

BRIGHT IDEA

You may think your tablet is nearly useless if you can't access the Internet when you're out and about. But here's how your home Wi-Fi network and a little preparation can help you do more.

- Download the Pocket app for your tablet, and you can save all sorts of Web articles for reading later, when you aren't connected to a network. Learn more at *getpocket.com*.

- Going somewhere? Take advantage of Google's offline map options, or find an app, like MapsWithMe, that offers this. You can download turn-by-turn directions before you go.

- Plan ahead and you can take your entertainment with you. Download movies, TV shows, e-books, magazines, news-papers, and games that can be played offline. Then enjoy yourself anywhere, even without a Wi-Fi connection.

Phablets are a fabulous two-for-one deal

You want a smartphone and a tablet, but can't afford both. Fortunately, a new device may put your gadget dreams within reach.

A "phablet" is a cross between a smartphone and a tablet. Its screen usually measures at least 5 inches diagonally, making it larger than a smartphone, but smaller than a tablet. Yet, this device can serve as your smartphone, mp3 player, e-book reader, and tablet.

That means you only have to pay for one device and one data plan, you only have to carry one device, and you get more screen real estate than a smartphone provides.

That extra space means you're less likely to squint at the screen or tap on the wrong spot when you try to navigate. Both text and images can be larger for easier reading or video viewing. You can also fit more content on the screen when surfing or doing other tasks.

Phablets are not perfect though. Their larger size can make them tricky to use as a phone, although a Bluetooth headset could solve that problem. Phablets may also be too large to use one-handed and may or may not fit in a pocket or purse.

Windows 7

tips & tweaks for your operating system

SIMPLE SETUP
FOR A SPEEDY START

Free tool tells if you're ready for Windows 7

Making the move to the Windows 7 operating system (OS) is a no-brainer. It's safer than XP and faster than Vista. Microsoft put a lot of money into making this system more secure. It's now much harder for bad guys to infect your computer with a virus, steal your personal information, or secretly take control of your machine.

The only question is — can your current computer handle it? Windows 7 needs more memory and a faster processor than past systems like XP. Machines made before 2005 probably aren't up to the task. At a minimum, your computer needs:

- a 1-gigahertz processor.
- 1 gigabyte of memory.
- 16 gigabytes of space available on your hard disk.

Luckily, you don't need to poke around the computer yourself to see if it's up to snuff. If you have Internet access, Microsoft will do it for you, free. Head to the website *windows.microsoft.com/en-US/windows/downloads/upgrade-advisor* and download Windows 7 Upgrade Advisor. Save it to your desktop, then double-click on its icon to open it.

Windows shopping made simple

Choosing which version of Windows 7 to buy can make your head swim. Relax. Microsoft sells six different ones, but you only need to consider two or three.

Home Premium. The average computer user will do just fine with Windows 7 Home Premium. It's what most people buy, and it likely does everything you need.

Professional. For more money, you can get the next step up. Windows 7 Professional packs all the same features as Home Premium, along with a few extras geared toward business people and office workers.

It lets you encrypt files and folders for an added layer of security, so other people can't read them. And it's a little better at backing up your computer and working with old programs. A few programs that worked in Windows XP may not work in Windows 7, but the Professional edition has ways of getting around that.

Ultimate. For even more money, you can buy Windows 7 Ultimate. It lets you encrypt your entire hard drive and offers even more business-friendly features like advanced networking. For the average person, this version is overkill.

MONEY-SAVER

Consider the Starter edition if you have a netbook rather than a computer. It won't let you play DVDs, and it lacks fancy graphics — but it costs less and still allows you to email, surf the Internet, and edit digital photos.

Upgrade OS with a few quick clicks

Buy the wrong version of Windows 7? No problem. Microsoft offers a no-sweat way to upgrade. Each Windows 7 disc actually contains all of the versions, from the bare-bones Starter edition to the bells-and-whistles Ultimate. For a few dollars more, you can upgrade instantly.

From your desktop, click on the Start button. Type "Anytime Upgrade" into the search box on the Start menu, and click on **Windows Anytime Upgrade** in the results that appear. This opens the upgrade program. From here, you can go online to the Microsoft website and pay by credit card for a fancier edition.

Microsoft makes it so easy that you may want to start out with the inexpensive Home Premium version, knowing you can upgrade later.

Save a wad of cash on Windows 7

Keep more money in your pocket. Buy the upgrade version, rather than the full version, of Windows 7 if you're switching from XP or Vista.

Upgrading means the new operating system builds on the framework of the old one, sort of like remodeling your house rather than building a new one from scratch. The alternative is a "clean install," the equivalent of tearing down the old house and putting up a new one. For a clean install, you need the full version of Windows 7.

Upgrading from most Vista editions is easy. Just pop in the Windows 7 DVD and follow the instructions. For XP, however, you must do a Custom installation. You'll need to back up all of your files and settings first.

If your computer is prone to glitches or general slowness, a clean install may be best. This clears the slate, giving your computer a fresh start. But as with a Custom install, you'll need to back up your files and settings first.

For step-by-step instructions on installing Windows 7, visit the Microsoft website at *windows.microsoft.com/isIS/windows7/Installing-and-reinstalling-Windows-7*.

3 steps to breeze through an upgrade

Follow this three-step process the day before installing your new operating system (OS). It will make upgrading your old computer or moving your files to a new one safe and simple.

- Update your anti-virus program, then run a full scan of your computer to make sure you don't move any infected files to the new machine or new OS.

- Create a full backup of your computer. It's a must if you are upgrading from Windows XP. It's optional if you upgrade from Vista, but you'll be happy to have it should something go wrong.

- Find the discs for any programs you have. You will need to reinstall them if you're upgrading from XP, or if you're moving your things from an old computer to a new one.

You're almost done. A few minutes before you begin the upgrade:

- turn off your anti-virus software and any firewall not made by Microsoft if you are upgrading the operating system on your current computer.

- unplug any nonessential gadgets from the computer, like printers, scanners, cameras, or external hard drives. You can plug them back in once you finish installing the new operating system.

- make sure your computer is hooked up to the Internet, if you have Internet access. Write down the phone number your computer dials to connect to the Internet, if you use a dial-up modem, along with your user name and password.

Painless way to move your files

Time for a new computer? Windows Easy Transfer is the best way to transfer your old files onto your new machine. This program gives you two ways to move them.

- Buy the Easy Transfer Cable, hook one end to each computer, and move files between them.

- Save your files to an external hard drive or USB flash drive, then copy them to the new computer using the free Easy Transfer software.

People upgrading from Windows Vista already have a copy of Windows Easy Transfer on their computer. Just click on the Start button, then on **All Programs** > **Accessories** > **System Tools**.

XP-users will need to install the program from the disc that comes with the transfer cable or download it from the Microsoft website at *http://bit.ly/9rt8eg*. Save the file to your old computer, then double-click on its icon to install it. When you're ready to move your files, open Windows Easy Transfer from the Start menu and follow the instructions.

 BRIGHT IDEA

You can also use Easy Transfer to upgrade your existing computer to Windows 7.

Open the Easy Transfer program, tell it **This is my old computer** when it asks, then save your files and settings to an external hard drive or flash drive.

Install your new Windows 7 operating system. When you finish, open the Start menu again, click on **All Programs**, then **Accessories**, **System Tools**, and finally **Windows Easy Transfer**. This time, choose **This is my new computer**. Follow the prompts to find your files and move them back.

Activate new OS with or without the Internet

You must activate your copy of Windows 7 within 30 days of upgrading your old computer. It's easier if you have Internet access, but you can do it by phone if necessary.

Open the Start menu and type "Activate" into the search box at the bottom. Choose **Activate Windows**, then **Show me other ways to activate**. Type in your product key, click on **Next**, and choose **Use the automated phone system**. You'll soon see a list of locations. Select the one closest to where you live, click on **Next**, and dial one of the phone numbers given.

An automated system will answer and guide you through activation. Be sure to write down the confirmation ID that the phone system gives you. Type this into your computer to finish the process.

If you bought a computer that came with Windows 7, you don't need to do anything. The manufacturer will have activated it for you.

Hook up gadgets with ease

Every gadget you plug into your computer needs a tiny program, called a driver, to run it. Windows 7 has a library containing thousands of them, so it's easier than ever to connect new devices.

Plug your printer, scanner, and other gadgets into the computer once you finish installing Windows 7. Turn them on, and the computer will search its library, automatically matching the right driver to each gadget.

Every once in awhile, Windows has trouble finding a driver. Learn how to find them yourself by reading *Get grumpy gadgets working again* in *SOS: everyday troubleshooting tips*.

No need to set computer clock

You'll never need to set the time and date on your computer, if you have Internet access — not even for Daylight Savings time. Windows 7 will fetch the information online once a week. Just be sure to choose the right time zone when you install Windows 7.

Don't have Internet? You can set it manually. Look for the time and date in the bottom-right corner of your computer screen. Click on this once to open the settings, then click on **Change date and time settings** at the bottom and follow the prompts.

 A CLOSER LOOK

Missing your calendar and built-in email? Unlike past operating systems, Windows 7 does not come with an email, address book, instant messaging, or video or photo editing program.

Thankfully, however, you can get them all online for free as part of a package called Windows Live Essentials. Head to the website *windows.microsoft.com/en-US/windows-live/essentials-home* and click on **Download now**. Some computer makers, like Dell, install this package of programs for you, so check first.

Slash electric bill with Sleep mode

Computers can eat up a lot of electricity, particularly when you aren't using them. Pull the plug on outrageous electric bills.

Walking away for an hour or less? Consider putting the machine to sleep. A sleeping desktop computer uses 90 percent less power than one left on.

Sleep mode puts the computer to rest without totally turning it off. It saves your place in whatever program or file you're working, much like a bookmark does in a book. Just move the mouse or press a key on the keyboard to wake up the machine and get right back to work. You can put the computer to sleep in a couple of ways.

- Send it to sleep manually by clicking on the Start button, then on the arrow beside the words **Shut down** on the Start menu. Choose **Sleep** from the small menu that pops up.

- Have it put itself to sleep automatically after it sits idle for awhile. Click on the Start button again and select **Control Panel** from the menu. In the window that opens, click on **Hardware and Sound**, then **Power Options**.

  To save the most electricity — and money — choose the **Power saver** plan. Click on the arrow next to **Plan settings** to adjust how long the computer idles before going to sleep.

Of course, if you'll be away for several hours, you may want to turn the computer off. Simply click on **Shut down** on the Start menu.

A CLOSER LOOK

Some people won't see **Sleep** as one of their options in the **Shut down** menu. They'll see **Hibernate** instead, which does much the same thing.

Sleep at the push of a button

Maybe you'd like your computer to go to sleep instead of turning off when you press the machine's power button. Change that with just a few clicks.

Return to the **Power Options** window that you opened through the **Control Panel**. In the left side, click on **Choose what the power button does**. A new window will appear, with the phrase **When I press the power button** in the center. The button beside this probably says **Shut down**. Click on the arrow to the right to choose a different option, like **Sleep**.

WINDOWS DESKTOP
Make it work for you

Return to the classic look of XP

Do you miss the look of your old Windows XP operating system? It's easy to take a trip down memory lane when you configure the **Control Panel** to have that classic look.

Click the **Start** button then select **Control Panel**. Notice the upper-right area of this window that says **View by: Category**. Click on the small down arrow. From the drop-down menu select either **Large Icons** or **Small Icons**.

 A CLOSER LOOK

> In Windows 7, the **Start** button in the lower-left corner of the **Taskbar** has been replaced with this icon. However, this book will still refer to it as the **Start** button.

Expand your Control Panel view

By default, when you click on **Control Panel** from the **Start Menu**, it opens in a new, separate window. Here you'll find programs and utilities grouped under categories. Some find it inconvenient to navigate this way and would prefer a complete alphabetical listing of all the **Control Panel** options.

To change your **Control Panel** view:

1. Right-click the **Start** button then choose **Properties**.
2. Under the **Start Menu** tab, click on **Customize**.
3. Find **Control Panel** in the list and change its display by clicking inside the circle next to **Display as a menu**. Click on **OK**.

Control Panel displayed as a menu

Pinned to Start Menu

Start button   *Programs pinned to Taskbar*

Windows 7 Smart Menu

Find things fast with built-in searching

Perhaps the handiest feature on your **Start Menu** is the **Search** box. Use it to find messages, pictures, files, programs, or folders — in fact, anything that is stored on your computer.

Simply start typing and you'll immediately see search results appear above the **Search** box. These results are organized by type, so you may see a suggested list under headings like **Programs**, **Control Panel Tasks**, **Pictures**, **Documents**, and more. Click on the result you wish to open or right-click it for additional options.

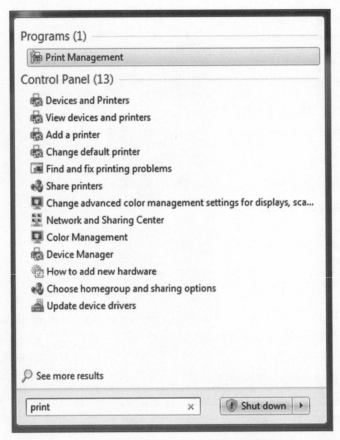

Search results organized by type

Bright idea

Customize your computer. It's easy to get exactly what you need, right on your screen. The **Quick Launch** toolbar from earlier versions of Windows is replaced in Windows 7 by a friendlier **Taskbar** that handles drag-and-drop like a pro. Just click on and drag a program, file, or folder icon to the **Taskbar**. Pin it to keep it there. Click on it to open.

Let the Start Menu lend a helping hand

Are you new to Windows 7 or have you been using it awhile but feel like you may still be missing some of the basics of this operating system? If so, you need look no further than the **Start Menu** for help.

There you'll find an entry titled **Getting Started**. Hover over or click on its arrow to see a list of useful topics. Each will take you directly to a **Control Panel** window, website, dialog box, or other informative location.

Jump right to work with Jump Lists

You can go straight to items you use most often with a feature new to Windows 7 called Jump Lists.

These are similar to the **Recent Items** lists you may be familiar with from older versions of Windows, but with more options.

These pop-up menus appear when you right-click an application icon in your **Taskbar**. Depending on the application, Jump Lists can show frequently opened items, a list of recent items, or even recent Web pages.

And by clicking on any of these choices, the application is opened — if it isn't already — and you jump straight to it.

You also have the option to close the application, pin or unpin it from the **Taskbar** or **Start Menu**, or open the application.

To set the number of items displayed in your Jump Lists, right-click the **Start** button then click **Properties > Start Menu > Customize**.

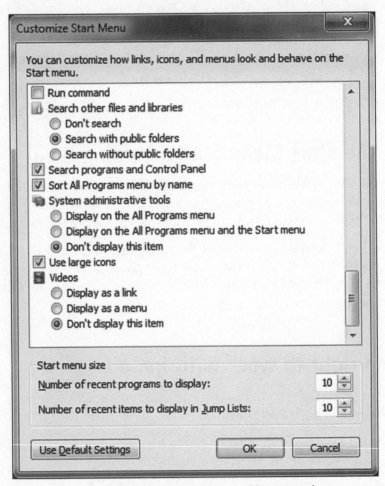

"Jump" to frequently opened items and recent Web pages with Jump Lists

Add a quick link to your Video library

Your **Start Menu** automatically has links to your Documents, Pictures, and Music libraries. But there's no quick link to your

Video library. If you love home movies and video clips, you'll want to remedy this right away. Here's how.

1. Right-click the **Start** button then click on **Properties**.

2. Select the **Start Menu** tab then click **Customize**.

3. Scroll down the alphabetical list until you get to **Videos** and click on **Display as a link**.

4. Click on **OK**. In the next dialog box, click on **Apply**.

A CLOSER LOOK

You've got plenty of ways to customize the **Start Menu**, **Taskbar**, and various toolbars. To view them all, right-click the **Start** button, and choose **Properties**. Work your way through the tabs in the dialog box, testing various options to see what customizations work best for you.

Flip your way through open windows

At the movie theaters, 3D is all the rage. And now 3D is playing on your local computer — Flip 3D, that is.

You'll flip over the way Flip lets you browse through your open applications and windows. Press the **Windows Logo (WIN)** key plus the **Tab** key to instantly bring up a parade of miniature windows, representing everything you have open. While still holding the **WIN** key down, tap the **Tab** key and your windows cycle across your desktop. To flip backward, press **WIN + Shift + Tab**.

The images are big enough so you can tell generally what is in each window. When the one you want cycles to the front, release the **WIN** key and that window expands, front and center.

Using Flip cuts down on mousing and helps you easily find windows that may seem buried in your **Taskbar**.

But maybe holding and pressing all those keys is just too much for you. You can turn Flip 3D on by pressing WIN + Ctrl + Tab. Let go. All your windows stay in Flip mode and you can cycle through them at your leisure by pressing either the Tab key or any of the arrow keys. Open the window on top by pressing Enter. The Escape key (**Esc**) takes you out of Flip.

New feature auto-arranges windows

Aero Snap, new in Windows 7, makes viewing multiple windows — well — a snap.

Let's say you need to work in a word processing document but also need to see information on a specific Web page at the same time.

Grab hold of your document's **Title Bar** and drag it until your pointer reaches the left edge of your screen. Let go and Snap automatically resizes it to take up the left half of your desktop.

Then drag your Web page to the right and, snap, you've got these two windows arranged side-by-side for perfect viewing. To reset a window, click on and drag the **Title Bar** down from the top of the screen. As soon as it resizes, release your mouse button.

This fun tool makes it easy for you to organize, read, and compare different windows. But if you want to turn off this feature, you can.

1. **Start button > All Programs > Accessories > Ease of Access > Ease of Access Center > Make the mouse easier to use**.

2. Under **Make it easier to manage windows**, check the box **Prevent windows from being automatically arranged when moved to the edge of the screen**.

BRIGHT IDEA

Snap is even easier with a keyboard shortcut. Select a window and press the **WIN** key plus a right or left arrow. Like magic, your window snaps to that half of the screen.

Aero Shake cleans up a cluttered desktop

Here's a nifty new feature in Windows 7 that's not only useful when your desktop becomes littered with open windows, but fun, too. You can keep one window up and running while minimizing all the others with one little shake.

Place your cursor on the **Title Bar** of the window you want to keep on your desktop, click and hold your left mouse button, then move your mouse quickly back and forth — just like you were shaking the window. All the open windows except the one you're shaking will minimize to the **Taskbar**. Shake again and all your windows are back.

> CAUTION
>
> You'll enhance your computer's performance, says Microsoft, by keeping a clean desktop. That means, don't store things like files or pictures or music directly on your desktop. Store them in the appropriate Library folder and access them either through the **Start Menu** or a shortcut.

Get a peek at your desktop with Aero Peek

You have another tool that will make navigating your computer simpler than ever. It's the small rectangle in the lower-right corner of your **Taskbar** called **Show Desktop**.

Hover over it when your desktop is full of layered windows, and they all instantly become transparent. Now you can take a peek at all those previously hidden icons, gadgets, folders, and whatever else resides on your desktop. Move your mouse and everything reappears. Click on this same area, the windows completely disappear, and you can move about your desktop.

For a keyboard shortcut to Peek, press the **Windows** key plus the Spacebar.

Preview open windows from the Taskbar

Now there's no need to open every window you've minimized to your **Taskbar** in order to view, switch, or close them. Simply hover your mouse over a **Taskbar** button and thumbnail images appear on your desktop.

You'll see a preview of all the Word documents you have open, for instance, if you hover over the Microsoft Word **Taskbar** button.

Move your mouse onto a thumbnail and you can click on it to open it or close it by clicking on the red X.

In addition, by moving your mouse onto a thumbnail, you get a temporary, full-size image of the window. That lets you read the details of a window before choosing it.

Hover your mouse over a Taskbar button and thumbnail images appear

Launch email with easy icon

Email is a huge part of the computing experience — perhaps the main reason you have a computer at all. So why not make accessing your email easier than ever?

It will take you just a few seconds to pin a Web mail icon to your **Taskbar**, allowing you to go directly to your online email account with a single click. Here's how to do it.

1. In your Web browser, navigate to your online email — Gmail or Hotmail, for instance — but don't sign in to your account.

2. Look to the top of your browser window and find your mailservice's logo located just to the left of the **Address Bar**.

3. Click and drag this logo to your desktop where it becomes a shortcut icon.

4. Close or minimize your Web browser window.

5. Drag and drop the icon onto your **Taskbar**.

You can delete the shortcut icon from your desktop if you like, just to tidy things up. Now, whenever you want to go to your email, single-click on your **Taskbar's** mail icon. It will open even if your Web browser is not.

 BRIGHT IDEA

Are you partial to working with keyboard shortcuts? Then you'll love this fast way to launch any of your **Taskbar** icons. Skipping the **Start** button, count off each icon in your **Taskbar**, left to right. Now press the **WIN** key plus an icon's corresponding number.

Make the Notification Area suit your needs

A great enhancement in Windows 7 is the ability to customize the **Notification Area**. This is, remember, the small section to the right of the **Taskbar** that houses special system icons. They alert you to changes, events, and updates.

To choose which icons are displayed and which are hidden, click on the small up arrow on the far right end of the **Taskbar**.

A small window will appear with perhaps one or two icons on top and the word **Customize** below. Any icons you see in this window are the ones that are hidden, meaning they do not appear in the **Notification Area**.

Click on **Customize** and a dialog box will open up. Here you can select whether or not you want to see an icon and its notifications. When you're through, be sure to click on **OK** to save your choices.

A quick way to simply change an icon from visible to hidden is to click on it and drag it up slightly. The same small window appears, and you can drop the icon into its top portion. You can also drag an icon out of this window and into the **Notification Area** to make it visible.

Choose to hide or show your notifications by making selections in this area of the Control Panel

Read notifications at your leisure

Every once in a while, your computer needs to tell you something. Often this comes in the form of a notification message. These little dialog boxes, attached to the **Notification Area** of your **Taskbar**, can look like cartoon text bubbles, but the information they are passing on is no laughing matter. Sometimes you need to act on a message immediately — install an update or repair a network error, for instance.

The problem is, by default, these messages appear for only about five seconds then disappear. It can be tricky to read and act on a message in that short amount of time. If you'd like a little more flexibility, adjust your settings like this:

1. Click on the **Start** button.

2. Select **All Programs > Accessories > Ease of Access > Ease of Access Center**.

3. Inside this window, click on the option **Make it easier to focus on tasks**.

4. Scroll down until you see the entry **Adjust time limits and flashing visuals**.

5. Click on the drop-down menu underneath **How long should Windows notification dialog boxes stay open**, which is probably set to **5.0 seconds**.

6. Now you can choose a longer notification time, up to five minutes.

Let Sticky Notes help you remember

Who doesn't need a handy way to jot down telephone numbers, Web addresses, or shopping lists? But all those tiny scraps of paper floating around your desk are so 20th century. Step into the future with Windows 7 virtual Sticky Notes. Here's how to get this little utility up and running.

1. Click on the **Start** button.

2. Type "Sticky Notes" into the **Search** field.

3. Click on **Sticky Notes** under the **Programs** heading.

The Sticky Notes icon is now in your **Taskbar** and a new empty note has appeared on your desktop. If this looks like something you'll use frequently, go ahead and pin the icon to your **Taskbar** by right-clicking it and selecting that option. Now you can launch this program as soon as you boot up.

Play around with the note on your desktop. Type an important reminder to yourself. Drag it to a different location. Practice copying and pasting text into your note or from your note to another program. Right-click it to change its color. Resize it by dragging the lower-left or lower-right corner.

Here are some handy keyboard shortcuts to help you format your note text. Select the text you want to change, then press the key combinations.

Bold	Ctrl + B
Italic	Ctrl + I
Underlined	Ctrl + U
Strikethrough	Ctrl + T
Larger font	Ctrl + Shift + >
Smaller font	Ctrl + Shift + <

You can also cycle through different list formats by selecting text then holding **Ctrl + Shift** and pressing the **L** key repeatedly.

Best of all, the next time you start your computer, your note will be sitting on your desktop waiting for you.

A CLOSER LOOK

You may notice your Sticky Notes don't have a minimize button as most windows do. But it's easy to remove all your open notes from the desktop by double-clicking the Sticky Notes program button in your **Taskbar**. Double-click again to return them to your desktop.

Get going with Gadgets

Gadgets are mini-programs that put information and entertaining options on your desktop. They aren't new to Windows 7, but they are improved.

If you used these mini-programs in Vista, you'll recall they could only appear in a specific area of your desktop called the **Sidebar**. Windows 7 allows you to place them wherever you like.

Start out by right-clicking anywhere on your desktop, and click on **Gadgets.** The **Gadget Gallery** window will open and from here, you can choose to drag a clock, calendar, game, or other Gadget to your desktop. Hover over it to see ways to customize it or remove it.

Top Windows Logo key shortcuts

You don't need your mouse to move around after all. Just keep this list of keyboard shortcuts handy. Every Windows user should know them.

WIN + D	Minimize all windows and show the desktop
WIN + E	Launch Explorer with Computer as the focus
WIN + F	Launch a search window
WIN + L	Lock the desktop
WIN + M	Minimize the current window
WIN + T	Cycle through Taskbar opening Aero Peek for each running item

CUSTOMIZE YOUR DISPLAY

Design your own desktop

Redecorating your computer is a whole lot easier than redecorating your house. Everything you see on your screen is part of a theme — a collection of colors, images, and styles that create an overall look in Windows 7.

Think of yourself as an interior decorator, picking a paint color, wallpaper, furniture, rugs, and art that give a room a cohesive look. You can do the same thing in Windows, but faster and for a lot less money.

Change everything from one location. Simply right-click your desktop and choose **Personalize** from the short-cut menu. Here, you have three main choices.

- Choose one of the themes that came with your computer, then personalize it with small changes.

- Go online and download a new theme from **Themes** or **Personalization Gallery** on Microsoft's website.

- Create a brand-new theme using your own photos as wallpaper, and design a look all your own.

To select one of the themes already on your computer, simply click on one of the images under **Aero Themes**. The wallpaper on your desktop will change instantly, so you can decide then and there if you like it.

Tweak your chosen theme to personalize it a bit. Click on one of the icons along the bottom of the **Personalization** window, such as **Window Color**. Here you can change the border color of your windows. Click on **Advanced appearance settings** beneath these color choices to make even more adjustments.

Return to the main **Personalization** window by clicking on either the left-pointing arrow in the window's upper-left corner, or on the word **Personalization** in the window's address line at the top. Have fun clicking on the rest of the icons at the bottom of this window to tweak the **Desktop background**, **Sounds**, and **Screen saver**.

Remember to save your changes when you finish. The theme you've personalized will show up as **Unsaved theme** under the heading **My Themes**. Just click on **Save theme** to the right of this icon and give it a name.

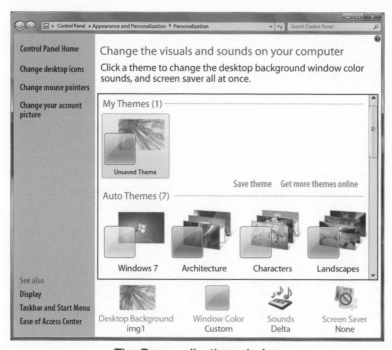

The Personalization window

Unearth amazing hidden themes

Have you ever wanted to travel to Australia or South Africa? Now you can, without leaving home, with exotic themes hidden in your computer. You won't see these in your list of choices. Instead, you'll need to do a little digging.

1. Click once in the **Address bar** of the **Personalization** window to highlight the current address. Then type "C:\windows\globalization\mct" in its place and press the **Enter** key.

2. Several folders will appear in the window, with endings like **AU**, **CA**, and **ZA**. Double-click one to open it.

3. Double-click the **Theme** folder, then double-click again on the Theme file inside.

The next time you open the **Personalization** window, you'll see the new theme under **My Themes**.

BRIGHT IDEA

Downloading files from a website can be risky business, since some carry viruses. But there's one guaranteed-safe place to get new themes for your computer — the Microsoft website.

Microsoft offers more than a dozen eye-catching themes for free at *http://windows.microsoft.com/en-US/windows/themes*. Simply click on the **Download** link below one, then choose **Open** in the dialog box that appears. The new theme will show up under **My Themes** in the **Personalization** window.

Make items on your screen easier to see

Windows 7 likes to show off its fancy new visual effects, but they can get distracting — especially if you have vision problems. Here's how to cut the visual clutter.

- Press the Windows key and the U key simultaneously. Click on **Make the computer easier to see** in the window that appears. Scroll to the bottom of the next window and click on the check box beside **Turn off all unnecessary animations (when possible)**.

- Make icons super-easy to see on your desktop by using a basic, black background. Click on the check box next to **Remove background images (where available)** in the same window as above. Click on the **Apply** button to see your new desktop. If you like it, click on **OK** to keep it that way.

BRIGHT IDEA

Fancy wallpaper is all well and good, but a busy background pattern can make it hard to spot the icons on your desktop. Go easy on your eyes by choosing a solid-colored background for your desktop.

In the **Desktop Background** window, click on the drop-down menu next to **Picture location** and select **Solid Colors**. Simply click on the color you like, then on the **Save changes** button at the bottom.

Liven up your computer with custom slideshows

Do more than change your desktop wallpaper. Create a slideshow to keep things interesting. You can even use your own photos.

Test drive an existing slideshow. First, try turning a Windows theme into a slideshow. Right-click the desktop and select **Personalize** from the shortcut menu. Choose a theme from **My Themes** or **Aero Themes**, then click on the **Desktop Background** icon at the bottom. The next screen will show you all the images that are part of this theme.

Windows assumes you want them all in your slideshow. You can tell it which ones to leave out by removing the check mark next to those images.

Create one from your photos. Skip the canned themes altogether. In the same **Desktop Background** window, click on the button next to **Picture location**. Choose **Pictures Library** from the drop-down list. This shows every image in your photo library. Don't see the ones you want? Click on the **Browse** button and poke around your hard drive to find the right folder.

Create a custom slideshow in the Desktop Backgrounds window

Set the slideshow to cycle through all of your photos, or pick only a handful to include. If you have loads of photos and only want a few, click on the **Clear all** button to remove all the check marks. Place your mouse pointer on the photos you want to keep and click on the check box that appears next to each. Once you have your slideshow set:

- decide how often you want the wallpaper to change. Click on the drop-down menu under **Change picture every** to select an interval.

- click on the check box next to **Shuffle** if you'd like them to appear in random order.

- choose how you want the images to look on screen under **Picture position**.

- click on **Save changes** to see your new slideshow in action.

Make small type easy to read

Forget about blocky, hard-to-read type. ClearType can make the letters and words on your screen as sharp and smooth-looking as in any book. This little program smoothes the edges of letters on the screen, making them easier to read. Adjust ClearType until it looks best to your eyes.

1. Click on the **Start** button and type "clear" into the **Start Menu** search box. Click on **Adjust ClearType text** in the results that appear.

2. Place a check mark in the box beside **Turn on ClearType**, if there isn't one already. Then click on the **Next** button in the bottom right corner.

3. Walk through the prompts, answering the questions about which groups of words are easiest to read. This subtly tweaks ClearType to suit your eyes.

Swap beeps and dings for more pleasing sound

Silence those annoying computer sounds or switch them to something more pleasant. Click on the **Sounds** icon at the bottom of the **Personalization** window, then click on the **Sounds** tab in the dialog box that opens.

To turn off all the computer's alert sounds, click on the drop-down menu beneath **Sound Scheme** and choose **No Sounds**. Or choose a different set of sounds that's easier on your ears by choosing another scheme from the list. Next, make a selection from the **Program Events** list and click on the **Test** button to see what the alert sounds like in the new scheme.

Maybe you don't mind the other dings and beeps, but you can't stand the noise Windows makes when starting. In that case, turn off just the startup sound. Remove the check mark beside **Play Windows Startup sound** by clicking on the box. Satisfied? Click on the **OK** button to put your changes in effect.

Amp up the fun-factor with screen savers

Screen savers were once a must-have to protect your monitor. Images on your screen could get permanently burned into the surface of big, bulky cathode-ray tube (CRT) monitors. That's not the case with the newer flat-panel, liquid crystal display (LCD) monitors.

Still, plenty of people love screen savers for the sheer fun of them. Here's how to set up yours.

Right-click the desktop and choose **Personalize** from the shortcut menu. Click on the **Screen Saver** icon at the bottom of the window to open the **Screen Saver Settings** dialog box. Pick an image from the drop-down list underneath the words **Screen saver**. Next, click on the arrows by the **Wait** box to change how long the computer waits before turning on the screen saver.

Some screen savers have lots of settings to play with. For instance, choose the **Photos** option, then click on the **Settings** button to the right. Here, you can:

- click on **Browse** to find a folder of photos to use as your screen saver.

- decide how long you want them to stay on screen with **Slide show speed**.

- have them appear in random order by clicking on the **Shuffle pictures** box.

- get even more guidance by clicking on **How do I customize my screen saver?**

The options you see under **Settings** change with each screen saver. Click on the **Preview** button in the main dialog box to get a sneak peak at how it will look, then press the **Esc** key to return to the screen. When you're satisfied, simply click on the **OK** button at the bottom.

CAUTION

You aren't limited to the screen savers that come with Windows 7, but beware where you get others. Plenty are available online for free, but hackers love to use them as a vehicle for viruses. Even innocent screen savers that aren't infected can slow down or freeze up your computer.

Scan everything you download with an anti-virus program before installing it. Watch for changes in your computer's performance or behavior after you begin using a new screen saver. Learn how to download safely from the Internet in the *Safe & secure surfing* chapter.

EASY ACCESS
Fine-tune Windows settings

Enlarge fonts and icons for squint-free reading

Lowering your screen's resolution used to be the only way to make text and other items bigger, but it had drawbacks. The lower the resolution, the bigger things got — but the more jagged and blurry letters and words became. That could actually make things harder to read.

Windows 7 fixes the problem with a new feature called scaling. This handy tool enlarges the words and images on your screen while keeping them sharp, clear, and very readable.

1. Right-click your desktop and choose **Screen resolution** to open a new window.

2. Click on the drop-down list next to **Resolution**. Move the sliding bar by dragging it with your mouse until it rests beside the number that says **(recommended)**.

3. Next, click on **Make text and other items larger or smaller** in the same window.

4. In the **Display** window that opens, click on the button beside **Medium - 125%** or **Larger - 150%**. Then click on **Apply**.

You'll see a message from Windows that **You must log off your computer to apply these changes**. You can choose to **Log off now**, or wait until you **Log off later** to make these changes.

If the text or images on your screen still aren't large enough for you to read comfortably, go back in and create a custom setting. Follow the instructions to reopen the **Display** window. This time click on **Set custom text size (DPI)** on the left.

This opens a **Custom DPI Setting** dialog box. Grab any part of the ruler with your mouse and drag it to the right. You can blow up the items on-screen as much as 500 percent. Click on the box beside **Use Windows XP style DPI scaling** to put a check in it. This should prevent older programs from looking blurry in the new scale. Log off, then back on, for your changes to take effect.

CAUTION

Scaling works great, most of the time. Nearly all programs made by Microsoft, like MS Word, look fine when scaled. Older, non-Microsoft programs may balk, however. Turn off scaling just inside these programs if the text in them looks blurry.

Right-click the program's icon on the **Start Menu** and select **Properties** from the shortcut menu. Click on the **Compatibility** tab. Under **Settings**, place a check mark in the box beside **Disable display scaling on high DPI settings**, and then click on **Apply**.

Blindness no barrier with Windows Narrator

Nowadays, you don't even need to see the screen to know what's on it. Windows Narrator will read aloud the text in any window or dialog box, which makes it perfect for people with poor vision.

To give it a whirl, press the **Windows (WIN)** key and the letter **U** on your keyboard simultaneously. This opens the **Ease of Access Center**. Click on **Start Narrator** beneath the heading **Quick access to common tools**. The **Microsoft Narrator** dialog box will open, and Windows will begin reading the text inside of it.

From here, you can change all sorts of Narrator settings, from how fast the voice talks to whether the program turns on when your computer does. To have Narrator:

- speak the names of keys aloud as you press them on the keyboard, place a check mark in the box beside **Echo User's Keystrokes**.

- read computer error messages and alerts when they pop up, place a check mark in the box beside **Announce System Messages**.

- turn on automatically when you start your computer, click on the link **Control whether Narrator starts when I log on**. Place a check mark in the box beside **Turn on Narrator** in the window that opens and click on **Apply**.

- slow down or speed up its speech, click on the **Voice Settings** button at the bottom of the **Microsoft Narrator** dialog box. Then click on the drop-down list beside **Set Speed**. Choose a higher number for faster speech or a lower one for slower. You can also control Narrator's volume and pitch from here. Click on **OK** when finished.

Learn Narrator's handy keyboard shortcuts for the best experience. You can have them read aloud by clicking on the **Quick Help** button at the bottom of the **Microsoft Narrator** dialog box. Or you can print a list of them by pressing the **F1** key on your keyboard.

The Narrator program has a few quirks. It may mispronounce words occasionally, and it can take a few moments to translate all the text in a window into speech. But it's a breakthrough for people who want to use a computer without relying on their eyes.

Choose contrasting colors for better vision

The soothing colors that decorate your windows, desktop, and icons can also make them hard to see. Put an end to that problem by dumping the pretty colors for a high-contrast look.

Right-click the desktop and choose **Personalize** in the shortcut menu. Note the attractive, color-coordinated themes in the center of the window that opens. Scroll past these until you reach the category labeled **Basic and High Contrast Themes**.

They're not as pretty, which is probably why Microsoft put them at the bottom, but they can make everything on-screen easier to read. Select one, and the computer screen will instantly change to show you how it will look. When you find a theme your eyes can live with, simply close the window.

Do you share this computer with someone who hates the high-contrast look? The two of you can switch back and forth between the old and new themes by pressing the left **Shift**, left **Alt**, and **Print Scrn** keys simultaneously. Choose **Yes** when Windows asks you to confirm the switch.

BRIGHT IDEA

Does your mouse have a scroll wheel in the middle of its back? If so, you can blow up all the icons in a window or on the desktop without a single click. Simply hold down the **Ctrl** key on your keyboard and roll your wheel forward, toward the top of the mouse. The icons will get larger the more you scroll.

Pick a pointer that's easy to find

Trying to find that pesky mouse pointer can leave you feeling like Tom chasing Jerry. Make it easier to spot with a few quick clicks.

1. Right-click an empty spot on your desktop and select **Personalize** from the shortcut menu.

2. Click on **Change mouse pointers** on the left side of the window to open the **Mouse Properties** dialog box.

3. Under the **Pointers** tab, click on the **Scheme** drop-down list and select one labeled **large** or **extra large**, such as **Windows Aero (extra large)**.

You can see how the new pointer will look in the preview to the right. When you finish, click on **OK** to save your changes.

Adjust sound for special hearing needs

Sure, you can crank up the volume if you're hard of hearing. But you can also make one speaker or earphone louder than the other to compensate for hearing loss in just one ear.

Click on the **Volume** icon in the Notification Area of your Taskbar. You can increase the volume of all your computer's sounds by dragging the slider up, but that's just the beginning.

1. Click on the **Speakers** icon at the top of the scale to open the **Speakers Properties** dialog box.

Volume control

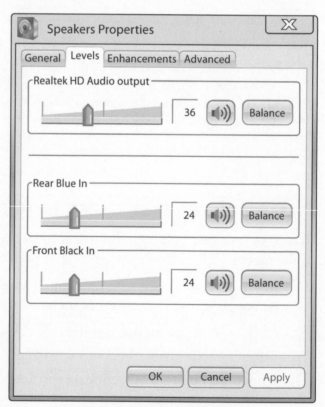

Speakers Properties dialog box

2. Click on the **Levels** tab. The top volume control (in this case, **Realtek HD Audio output)** should represent your computer speakers or headphones. Click on the **Balance** button beside it.

3. The tiny dialog box that opens shows separate volume controls for the left **(L)** and right **(R)** speaker or earphone. Drag one slider to the right to boost the volume on that side, then click on **OK**.

Finger-friendly keyboard shortcuts

Regular keyboard shortcuts can save you a lot of mousing, too. Combinations like **WIN + U** to open the **Ease of Access Center** or **Alt + Tab** to flip between windows can skip many clicks. But pressing these key combos simultaneously is easier said than done, especially if your hands are stiff. That's where Sticky Keys come in. Turn it on, and you can press the keys one at a time instead of all at once.

Press **WIN + U** to open the **Ease of Access Center**, then click on **Make the keyboard easier to use**. In the next window, place a check mark in the box beside **Turn on Sticky Keys**. Click on **Set up Sticky Keys** and place a check mark in the box next to **Turn on Sticky Keys when SHIFT is pressed five times**. Now pressing the **Shift** key five times in a row will turn this feature on and off. Click on **Apply** and close the window.

Ditch the mouse for good

Mouse Keys are back and better than ever in Windows 7. This tiny tool virtually eliminates the need for a mouse. Instead, you move the pointer across your screen with a numeric keypad. That's the separate set of number keys on the right side of most keyboards. First, turn on Num Lock by pressing the **Num Lock** key. Then get ready to go mouse-free.

Open the **Ease of Access Center** by pressing **WIN + U** on your keyboard. Click on **Make the mouse easier to use** and look for the heading **Control the mouse with the keyboard**. Click on the box beside **Turn on Mouse Keys** to place a check mark in it, then on **Apply**. Use this cheat sheet to control your mouse.

Key	Pointer action
1	move down and left diagonally
2	move straight down
3	move down and right diagonally
4	move left
5	click on an item
6	move right
7	move up and left diagonally
8	move up
9	move up and right diagonally
+	double-click an item
/	select an item, the same as pressing the left mouse button
-	right-click
Insert	hold down an item to drag it
Delete	release an item after dragging

Under the check box that turns on Mouse Keys lies another link, **Set up Mouse Keys**. Click on this to fine-tune the feature. Maybe the pointer moves too slowly for your taste. No problem. Click on the box beside **Hold down CTRL to speed up and SHIFT to slow down**. Now you can adjust the pointer speed by pressing those keys.

5 minutes to easier computing

You could spend all day poking around the Ease of Access Center, trying to make your computer more user-friendly. Why not let Windows do the work for you in just five minutes?

Press **WIN + U** on your keyboard to open the **Ease of Access Center**. Look for a small light bulb, and click on **Get recommendations to make your computer easier to use** next to it. This opens a wizard that asks you a series of questions about your eyesight, hands, hearing, speech, and mental ability. Place a check mark next to the statements that apply to you, then click the **Next** button.

At the end of the questioning, the wizard will suggest features to make the computer easier for you to use. There you can turn on features like Narrator and Sticky Keys, as well as change the contrast on your screen or the size of the mouse pointer. When you've made your choices, click on **OK** or **Apply**.

Free program lets you talk to computer

Kiss your keyboard goodbye and kick your mouse to the curb. Speech Recognition, a new feature of Windows 7, lets you control the computer with your voice, as well as dictate documents and emails.

It's not as fancy as programs like Dragon NaturallySpeaking, but unlike them it's free. You will need a microphone, however. Some computers have one built-in, but for the best results get a headset-style microphone.

Open the **Start Menu** and click on **Control Panel**. Select **Ease of Access**, then **Speech Recognition**. This opens the **Speech Recognition** window, where you can set up an external microphone and learn to use this powerful program.

- First, plug in your external microphone, if you have one, then click on **Set up microphone**.

- Once your mike is working, practice using it to control the computer. Click on **Take Speech Tutorial** and follow the prompts.

- Teach the computer to better understand your words, so you get the most accurate results during dictation. Click on **Train your computer to better understand you.**

- Finally, click on **Open the Speech Reference Card** to learn **Common commands in Speech Recognition**. Click on topics like **Dictation** to open them, then click on the printer icon at the top to print the list of commands.

Turn on the program and get talking. Click on **Start Speech Recognition**. The wizard will walk you through setting up and fine-tuning the program.

Click, drag, and drop with just your voice

With Speech Recognition, you can click on any icon by saying its name — but what if you don't know it? That's easy. Simply say "Show numbers," and a number will appear on every clickable object. Speak the number you want to click and watch it turn green. If it's the right one, say "OK." This feature also works on Web pages.

Mousegrid works much the same way. Use it to drag items with your voice.

1. Say "mousegrid," and a numbered grid will cover your screen. Speak the number of the section where item is, and the grid will zoom in, with more numbers.

2. Keep picking numbers and zooming the grid until you can grab only what you want to drag.

3. Say "mark" to grab the item, and a new grid will appear. This time, zoom in on the place you want to drop it. When you reach it, speak that square's number, then say "click."

No-click way to switch windows

No more clicking to move between windows. Do it just by pointing your mouse. Press **WIN + U** to open the **Ease of Access Center**, then click on the link **Make the mouse easier to use**. In the next window, click on the box beside **Activate a window by hovering**

over it with the mouse to place a check mark in it. Now when you hover the mouse pointer over any window, it will immediately jump to the front.

You can open the menus within the **Start Menu** by hovering, too, saving you a few more mouse clicks. Right-click the **Start** button and choose **Properties** from the shortcut menu. Then click on the **Customize** button under the **Start Menu** tab. Scroll through the list of options and place a check in the box next to **Open submenus when I pause on them with the mouse pointer**.

BRIGHT IDEA

Are you tired of searching for the **OK** or **Apply** button in a box? Turn on the Snap To feature, and your mouse will automatically jump to the default button.

Right-click the desktop and choose **Personalize** from the shortcut menu. Click on **Change mouse pointers** on the left side of the **Personalization** window to open the **Mouse Properties** dialog box. Here, click on the **Pointer Options** tab. Under the heading **Snap To**, place a check mark in the box beside **Automatically move pointer to the default button in a dialog box**. Then click on **Apply**.

Tweak mouse to suit your needs

Make common moves like dragging and double-clicking a whole lot easier with a few tweaks to your mouse.

Right-click on the desktop and select **Personalize** from the shortcut menu. Then click on **Change mouse pointers** on the left side of the **Personalization** window to open the **Mouse Properties** dialog box.

Turn on ClickLock. Simplify the finicky art of dragging and dropping with this handy feature. Under the **Buttons** tab, place a check mark next to **Turn on ClickLock**, and click on **Apply**.

Place your pointer on an item and press the mouse's left-click button for one to two seconds. This grabs the item and locks the button in place. Just move your pointer to the new location and click again to drop it.

Give your finger a break. Double-clicking isn't easy, especially if you suffer from arthritis. Get the computer to recognize a slower double-click.

Under the **Buttons** tab, look for the heading **Double-click speed**. Drag the slider to the left, then try double-clicking on the folder to the right. Keep adjusting the slider until you can comfortably double-click and open the folder.

Move the mouse farther, faster. Do you have a big computer screen, or a tiny mousepad? Then you're probably tired of picking up the mouse and putting it down to move your pointer across the screen.

Make it dart farther with each nudge. In the same **Mouse Properties** dialog box, click on the **Pointer Options** tab. Move the slider under **Select a pointer speed** to the right. Click on **Apply** to put the change in effect.

FILE & FOLDER FUNDAMENTALS

Tidy up with new tools

Keep your files more organized than ever with Libraries, a new feature in Windows 7. Libraries house links to your files. The real files continue to live elsewhere on your computer, but Libraries give you a way to view them all in one place.

Take photos, for instance. You may have photos in lots of different folders scattered around your computer, but they all appear together in your Pictures Library. This lets you open them from one place, instead of tracking them down in their separate folders.

To see your Libraries, click on the icon on your Taskbar that looks like a stack of file folders. Windows 7 starts you out with four Libraries — **Documents**, **Music**, **Pictures**, and **Videos**. You can jump to them from any window by clicking on them in the Navigation pane to the left.

Begin by opening the **Pictures Library**. In the main window, you'll see most, if not all, of the photos stored on your computer, regardless of where they actually live on the hard drive.

Find the source. You can also see which folders a Library is pulling from. Click on the **locations** link beneath the heading **Pictures**

Library. By default, it includes photos from the **My Pictures** and **Public Pictures** folders.

Add another. But what if you have more pictures elsewhere? Tell the computer to include additional folders in that Library. Right-click on the folder you want to add, hover over **Include in library**, and pick a Library from the list that appears.

Delete a few. You can remove folders from a Library, too. Open the relevant Library and click on **Includes: 2 locations** (yours may have more) beneath the Library's name. In the **Library Locations** box that opens, click once on a folder, then click on **Remove**.

Sort to suit you. Click on the button next to **Arrange by** to group the files in your library differently. It's especially handy with photos and music.

In the **Pictures** library, for instance, you can group them by month or day. The **Music** library lets you arrange by album, artist, or genre.

A CLOSER LOOK

You can add folders from an external hard drive and or USB flash drive to Libraries, too. Plug the device into your computer. If it appears underneath **OS (C:)** in the Navigation pane, you can add its folders to a Library.

Add its folders to a Library the same as any other folder. Keep in mind, the items inside it will only show up in the Library when the device is plugged into your computer.

Tweak Libraries to meet your needs

You're not stuck with the Libraries that come with Windows 7. You can create your own, organizing your documents, photos, and music any way you want.

Turn an existing folder into a Library. Right-click the folder to open the shortcut menu. Hover your pointer over the option **Include in library**, then select **Create a new library** from the pop-up menu that appears.

Build a new one from scratch. You don't have to start with an existing folder. Rather than clicking on a specific Library, right-click the main heading, **Libraries**, in the Navigation pane on the left. Hover over **New** in the shortcut menu, then choose **Library**.

Once you've created your Library, tell Windows what you plan to put in it. This controls the options you see when you click on **Arrange by**. Right-click the Library's folder in the Navigation pane and select **Properties** to open the **Properties** dialog box. Click on the button beneath **Optimize this library for** and choose the type of files you plan to keep here.

You can also delete Libraries that you don't use, a good idea if things get cluttered. In the Navigation pane, right-click a Library and choose **Delete** from the shortcut menu. A dialog box will appear, asking if you're sure you want to do this. Click on **Yes**.

Did you accidentally delete one of the built-in Libraries, like **Pictures**? You can bring it back in a snap. Right click the main **Libraries** heading in the Navigation pane and select **Restore default Libraries**.

CAUTION

Don't confuse Library folders with the folders living on your hard drive. Both show up in the Navigation pane. Library folders, however, don't house any real files. They house shortcuts to files.

The real files actually live in your hard drive folders. Click on the heading **Computer** in the Navigation pane. Its contents will appear in the main window. Double-click the **OS (C:)** icon then the **Users** folder inside. Look for a folder labeled with the name you use to log in to your computer. All of your items live inside.

Make windows work for you

Learn your way around folder windows, and you'll find files faster and with less frustration. Microsoft has hidden a few features that can help.

Rearrange the view. Change what you see when you open a folder window. Click on the downward-pointing arrow beside the **View Options** button to see the many ways you can view your files.

Some show you just the icons. Others, like **Details** and **Content**, give you information about those files at a glance.

If your mouse has a scroll wheel, there's an even easier way to change the view. Hold down the **Ctrl** key on your keyboard while rolling the wheel forward or backward to cycle through all the available views.

Leave a trail. The folder tree on the left side of the window, in the Navigation Pane, hasn't changed much in Windows 7 — with one exception.

In past operating systems, like Vista, the folder tree would expand as you opened folders in the main window. That won't happen now unless you tell it to.

- Click on the **Organize** button in the window's upper-left corner and choose **Folder and search options** from the drop-down list.

- Click on the **General** tab of the dialog box that opens. In the Navigation pane section, place a check mark in the box beside **Automatically expand to current folder**.

Get a sneak peak. The Preview pane may be the best way to look through photos, music, and documents. It actually shows what's inside a file without you opening it.

That's perfect, for instance, when you know what a photo looks like but can't remember what you named it.

To turn it on, click on the **Hide/Show the Preview pane** button in the window's upper right corner. Now when you single-click on a file, a picture of its contents will appear on the right.

You can even play music using the Preview pane without opening Windows Media Player. Select an album or song file, then click on the **Play** button in the Preview pane.

Bring back menus. You may notice at some point that the Menu bar is missing in folder windows. No more **File**, **Edit**, **View**, and **Tool** options. Or are there?

They still exist. They're just hidden. Bring them back by clicking on the **Organize** button, pointing at **Layout** in the drop-down list, and clicking on Menu bar. The same instructions will also turn menus off again. To show them temporarily, press **F10** on your keyboard.

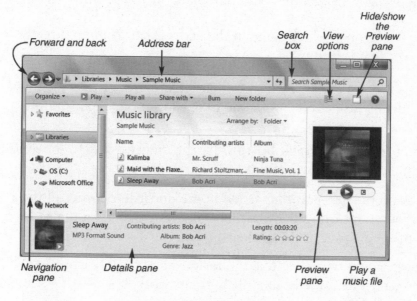

Windows Explorer window

3 quick tricks to move between folders

Moving among folders is easier than ever. Here are three quick ways to jump from place to place in a folder window.

Use the Navigation pane. The folder tree on the left side of the window lets you hop from one folder to another with a couple of clicks.

- Click on the arrow next to an item to see what's stored inside it.

- Click on the icon or name itself to see the folder's contents in the main window.

Drive with the Address bar. The Address bar at the top of a window shows you where you're looking in your computer.

- Click on a folder name in the address bar to jump directly to that location.

- Click on the arrow next to that folder's name to see the items living inside it. Choose one to open it in the main window.

Don't forget the Back button. It's the quickest way to move back and forth between windows.

Click on the left-pointing arrow in the upper left corner of the window to return to your last location. Then click on the right-facing arrow to leap forward again.

These arrows work just like the forward and back buttons in Web browsers. The same keyboard shortcuts work, too — **Alt + <** to go back, and **Alt + >** to move forward.

Quick access to Favorite places

The Favorites section of your Navigation pane may become your new favorite place. Do you find yourself visiting the same folders again and again?

Add them to your Favorites list so you can open them with one click from any window, without all the digging.

Hover over **Favorites**, then click on the arrow that appears to its left to open the list. You'll see that Windows has already put a few places here for you, like the **Desktop** and your **Downloads** folder. You can add more.

- Find the folder you want, either in the Navigation pane or in the main window. Grab its icon, then drag and drop it directly onto the word **Favorites**. This doesn't move the folder. It simply creates a shortcut to it.

- If you have trouble with dragging and dropping, open that folder in the main window. Right-click **Favorites** and choose **Add current location to Favorites**.

- Take an item off the **Favorites** list by right-clicking the item and choosing **Remove** from the shortcut menu. This doesn't delete the actual folder, only the shortcut leading to it.

Fast ways to find anything on your computer

All of the folders-within-folders that Windows uses to keep you organized can backfire when you can't remember where you stored something. Fortunately, finding a lost file is easier than ever in Windows 7, thanks to the handy Search feature.

Search in any window using the **Search box** in the upper-right corner. Or search directly from the **Start Menu** with the **Search programs**

and files box at the bottom. You can search based on all kinds of information. Try typing:

- part of the item's name.

- a word or phrase that appears inside a document or other item. Put quotation marks around phrases.

- the date you created the item, or the last date you saved changes to it.

Windows begins looking as soon as you start typing. You don't even have to press the Enter key. And don't worry about capitalization. It doesn't count.

Get started. Searches from the **Start Menu** search the entire computer, including files, folders, programs, email messages, address book entries, photos, Internet bookmarks, documents, and even calendar appointments.

Then it groups your results into categories, like **Documents**, **Programs**, or **Pictures**. Click on a category's name to see all the results in that group.

Start Menu searches only return the 15 most likely matches. If you don't spot what you're looking for, click on **See more results** at the bottom.

Throw open a window. Searches done in a window search only the files and folders in that window. Aren't sure where to start? Try looking in one of the main folders, like **My Documents**, or one of the Libraries, to cast your net a little wider.

Open the window's Preview pane for a glimpse at the contents of each file you select. It makes finding the right item even simpler.

Narrow searches even further

Sort through your search results in a snap with filters. Run your search using the **Search box** in any window. Then click on the **View options** button and choose **Details**. Several columns will appear with information about each file.

Hover your pointer over one of the columns and click on the drop-down arrow that appears beside it. This opens a set of filters you can apply to your search results.

Click on a check box to filter your results. Windows hides all the search results that don't meet the filter criteria, making it much easier to spot the item you want.

Say you want to find an email you started two days ago. Searching on the word "email" could return dozens of results. No sweat. Click on the drop-down arrow beside **Date Modified**, and choose the filter **Earlier this week**. Now you'll only see emails you wrote in the last seven days. To turn off the filter, remove the check mark.

Sort by date or date range

Tweak your filters even more by changing the columns you see in the **Details** view. Right-click one of the columns to see more options.

Click to put a check mark in the box next to any column you want to add. Still not satisfied? Click on **More...** at the bottom of this list to see 200 more columns. Each comes with its own filter options.

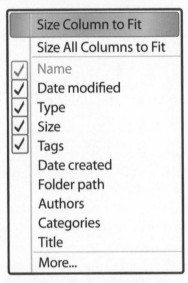

| Size Column to Fit |
| Size All Columns to Fit |
| ✓ Name |
| ✓ Date modified |
| ✓ Type |
| ✓ Size |
| ✓ Tags |
| Date created |
| Folder path |
| Authors |
| Categories |
| Title |
| More... |

Choose more filter options

Look for files stored elsewhere

What makes Windows 7 searches so fast? Indexes. Windows is constantly gathering information about the things stored on your hard drive.

It takes notes when you create or delete files or folders, and it memorizes exactly what's in them. In fact, it started taking notes the first time you powered up your computer.

It stores all this information in an index, which works a lot like the index at the end of a book. When you want to look up a topic in a long book, you don't reread the whole thing. You check the index to find the right page.

When you type a search into Windows 7, it doesn't read every file and folder right then and there. It did that a long time ago, then it added the important details to an index. This time, it merely checks its index and voila — nearly instant results appear.

Windows doesn't index everything on your computer. It skips programs and the software that runs the operating system. Nor can it index things on a CD, DVD, or flash drive.

It can, however, index items on an external hard drive, if you tell it to. Maybe you keep all of your music and photos on an external hard drive to save space on your computer. Add them to the index so you can search through them easily. You can either:

- add the folder you want indexed to one of your Libraries, which are automatically indexed.

- change the Index Options. Open the **Start Menu** and type "index" into the **Search box**. Click on **Indexing Options** in the search results, then click on **Modify**.

From here, you can add and remove folders from the index. Click on the arrows next to locations like **OS (C:)** to expand it, and click on the boxes to place or erase check marks. When you're finished, click on **OK**.

Tag files for easy finding

Tags give you one more way to sort files, group them together, or find them at a later date. Think of them as electronic sticky notes you can slap on a file.

Tags are one of the many bits of information you see in the Details pane of a window. Single-click on a file in the main window and watch the information change in the area below. Drag the top edge of the Details pane with your pointer and pull it up to expand and see even more information.

You can edit a lot of the details you see, like the title, comments, and tags. Hover your pointer just to the right of a category, like **Tags**, and click inside the box that appears. Type the new information then click on **Save**.

Consider adding keywords to the Tags field to help you find files again later. Tag photos from your Florida vacation with keywords like "Florida" or "Disney. When you want to find photos from that trip to send your family, type "Florida" or "Disney" into the **Search box** in any window. You'll pull up all the pictures from that vacation, without needing to dig through Libraries or folders.

To tag lots of files with the same keyword, highlight all the items you want to tag, type the keyword into the **Tag** field of the Details pane, and click on **Save**. Now each of those items will carry the same keyword. Use the sortable columns in the **Details** view to sort files by the tags you apply or any other information you add in the Details pane.

Save searches you do often

Do you often perform the same search? Then save it, and save yourself the hassle of setting it up each time.

Perform the search in a window, not from the Start Menu, and apply all your normal filters. Once you get your results, click on the **Save search** button below the Address bar. Give this search a name, then decide where to store it. Windows will suggest saving it in the **Saved Searches** folder, but you can put it anywhere — even on your desktop.

In fact, you could create a desktop folder for all of your searches, and open it when needed with a quick double-click. Or use the **Saved Searches** folder and pin it to your **Favorites** list.

Move and copy like a pro

At some point, you'll need to move or copy files from one place to another. Windows gives you just the tools you need to make it painless.

Drag and drop. Use the Navigation pane to rearrange your files and folders. Find the file or folder you want to move in the main window. Then expand the folder tree in the Navigation pane until you see the place you want to put it.

Drag the item from the main window and drop it on the destination folder in the Navigation pane. To copy an item instead of moving it, hold down the **Shift** key while dragging.

Stick with the keyboard. Of course, you can skip the drag-and-drop hassle altogether. Single-click on an item, then press either **Ctrl + X** on your keyboard to move it or **Ctrl + C** to copy it. Mouse your way to the new destination. When you get there, press **Ctrl + V** to place the item in its new home.

BRIGHT IDEA

Change the names of files, folders, and other icons in a flash. The usual way works — click once on an icon, wait a moment, then click again — but it takes practice. Here's a simpler solution. Click on the item then press the **F2** key on your keyboard and type the new name. Or right-click the item and choose **Rename** from the shortcut menu.

Super-simple way to select multiple files

Windows 7 hides check boxes everywhere, making it easy to move, copy, or delete lots of items at once. To turn on these check boxes, open a window and click on **Organize**, then on **Folder and search options**. Under the **View** tab, scroll down the list of **Advanced settings** and put a check in the box beside **Use check boxes to select items**. Click on **OK**.

Place a check mark in the box beside each item you want to select, then use the normal commands to copy, move, or delete them.

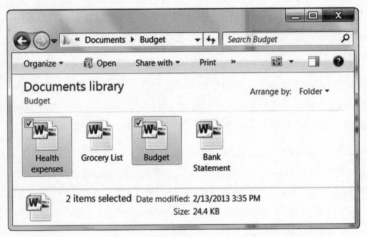

Check boxes make it easy to select multiple files

Cut the hassle of copying

Forget copying and pasting, or even dragging and dropping. Use Send To to quickly create copies of files and folders.

Right-click the file or folder, click on **Send to** in the shortcut menu, and choose where you want to put it. Windows will drop a copy of that item in the location of your choice. Press the **Shift** key when you right-click, and you'll see an even longer list of options under **Send to**.

With this handy command, you can also attach a file or folder to an email using your computer's mail program **(Mail recipient)**, burn something directly to a CD or DVD **(DVD RW Drive)**, and copy your files to a removable drive, like a USB flash drive or an external hard drive.

Foolproof tips to delete files for good

You pressed the **Delete** key and dumped that file or folder. But did you know it's not really gone for good? Yep. It's still there, lurking in the Recycle Bin of your computer.

Windows puts things you delete in the Recycle Bin for awhile, just in case you change your mind or deleted something by mistake. But you can get rid of them for good in two ways.

- Empty the Bin regularly, or even right after you trash something. Right-click the **Recycle Bin** icon on your desktop and choose **Empty Recycle Bin**.

- Tell the computer to skip the **Recycle Bin** altogether. Click on the item you want to delete, then press **Shift + Delete** on your keyboard. Answer **Yes** in the dialog box, and the file or folder will permanently disappear.

A CLOSER LOOK

Tired of the back-talk you get from your Recycle Bin, with its nagging "Are you sure" warnings? Tell it to pipe down by turning them off. Right-click the **Recycle Bin** icon, choose **Properties**, and click on the box beside **Display delete confirmation dialog** to remove the check mark.

Act fast to save deleted files

So you deleted a file by accident. Don't panic. It's not really gone. Deleted files still live on the hard drive for a little while, until the computer stores new information on top of them, a process called overwriting. That's why it's important to rescue your stuff as soon as possible. Take these steps to fix your mistake.

- Press **Ctrl + Z** on your keyboard immediately after you delete it. This will magically undo the last thing you did on the computer, including deleting a file or folder.

- Undo won't work on items you deleted hours or days ago. Look in the Recycle Bin, instead. Double-click the **Recycle Bin** icon on your desktop to open it. Right-click the item you want to rescue and choose **Restore** from the shortcut menu.

Don't see your lost item in the Recycle Bin? Either you emptied the Bin or it emptied itself when it got too full. Never fear. Some free programs on the Internet can still retrieve your files.

Try Recuva, available online at *www.piriform.com*. Plug a flash drive or external hard drive into your computer. Download the program directly to that drive, not to your computer.

Install the program on the same removable drive and run it on your main computer. As long as the deleted file hasn't been over-written, this little program will find it with no problem.

Shrink the Bin to save space

The Recycle Bin empties itself when it gets full, unlike your trash can at home. You decide how full it should be before it begins dumping files. Once it reaches that level, it will permanently delete older items as you put new ones in it.

If your computer has plenty of hard drive space, you can afford to let it get a little fuller before emptying. But if memory is at a premium on your computer, consider keeping the Bin small.

Windows automatically allots 10 percent of your hard drive to the Bin, but you can shrink that amount. Right-click the **Recycle Bin** icon and choose **Properties**. Under Custom size, change the **Maximum size** to a smaller number.

Keep in mind, the less space you give your Bin, the less time you'll have to rescue things you accidentally put there before they get permanently deleted.

CAUTION

You should never delete a file if you didn't create it or download it yourself. You could inadvertently throw away an important program or some tiny bit of information your computer needs to function.

Don't delete something if you don't know what it is. Learn how to safely delete programs you no longer need in *Add speed by removing old programs* in the *Software nuts & bolts* chapter.

WINDOWS SECURITY ESSENTIALS

Decode cryptic security warnings

A tiny white flag on your Taskbar could protect you from nasty viruses and malicious hackers. It's the gateway to Windows' Action Center, the place for managing all the security software and settings that guard your computer.

This flag lives on the right side of the Taskbar in the Notification area. Pay attention. When an X inside a red circle appears on the flag, you'll know your computer has something to tell you. If the message is really important, a small balloon will pop up, too.

Notification Alert flag

Don't ignore these warnings. The flag could be trying to tell you that your firewall isn't working or your anti-virus program is out of date. Problems like these leave your computer open to attack. Fortunately, fixing them is easy. Click on the flag to see the problems Windows wants you to address.

• Click on each problem in the list to open a window where you can fix it.

- If the list is long, click on **Open Action Center** at the bottom to open the main **Action Center** window where you can fix everything at once.

Warnings inside the **Action Center** are color-coded by urgency. Red alerts are the most important, so take care of them right away. Yellow ones are suggestions, which you can handle now or leave for later.

Some alerts deal with the built-in firewall (Windows Firewall), anti-virus (Microsoft Security Essentials), and anti-spyware (Windows Defender) programs that come with Windows 7. Learn how to set up this free security software and keep it up to date in the *Safe & secure surfing* chapter.

CAUTION

Watch out for a new twist on computer scams. Someone calls from out of the blue claiming to work for a big computer company like Dell, Microsoft, Norton, or McAfee. They say they've found a dangerous virus or spyware program on your computer. Luckily, they can remove it. Simply pay them a fee and download a program that lets them access your computer.

Don't believe it. The scam is called "scareware." Hang up the phone and file a complaint with the Federal Trade Commission. Call 1-877-FTC-HELP or visit the website *www.ftccomplaint assistant.gov*.

Thwart attacks with sign-on savvy

Make your computer instantly safer by doing one simple thing — log into your computer using a Standard account. Every computer has an Administrator account, but using it for everyday computing can put your machine at risk.

Logging in as an Administrator gives you complete control over security settings and allows you to install new software. Standard accounts let you change some settings, but not security ones, and it blocks you from installing software.

That's a good thing. If a virus or computer hacker attacks while you are logged in as an Administrator, then it also gains Administrator power. It can infect your entire machine, turn off your security, or install malicious software. That can't happen if you are logged in with a Standard account.

To find out which type of account you usually use, open the **Start Menu** and click on your account's picture at the top. This opens the **User Accounts** window. On the right side, you'll see your account name, and beneath that the words **Administrator** or **Standard user**.

User account picture on Start Menu

If your usual account is a Standard one, you're all set. If not, however, create a new Standard account for everyday use. In the **User Accounts** window, click on the link **Manage another account**. Click on **Create a new account** in the next window. Name the account, click to select **Standard user**, and click on **Create Account**.

When you try to make a change from a Standard account that requires Administrator privileges, the computer will ask you to authenticate yourself by typing in the password for the mighty Administrator account. This small hassle is well worth the added safety.

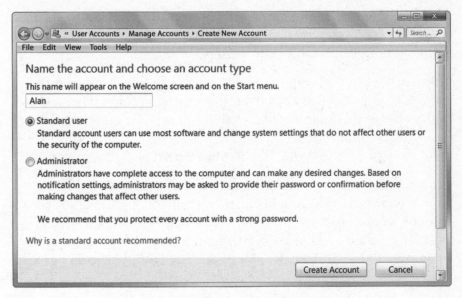

Create new user account

Give guests limited access

Protect your PC from hapless family members who visit for the holidays. Give them a Guest account if they ask to use your computer. This will stop them from changing your settings, accidentally deleting your files, or poking around in your personal folders. Windows 7 comes with a Guest account. You only need to turn it on.

1. Log into your Administrator account. Then open the **Start Menu** and click on your account's picture at the top to open the **User Accounts** window.

2. Click on **Manage another account** and look for the **Guest** account icon in the window that opens.

3. If the words beneath the account read **Guest account is off**, click on the **Guest** icon, then **Turn On** in the next window.

The next time your computer starts up, you'll see the Guest account option on the login screen. You don't have to restart it to let a guest jump on, however. Simply switch users.

Click on the **Start** button, then on the arrow beside the **Shut down** button. Choose **Switch user** from the shortcut menu. This will return you to the login screen, where you or your guest can log into a different account. Once they finish with the computer, ask them to click on the arrow beside **Shut down** and choose **Log off**.

You needn't close any programs in order to change users. Leave your Web pages or documents open. When you log back into your account, your programs and documents will be right where you left them. Be sure to tell your guest not to turn off the computer when they finish. If they do, you'll lose any work you didn't save.

Tighten security to beat bad guys

Keep malicious software from taking over your computer by adjusting your User Account Control (UAC) settings.

UAC alerts you when a program tries to make changes to the computer, for instance by installing software or adjusting your settings. Most of the time, these changes are innocent. But a UAC alert can help you block a nasty virus from installing itself, or a hacker from disabling your security settings. Tweak your alerts through the User Accounts window.

1. Open the **Start Menu** and click on your login picture at the top. Click on **Change User Account Control settings** in the window that opens.

2. Drag the slider on the left up to tighten security or down to loosen it.

3. The pane on the right tells you how the new setting will affect your computer. Experts recommend choosing to **Always notify**, the top-most slider setting, or **Default**, the next step down.

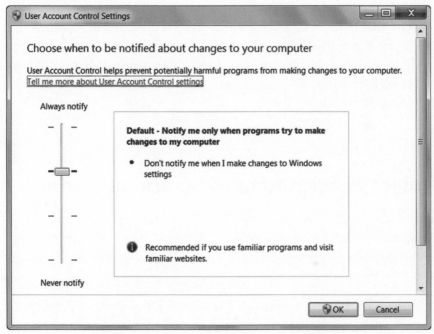

Tighten User Control Account settings

Now when you try to install software or tweak certain settings in your computer, a small UAC box will pop up, asking if you want to allow these changes. If you are the one making the changes or installing the software, click on **Yes**.

But if the box pops up on its own, or if you don't recognize the program trying to make a change, do a little investigating. You may end up clicking on **No**.

Delete old accounts without deleting files

A divorce or a death can be hard enough without having to figure out what to do with someone's electronic belongings. If a life change like this hits you, you can delete a User Account you no longer need and still retain the files that belonged to that person.

Open the **User Accounts** window. Click on **Manage another account**, then click once on the account you want to delete in the window that opens. Choose **Delete the account** in the options that appear on the left. The computer will ask if you want to keep the user's documents, pictures, music, and other folders. If so, click on the **Keep Files** button. These items will be packaged into a folder and placed on your desktop.

Protect PC with tough-to-crack password

Creating separate user accounts won't protect your computer if they aren't secured by passwords. Without one, a thief can get into your machine simply by selecting your account on the login screen.

At the very least, assign a password to the Administrator account, to keep strangers from fiddling with the guts of your computer.

Pick a strong password. Don't use your name or a series of numbers such as "1234." Remember, if a thief breaks into your home and steals your computer, the password could be the only thing standing between you and a stolen identity. Experts suggest making it at least eight characters long and using at least one uppercase letter and one number.

Get solid advice on creating a tough-to-crack password by reading *Successful tips for setting an ironclad password* in the *Safe & secure surfing* chapter.

Put it in place. Open the **User Accounts** window by clicking on your account's picture at the top of the **Start Menu**. Click on **Create a password for your account**. Type the new password into the first field, then again into the second one. From now on, the computer will ask you to type this each time you log into your account.

Create a password for your account

Guard against forgetfulness. Afraid you'll forget the new password? Give yourself a hint in the bottom field. Come up with a word, phrase, or sentence that will jog your memory. Don't make it too specific, however. It should be meaningful to you but vague enough that a thief won't guess the password from reading the hint.

117

First aid for forgotten passwords

Oh, no! It finally happened. You forgot your computer password and you're locked out. Never fear. These three tips are guaranteed to get you out of that jam.

Get a clue. Call up the hint you left yourself after creating your password. On the login screen, leave the password field blank and press **Enter**. Click **OK** on the error message that pops up. A new login screen will appear, this time showing your hint below the password field.

Log in as Admin. If the hint doesn't help, try this sneaky trick. You can reset the password on a Standard account by logging into your all-powerful Administrator account.

1. Log into your Administrator account, open the **Start Menu**, and click on the account's picture at the top.

2. Click on **Manage another account** in the **User Accounts** window, then click on the account you are locked out of.

3. Click on **Change the password** in the next window. Type the new password in the first and second fields, then include a hint in the third field. Click on the **Change password** button.

4. Log out of your Administrator account. Open the **Start Menu**, click on the arrow beside the **Shut down** button, and choose **Log off**.

5. Click on your Standard account on the Log in page, type the new password, and press **Enter**.

You will lose any passwords you saved for logging into websites or email. Resetting the account password erases them, but it's a small price to pay for unlocking your computer.

Pop in a password reset disk. Plan in advance, and you'll never need to worry about forgetting your password. A Password reset disk works like a key to unlock your computer.

Log in to the account you want to create a "key" for. Plug in a USB flash drive or insert a CD or DVD into your computer. Open the **Start Menu** and click on the account's picture at the top. On the left side of the **User Accounts** window, click on **Create a password reset disk** and follow the instructions. When finished, label it and store in a safe place.

If the time comes when you forget the password, leave the password field blank on the login screen. Press **Enter**, click on **OK** at the error message, then insert your password reset disk.

Click on **Reset password** on the new login screen and follow the instructions for creating a new password. The same disk will still unlock your computer in the future, even though you've reset the password.

A CLOSER LOOK

So your computer doesn't like the password you typed in. Make sure the Caps Lock feature is off. Most keyboards display a light when you turn on Caps Lock. Press the **Caps Lock** key on your keyboard until the light turns off, then retype the password.

Windows 7 tools
Update, maintain & protect

Tune up your computer with free tools

Computers get slow. The older they get, the slower they get, just like people. Chances are, all your computer needs is a little tune-up. Windows comes with free tools that will have it working like new again.

So how do you know if your computer is slowing down because your hard drive is full, or it's time to reorganize your files, or your memory is running low?

Pop the hood on it. Open the **Start Menu** and click on **Computer**. Under **Hard Disk Drives**, right-click the hard drive labeled **(C:)**, then choose **Properties** from the shortcut menu. This opens a dialog box that houses all the tools you need to tune up your computer.

Clean up the clutter. Clear the cobwebs from your computer's memory and file system. Under the **General** tab, you can see how much memory, or "space," is left on your hard drive, and how much is full of stuff you've stored. The results are color-coded.

Websites and programs leave little crumbs all over the hard drive. Just like at home, you need to sweep. In this case, cleaning can free up a substantial amount of space.

Put Windows on the job by clicking on the **Disk Cleanup** button beside the pie chart. Windows will take a quick look to see which crumbs it can safely throw away then tell you how much memory you'll gain.

Next, it will ask which types of files you want to delete. Click on each category to learn more about it in the **Description** below, and place a check next to those you'd like to trash. Click on **OK** to send Windows to work.

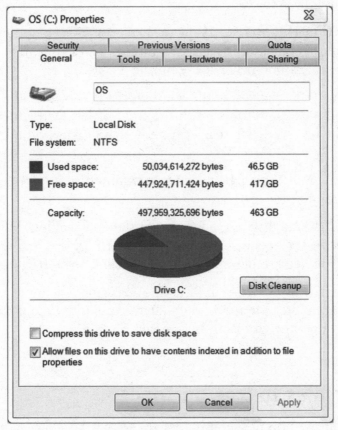

Hard drive properties

Check for errors. Hard drives get damaged when the computer turns off without warning, say, after a black out, or during power surges and voltage spikes. A damaged hard drive can damage your files. Fortunately, Windows can fix most problems.

Click on the **Tools** tab of the same dialog box, then click on **Check now**. This opens the **Check Disk** box. Put check marks beside **Automatically fix file system errors** and **Scan for and attempt recovery of bad sectors**. Click on **Start**.

Windows will tell you it can't check the disk right now, but don't worry. Simply click on the button **Schedule disk check**, and Windows will do its thing the next time you turn on your computer. Check for errors every three to six months.

Put together the puzzle. Want to speed up your computer? Defragment your hard drive once a month. Over time, bits of files get scattered around it like loose puzzle pieces.

Every time you open a file, the computer sifts through all those pieces and puts them together in the right order. Defragmenting groups the bits so they're closer together and easier to find.

This little bit of organizing can dramatically speed up your computer. Under the same **Tools** tab, click on **Defragment now** to open the **Disk Defragmenter** program.

Click on **Analyze disk** at the bottom of the new window. Windows will check to see how disorganized your hard drive is and tell you whether you need to defragment it. If so, click on **Defragment disk**.

Start the process before bed, or at another time when you won't need the computer for a few hours. Defragmenting can take awhile. Close any open programs to help speed it up.

Shrink files to free up space

The hard drives on new computers are so big these days you're unlikely to fill them up. But if you own an older machine, that possibility is all too real.

Emptying the Recycle Bin and defragmenting are all well and good, but they may not do enough if you're burdened with a tiny drive. In that case, compression is for you.

Windows 7 is a wiz at compressing files to make them smaller. It can then reinflate them when you open them. It happens so fast and seamlessly that you may not even notice.

You can compress individual files, whole folders, or the entire hard drive and still use your computer normally.

Some things compress smaller than others. Photos don't compress very much, but text files compress a lot. How much space you regain depends on what's stored on your hard drive.

Start small. Tidy up by compressing a few folders at first, if you're worried about the process.

1. Right-click a folder and choose **Properties** from the shortcut menu.

2. Click on **Advanced** under the **General** tab.

Compress folder dialog box

3. Place a check mark in the box beside **Compress contents to save disk space** in the dialog box that opens, and click on **OK**.

4. Click on **OK** back in the main **Properties** dialog box.

Windows will ask if you want to compress just this folder, or all the folders stored within it. Why not? Click on **Apply changes to this folder, subfolders and files**, then click on **OK**.

Go big. Create even more space by compressing the whole hard drive. The process may take several hours, so do it when you won't need the computer for awhile.

Open the **Start Menu** and click on **Computer**. Under **Hard Disk Drives**, right-click the hard drive labeled **(C:)** and choose **Properties**.

Under the **General** tab, place a check mark in the box beside **Compress this drive to save disk space**, then click on **OK**. Choose **Apply changes to drive C:\, subfolders and files** to compress everything on the hard drive.

Don't walk away from the computer just yet. Some files can't be compressed, and Windows will show you an error message when it finds one. At the first one, click on **Ignore all**.

Now Windows will simply skip over those files, instead of waiting for you to approve each one.

Caution

You'll know without a doubt that it's time to clear the clutter on your hard drive if you get a Low Disk Space message from Windows.

It's polite, of course — **You are running out of disk space on Local Disk (C:)**. The ever-helpful Windows 7 then offers to make some room on your hard drive.

Do what it tells you, then put your PC on a regular clutter-clearing schedule to avoid future warnings.

Ditch the flashy looks for a faster computer

The nicer you look, the longer it probably took you to get ready. Getting dressed up takes time, and Windows 7 is no exception. It comes with lots of fancy graphics and snazzy special effects. Unfortunately, the nicer it looks, the slower your computer.

All those visual effects suck up memory and processing power. You may not notice with a new machine, but you certainly will with an older one. If your computer barely creeps along, speed it up by turning off some of these frills.

1. Open the **Start Menu** and type "visual effects" into the search box.

2. Click on **Adjust the appearance and performance of Windows** in the results list.

3. Click on the **Visual Effects** tab of the **Performance Options** dialog box.

4. Click on the button beside **Adjust for best performance**. This turns off all of Windows 7's special effects.

5. Click on **OK** or **Apply**. Your computer screen will go black for a moment as Windows adjusts itself. When it returns, you'll see a bare-bones version of your desktop.

Eventually, you may realize you've turned off a feature you love, like the shadow on your cursor that makes it easier to see. No problem. You can turn on individual effects like this from the same **Performance Options** dialog box.

Reopen it, click on the **Visual Effects** tab, then on the button next to **Custom**. Place a check mark beside each effect you want to keep and click on **OK**.

Easy upgrade amps up speed

One little upgrade can crank your computer's speed to greased lightning. Best of all, you can do it yourself. All you need is a USB flash drive or memory card. You may even have an extra one lying around.

Put it to work with ReadyBoost, a feature that lets your computer "borrow" memory from a flash drive or memory card. Simply insert the memory card or plug in the USB drive. This opens the **AutoPlay** window. Scroll to the bottom and choose **Speed up my system**, under **General options**.

A **Properties** box will open. Unless you plan to store more files on this device, go ahead and let Windows use it all. Under the **ReadyBoost** tab, click on **Dedicate this device to ReadyBoost**, then on **OK**.

You can plug in up to eight flash drives or memory cards all at one time for ReadyBoost to use. Just remember that each device needs to have at least 1 gigabyte (GB) of storage space available. Otherwise, it won't speed up your computer.

Not all devices will work with ReadyBoost. Some flash drives, especially older ones, are too slow or don't have enough memory. You'll find out as soon as you plug it in. If it's not compatible, you will not see the option **Speed up my system** in the **AutoPlay** window. When shopping for a device that will work with ReadyBoost, look for one of these.

- the words "Enhanced for ReadyBoost" on the package

- a flash drive labeled as USB 2.0 or higher

- a flash drive with a read speed of 2.5 megabytes per second (MBps) and a write speed of 1.75 MBps

Top 10 reasons for a slow computer

Stop putting up with a slow computer. Try these tips to get back the lightning speed you crave without spending a cent.

Cause of slowdown	Free, simple solution
fragmented hard drive	clean it up with Disk Defragmenter
visual effects sap computer memory and processing power	turn off fancy visual effects
spyware infection	learn to scan for and remove spyware with Windows Defender in the *Safe & secure surfing* chapter
clutter left from deleted files and uninstalled programs	run Disk Cleanup
too many programs start when you turn on computer	remove unnecessary programs from the Startup list
computer virus infection	learn to scan for and remove viruses with Microsoft Security Essentials in the *Safe & secure surfing* chapter
damaged hard drive	fix it with Check Disk
too little RAM memory	add more with ReadyBoost
too little hard drive space	compress some files
outdated Windows 7 software	run Windows Update and allow automatic updating

Turn off programs for faster start

New computers come fresh from the factory loaded with programs, and many of them start up every time you turn on your computer. That flurry of activity can make your new machine as slow as molasses when it comes on.

Tell unnecessary programs to stop starting themselves. Open the **Start Menu** and type "system configuration" into the search box. Click on **System Configuration** in the results list, then click on the **Startup** tab in the dialog box that appears.

Here you'll see a list of all the programs that scramble to open when you start your computer. Some are necessary, like your anti-virus and firewall software. Others aren't.

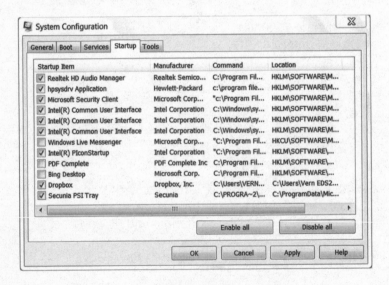

Turn off autoloading programs

Scroll down the list and uncheck the box beside those you don't want running automatically. If you aren't sure what something does, play it safe and leave it checked. You can also look up programs online to find out what they do. Type the name of the **Startup Item** into the search box of your Web browser.

Pay attention the next time you turn on your computer. If it balks or doesn't start properly, you may have unchecked an important program. Reopen the **System Configuration** box to look for the culprit.

Update your operating system automatically

Why rush out and spend thousands on a computer when all it might take to get your old machine working like new is a simple three-step update? Avoid crashes, viruses, and frustrating error message by setting Windows 7 to update itself automatically.

Keeping your operating system up-to-date is like changing the oil and filters on your car. The only difference is, it doesn't cost you anything. Like a car, many things can go wrong with your operating system. The smart folks at Microsoft are constantly trying to head off new problems and fix existing ones by releasing free software updates. All you need to do is make certain you get them. Luckily, Windows comes with a program that finds them for you.

1. Open the **Start Menu** and click on **Control Panel**, then click on the heading **System and Security** in the window that appears.

2. Make updates automatic, so you never have to think about them. Click on **Turn automatic updating on or off** under the heading **Windows Update**.

3. Click on the drop-down list beneath **Important updates** and choose **Install updates automatically (recommended)**.

Decide when you would like Windows to install any updates it finds. Pick a time when your computer is likely to be turned on, but when you aren't likely to be using it. Click on the drop-down lists beside **Install new updates** to set a day and time.

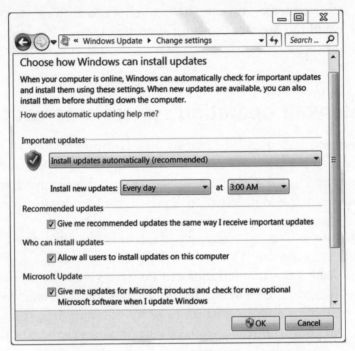

Schedule automatic operating system updates

Place a check in the box beneath **Recommended updates** to apply the same settings. While you're at it, mark the box beneath **Microsoft Update** to ensure you get updates for Microsoft Office and other Microsoft programs. Click on **OK** when you're finished.

Track down trouble with Windows Update

Not every update will download smoothly. You're bound to get the occasional hiccup. First, make sure your computer is connected to the Internet. If that doesn't solve the problem, try these tricks.

Do it by hand. Some errors occur because of busy websites or Internet connections. Try installing the update manually. Click on **Control Panel** in the **Start Menu**, then on **System and Security**. Under the **Windows Update** category, click on **Check for updates**.

Click on a result, and place a check in the box by the updates you want to install.

Click on **OK** to return to the previous window, then on **Install updates**.

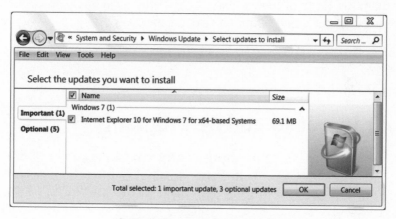

Install the update manually

Say yes to the license. You have to agree to the license terms in order to install some updates. Try manually updating, as described above, and be sure to accept the license terms if you're asked.

Make space. You may not have enough room to download an update if your hard drive is chock-full. Run **Disk Cleanup** and then defragment the drive to create room.

Let Windows fix it. For stubborn problems, download a fix-it tool directly from Microsoft. Visit the website *support.microsoft.com/kb/ 971058*, and click on the green **Run now** button. If a box appears at the bottom of your screen, asking whether to run this program or save it, choose **Run**.

This opens the Microsoft Fix it window. Click on the **Accept** button to install the troubleshooting program. In the next window, select the option **Detect problems and apply the fixes for me**. Windows will do all the work.

A CLOSER LOOK

Some recommended updates that don't install properly deal with your computer's drivers — tiny pieces of software that help run parts of the machine. Learn how to fix fussy drivers in the chapter *SOS: everyday troubleshooting tips*.

Don't forget to update programs

Windows does a great job of protecting your operating system with the latest updates. And if you checked the box beneath Microsoft Update, it will keep Microsoft programs like MS Office up-to-date, too.

It won't, however, update programs made by other companies. That's up to you. Get a helping hand from free third-party software such as Secunia's PSI Scanner.

1. Go to *secunia.com/vulnerability_scanning/personal/* and click on the green **Download** button.

2. Choose **Run** when Windows asks you what you want to do with this file. The Secunia program will walk you through setting it up.

After it installs itself, the software will ask if you would like to launch Secunia PSI. Close any programs you have open, including your Web browser, then click on **Yes**. A moment later, you'll see a list of **Programs that need updating**. Click on one to fetch the update from the Internet, then click on **Run** to install it.

You can scan for more updates at any time. Just open the **Start Menu**, click on **All Programs**, and choose **Secunia PSI**.

Guard against computer crashes

Losing your files in a computer crash is no fun, but you won't need to worry if you stashed a copy of them somewhere safe. The free Windows Backup program makes it so easy there's no excuse not to do it. It copies the files of everyone who uses the computer. All you have to do is tell Windows where to store them.

Plug in a flash drive or external hard drive, or insert a CD or DVD. Click on the **Start** button, then on **Control Panel**. Under the **System and Security** category, click on **Back up your computer**. The first time you create a backup, you'll see the message **Windows Backup has not been set up**. Click on **Set up backup** to do that now.

Pick a spot. Windows will scan your system for storage devices and then suggest a place to save your backup. Click on **Guidelines for choosing a backup destination** for advice on choosing a location.

Don't save it to your computer's hard drive. If the computer crashes, it will take your backup with it. And while you can save to rewritable CDs (CD-RW), they won't hold much. You may need several discs to do a backup. Rewritable DVDs (DVD-RW) offer more storage.

Choose your files. Choose where you want to put your files, then click on **Next**. Windows will ask which files, in particular, you want to back up.

- The first option, **Let Windows choose**, will back up your Libraries, desktop, and email, among other things.

- The second option, **Let me choose**, allows you to pick the exact folders you want backed up.

Pick an option and click on **Next**. If you're choosing the files yourself, do that in the next dialog box.

Set a schedule. Look over the choices you've made so far under **Review your backup settings**. To make changes, click on the window's **Back** button.

Check the schedule while you're here. Windows will offer to back up your files automatically from now on — for instance, every Sunday at 7 p.m. Click on **Change schedule** to pick a different day and time. Then click on **Save settings and run backup**. On the day of your scheduled backup, remember to:

- leave your computer turned on. It can't back up if it's turned off.

- insert the disc or plug in the flash drive or external hard drive that holds your last backup. Windows will simply update the last backup with any new information or changes.

Keep in mind if your first backup required multiple CDs or even DVDs, then automatic backups won't work unless you are there to feed discs to the computer. If that's not possible, tell Windows not to back up your stuff automatically. In the **Review your backup settings** window, click on **Change schedule**. Simply remove the check mark beside **Run backup on a schedule**.

CAUTION

Opt out of automatic backups, and it will be up to you to back up your stuff on a regular basis. Experts recommend backing up a home computer at least once a month — more often if you have a home-based business.

Open the **Control Panel** and click on **Back up your computer** under **System and Security**. Click on **Create new, full backup** on the left and follow the instructions.

Prepare for the worst before it happens

At the end of your first backup, Windows will ask if you'd like to create a repair disc while you're at it. By all means, say yes.

A repair disc can get your computer up and running when it refuses to start. Plus, it's an electronic toolbox, equipped with everything you need to fix a sick machine.

The Windows 7 installation CD acts as a system repair disc, so if you have one, you're all set. If not, or if you're not sure what you have, take a moment to make one now.

1. Return to the **Back up or restore your files** window by opening the **Start Menu**, clicking on **Control Panel**, then on **Back up your computer** under **System and Security**.

2. Click on **Create a system repair disc** on the left.

3. Pop a blank CD or DVD into your computer, then click on **Create disc**. If a box appears asking what to do with the blank disc, click on **Format**.

The computer will whir, then tell you when it's finished. Close the dialog boxes and eject the disc. Take Windows' advice and label it right away. Write on the top of the disc with a permanent marker, naming it something like "Emergency Computer Repair Disc, Windows 7."

Tuck it somewhere safe, where you'll remember to look when you panic and need it. Learn how to use this repair disc in the *SOS: everyday troubleshooting tips* chapter.

Never lose another file or program

Make both a backup and a system image, and you're virtually guaranteed not to lose anything important if your computer one day bites the dust.

Microsoft created these two programs to work hand-in-hand, safe-guarding your stuff from almost any mishap.

- Backups contain copies of individual files and folders, but not programs or the operating system itself. If a specific file gets damaged or deleted, you can grab a copy of it from your backup.

- A system image is a copy of the entire computer — not just documents, photos, and music, but all of your programs and carefully crafted settings. If your whole hard drive dies one day, you can rescue everything with a system image.

Let Windows do it for you. You can make a system image at the same time you perform a regular backup, but only if you are saving that backup to an external hard drive. Simply let Windows choose which items to back up, and it will automatically make a system image, too.

If you prefer choosing the files and folders yourself, put a check in the box beside **Include a system image of drives** in the **What do you want to back up?** window.

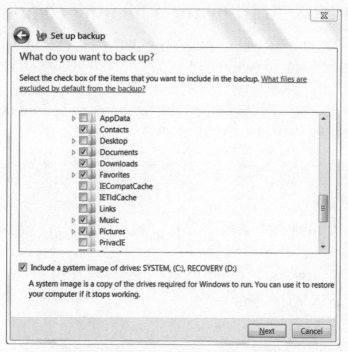

Make a system image during back up

Make one manually. Don't have an external hard drive? Then create the system image separately from the backup and save it on DVD, CD, or USB flash drive. Keep in mind that system images are big. After all, they're a copy of your entire computer. You'll need multiple CDs or DVDs, or a really large flash drive, to make just one copy.

Open the **Start Menu** and click on **Control Panel**, then on **Back up your computer** under the **System and Security** category. In the **Back up or restore your files** window that opens, click on **Create a system image** on the left. Windows will walk you through the process.

Experts suggest making a new system image every few months. Save money by using rewritable DVDs (DVD-RW) or CDs (CD-RW) and reusing them each time.

Can't-miss strategy for a healthy computer

People with the fastest, healthiest computers have something in common — they stay on top of easy and often overlooked maintenance tasks.

Pick up their savvy habits, and your computer will be running like a top for many trouble-free years ahead.

Task	How often
scan for spyware	daily
check for operating system updates	at least once a week
scan for viruses	at least once a week
delete unnecessary files with Disk Cleanup	monthly
back up your files and folders	at least once a month
defragment the hard drive	every three months
check the hard drive for errors with Check Disk	every three months
dust the computer tower and vents	every three months
make a system image	every few months
change passwords on email, online banking, and other accounts	at least once a year, more often for sensitive accounts like banking

Plan 'B' guards against disasters

Windows 7 offers yet another built-in backup, called System Restore. Whereas Windows Backup safeguards your personal files, System Restore protects your operating system.

Windows periodically takes a snapshot of the operating system, then saves it as a "restore point." Should something go haywire, say after you update some software or install a new printer, you can use that restore point to undo whatever changes triggered the problem. Windows 7 automatically creates a restore point:

- once a week on a set schedule.

- when you install new hardware or new software.

- before installing a Windows Update.

- when you create a new backup.

These automatic restore points aren't foolproof. That's why experts recommend creating one manually before you do anything big, like install a new gadget or program — just in case the new item doesn't get along with your computer. Follow these steps.

1. Open the **Start Menu**, right-click **Computer**, then choose **Properties** from the shortcut menu.

2. Click on **System protection** in the left pane of the window that opens.

3. Under the **System Protection** tab, click on the **Create** button near the bottom.

4. Name the restore point. Pick something related to what you're about to do, like "Before New Printer," to help you find the right restore point should you need to rewind the computer. Then click on **Create**.

CAUTION

Here's one more reason to keep your hard drive decluttered with tools like Disk Cleanup. When the drive begins to get full, System Restore stops creating restore points. Eventually, it begins deleting them, and all without warning you first.

SOS
Everyday troubleshooting tips

Get help almost anywhere

Help is always close at hand in Windows 7. No matter where you are — on the desktop, in a window, and even in a dialog box — it's easier than ever to find answers.

Desktop. Call for help straight from the desktop. Open the **Start Menu** and click on **Help and Support**, or press the **F1** key at the top of your keyboard. Both open the **Windows Help and Support** program. Type a question or phrase into the search box at the top, then press **Enter**. Click on a result to get step-by-step help on that topic.

Windows. Click on the Get Help icon, shaped like a question mark in the upper-right corner of windows. The computer will show you a Help article related to whatever you're viewing in the main window.

Programs. Programs made by Microsoft have their own Get Help icon. Just look for a question mark in the upper-right corner. Click on it to open a Help tool made specifically for that program.

Dialog boxes. Some but not all dialog boxes also feature a handy Get Help icon. Clicking on this question mark opens a Help article that explains the dialog box as a whole. Also look for blue-colored links. Click on these to open a related Help article.

Master the art of Windows Help

A few clever tricks can help you get the most from Windows Help. Follow this advice to find everything you need fast.

- Look for links in Help articles. Click on green-colored words to see a definition. Click on blue-colored words to open another Help article.

- Move back and forth between articles by clicking on the **Back** and **Forward** buttons in the upper-left corner of a Help window.

- Click on the printer icon in the upper-right corner of a Help window to print the article you're viewing.

- Enlarge the text for easier reading by clicking on the **Options** button in the upper-right corner. Hover over **Text Size** and choose **Larger** or **Largest** from the menu that appears.

- Use quotation marks around exact phrases when searching in Help.

Typing a word or phrase into a Help search box will only unearth the right article if you call something by the same name Microsoft does. If the search box doesn't give you the results you want, start from the top.

Open the main Help window by clicking on **Help and Support** in the **Start Menu**. Then look at the links under the heading **Not sure where to start?**

For help with basics such as navigating windows or printing a document, click on **Learn about Windows Basics**. Or click on **Browse Help topics** to see a complete list. Click on a category and drill down through successive Help screens until you find what you need.

Easy fix for tough problems

Don't waste time and tears trying to solve a tricky computer problem yourself. Let Windows do it for you. Open the **Start Menu** and click on **Control Panel**. Under **System and Security**, click on **Find and fix problems**.

This opens the **Troubleshoot Computer Problems** window, where you can get help with:

- Internet connections.

- hardware and gadgets.

- older programs.

- Windows Update.

- a slow computer.

Click on a topic that describes what you're trying to do. Say you upgraded your computer from Windows XP to Windows 7, and now one of your old programs doesn't work. Click on **Run programs made for previous versions of Windows**.

This opens the **Program Compatibility** troubleshooter. Click on the **Next** button. Your computer will think for a minute, then return with a list of programs that could be causing problems.

Choose the one that isn't working and click on **Next**. Windows will ask if you'd like it to fix the program **(Try recommended settings)**, or if you want to fix it yourself **(Troubleshoot program)**.

Choose one and follow the instructions. Chances are, that pesky program will be up and running in no time.

The same process works for other problems, too. Clicking on a topic in the **Troubleshooting** window opens a tool for fixing it. To get the most from these tools, make sure you are connected to the Internet, then put a check mark in the box beside **Get the most up-to-date troubleshooters from the Windows Online Troubleshooting service** at the bottom of the main window.

 BRIGHT IDEA

Do yourself a favor. Create a folder in your computer files just for user manuals. Each time you install a new program or device, go to the manufacturer's website and download the instruction manual that goes with it. Save it in your specially designated folder.

The next time a glitch strikes, you'll have help close at hand. And forget about thumbing through the pages. Most will download as "pdf" files, meaning you can easily search them.

Do you own a scanner? You can even scan the pages of owner's manuals for your television, refrigerator, electronics, and tools. Save them in the same folder for fast searching.

No-sweat solution for sticky computer problems

Take the easy way out of solving a computer problem with Microsoft's Fix It tool. Head to the website *support.microsoft.com/fixit*. Here, you can look up common problems by type, whether it's with the Windows operating system, Internet Explorer, or something else. Narrow your search further by choosing from the **What are you trying to do** box.

This produces a list of fixes, each with a **Run Now** button. Click on that and Windows will leap into action, downloading a program to your hard drive that will diagnose and fix the issue.

When Windows begins the download, a small box will appear at the bottom of your screen asking what you want to do with the file. Click on **Run** to open Microsoft Fix it. Accept the license terms and select **Detect problems and apply the fixes for me**. Answer a series of questions about the trouble you're having, and Windows will make short work of fixing it for you. Fix It can't solve every problem, but it's a good place to start.

Discover the key to opening unknown files

What do you do if you try to open a file, but your computer doesn't know what program to use? Perhaps it's lost its file extension, like .doc or .jpg. Or maybe the file was created using an unusual type of program. You have a short-term solution and a long-term fix.

First, choose a program. When you attempt to open a file with no recognized file type, your computer will open a dialog box giving you two options.

- Use the Web service to find the appropriate program. If you select this option, Windows will open a browser window and help you look up the file extension on the Microsoft website.

- Select the program from a list of installed programs. If you pick this option, you'll see a list of programs installed on your computer. Click on the program you want to use.

Then, make it permanent. Assign file types to be automatically opened in certain programs so you won't have this problem repeatedly.

- Right-click a file and select **Open with**.

- You'll see a list of programs, along with the option to **Choose default program**. Click on that option.

- A list of **Recommended Programs** will open in a new window. Find the program you want to use, and check the box next to **Always use the selected program to open this kind of file**.

- Then click on **OK**.

Restore a lost file to save the day

You can check the **Recycle Bin** icon on your desktop for a file you accidentally deleted. But if the bin has already been emptied, you may be out of luck.

All is not lost. If you've used the Windows Backup feature available in Windows 7 to create a backup of your important files and folders, you can find a lost, changed, or accidentally deleted file in the backup you created. Here's how to get that one file you really, really need.

- Click on **Start** > **Control Panel** > **System and Security**. Then choose **Backup and Restore**.

- If you need only your own files and not those of other users on the computer, select **Restore my files**.

- Click on **Browse for files** to see the contents of the backup you created. Then you can search for your file by name or by file type.

- Once you find the file you need, highlight it and click on **Add files**.

- Click on **Next**, and choose a location for the restored file to be placed. Click on **Restore**, then on **Finish**.

Get grumpy gadgets working again

When Troubleshooter doesn't solve a device problem, you can do the dirty work yourself. First, make sure the gadget is plugged in, hooked up to your computer, and turned on. If it's still not working properly, it's time to dig into the driver.

Drivers are the tiny pieces of software that allow devices to talk to your computer. When something goes wrong, you can often blame a buggy or outdated driver. Log in to your computer as an Administrator, and try these steps to get it working again.

Find an update. Sometimes a driver just needs updating. Open Windows Update to find out if the gadget's manufacturer has released any new software.

Click on the **Start Menu**, then on **Control Panel** and **System and Security**. Next, click on **Check for updates** under the category **Windows Update**. Your computer will tell you how many, if any, **important** and **optional** updates are available.

A driver update could appear as either type. Click on the link for **important updates** first, and put a check in the box beside any that look like a device or driver update. Do the same with **optional updates**. Click on **OK** then **Install updates**.

Undo an update. Maybe a recent update is the cause of your problem, not the solution. In that case, undo it.

1. Open the **Start Menu** and type "device" into the search box at the bottom. Click on **Device Manager** in the list of results.

2. Click on the arrow beside each type of device to see all the drivers in that category.

3. Look for a driver with a yellow exclamation point (!) next to it. Double-click it to open its **Properties** dialog box.

4. Click on the **Driver** tab, then click on the **Roll Back Driver** button to undo the most recent software update. If there hasn't been an update recently, the button won't be available.

Reinstall a stubborn driver. A corrupt bit of software could be behind the snag. If updating the driver doesn't take care of it, try downloading a new one directly from the manufacturer's website.

1. Use the **Device Manager** to open the **Properties** dialog box for your grumpy gadget.

2. Click on the **General** tab and write down the name of the company listed beside **Manufacturer**.

3. Hop on the Internet and head to the company's website. Type its name into a search engine like Google for help finding it.

4. Look for the Support area of the website. From there, you should find a link to "Drivers," "Software Downloads," or something similar.

5. Choose the driver designed for Windows 7. You may see two options, one for 32-bit computer systems, and the other for 64-bit systems. Find out which type of computer you have by reading *Choose software that's right for your computer* in the *Software nuts & bolts* chapter.

6. Download the right version onto your computer, and save it on your desktop. Double-click the file to install the new software.

Rewind time to rescue your system

You could save a bundle of money fixing the computer yourself with System Restore. It's like a time machine for Windows. Use it to return to the moment right before you clicked "install" on that buggy program, or "download" on that infected Internet file.

System Restore can rewind your computer to a point right before you made that mistake, undoing any changes made to programs, drivers, and the operating system. That may also undo any glitches you're having. And it does all of this without affecting your documents, photos, or other personal files.

It relies on restore points, both the ones the computer creates and those you learned to create yourself in *Plan 'B' guards against disasters* in *Windows 7 tools*. Pick the right restore point for your rewind, and you just may save the day.

Before turning to System Restore, try uninstalling the program, driver, or Windows Update that you think started the trouble. If that doesn't work, follow these steps.

1. Open the **Start Menu** and type "restore" into the search box at the bottom. Click on **System Restore** at the top of the results list.

2. Read the instructions in the window that opens, and click on **Next**. Look through the list of restore points. The newest one is at the top.

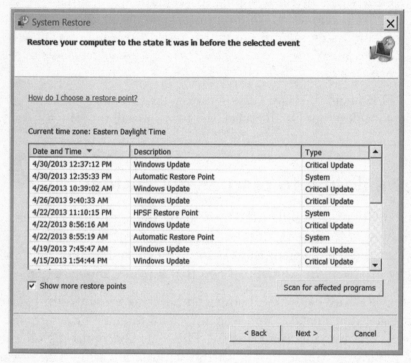

Choose a restore point

3. Try to remember when your computer began sputtering. Click on the restore point just prior to that. If you don't see the one you want, check the box beside **Show more restore points** to look further back in time.

4. Click on **Scan for affected programs** to see which programs and drivers will be affected by the rewind.

5. Click on **Next** and confirm your choices. Click on the link **Create a password reset disk** if you have changed your computer password since that restore point was made. Find out how to use this disc in *First aid for forgotten passwords* in *Windows security essentials*.

6. Click on **Finish**, then on **Yes** in the confirmation box that appears. Leave your computer alone while it works.

Your machine will automatically restart when it finishes rewinding. Put it through its paces to see if the old glitch returns. If so, return to **System Restore** and choose a different point. If turning back the clock actually made the problem worse, reopen **System Restore** and click on **Undo System Restore** on the first screen.

BRIGHT IDEA

System Restore can even thwart a computer virus, if the infection hasn't gone too deep. Rewind your computer to a time before you think you caught the virus. Then immediately install a good anti-virus program and run a thorough scan. See how in *Vaccinate your PC against nasty viruses* in *Safe & secure surfing*.

Troubleshoot a blank screen

A blank screen may not be as scary as you think. Before you panic, follow this advice to snap your computer out of it.

• Desktop monitors have a separate power button from the computer. The monitor may be off. Press its power button to turn it on.

• Is the computer asleep? Some are harder to wake up than others. Press the tower's power button to prod it awake.

- Loose connections could be to blame. Unplug then reconnect all the cables linking your computer to your monitor, and tighten any screws. Check the power cord connections while you're at it.

- Cables can go bad. Connect the computer to the monitor with a new cable. Still no luck? Switch out the old power cord and test again.

- The desktop monitor may have gone kaput. Test this by hooking up a different monitor. If the new one doesn't work either, then the problem is with the computer itself.

Thaw out a frozen computer

Frozen computers are no fun, but don't assume the worst. First, make sure it really is "frozen." It may simply be thinking hard. Look for flashing lights on the computer tower or laptop keyboard, and listen for sounds like the whirring of your hard drive. These suggest the computer is still working, although slowly.

Walk away for a few minutes — get some coffee or check the mail. When you return, your machine may have worked out the kinks itself. If it still shows no signs of movement, it's time to take action.

1. Disconnect your mouse and keyboard, reconnect them, and check to see if either works.

2. Unplug all the gadgets attached to your computer, including USB flash drives, cameras, and printers, and see if the system starts responding.

3. Still nothing? Press the Windows Logo (WIN) key on your keyboard to open the **Start Menu**, and click on the **Shut down** button.

4. Press the **Ctrl**, **Alt**, and **Delete** keys simultaneously. Click on the red **Shut down** button in the bottom-right corner of the window that appears.

5. Press **Alt + F4** on your keyboard to open a special **Shut Down Windows** dialog box. Select **Shut down** from the list of options and press **Enter**.

If all else fails, press and hold the power button for five seconds to forcibly turn off the computer. Pulling the plug may feel more satisfying, but it can damage the machine.

Solve startup problems with Safe Mode

Windows not behaving? Put it in Safe Mode. That should be your first step after Windows crashes, freezes, or refuses to start.

First, turn your computer on. Press the power button, then immediately begin pressing the F8 key repeatedly on your keyboard. Do this until the special **Advanced Boot Options** screen appears. If you see the Windows logo, it's too late. Restart your computer and try again.

The **Advanced Boot Options** screen is bare-bones, but it holds some powerful tools for fixing your computer. Use the up and down arrows on your keyboard to highlight **Safe Mode**, then press **Enter**. A Windows login screen should appear. Sign into your computer using an Administrator account. With any luck, you'll then see a basic-looking version of your regular desktop.

Safe Mode bypasses startup programs and drivers so you can fix glitches in a jif. Once in Safe Mode you can:

- scan for and fix hard drive errors with Check Disk. See how in *Tune up your computer with free tools* in *Windows 7 tools: update, maintain & protect*.

- check for memory problems. Open the **Start Menu** and click on **Control Panel** > **Administrative Tools**. Then double-click **Windows Memory Diagnostic**. Choose **Restart now and check for problems (recommended)**, then sit back and let the computer run its tests.

- look for faulty drivers using the Device Manager. Here, you can uninstall a new driver or roll back an update to one, if you suspect it's the source of your troubles.

- remove a newly installed program if you think it could be the culprit. Double-click **Programs and Features** in the **Control Panel** window. Click on a program in the list to select it, then on **Uninstall**.

- run Windows' built-in troubleshooters. Double-click **Troubleshooting** in the **Control Panel** window.

You may discover that you need to go online in order to download a new driver or use a troubleshooting tool. In that case, restart your computer, press **F8** to open **Advanced Boot Options**, and choose **Safe Mode with Networking** instead.

Restart your computer after each fix to see if it worked. Let Windows try to boot normally. If the problem persists, restart again, enter **Safe Mode**, and try another repair.

What to do when Windows won't start

A truly cranky computer may even refuse to enter Safe Mode. Never fear — you still have options.

Restart your computer, press the **F8** key to enter **Advanced Boot Options**, and select **Last Known Good Configuration**. The computer will revert to the settings it used the last time it was able to start successfully, without affecting your personal photos, documents, or other files.

If that doesn't work, it's time to break out the big gun, known as Startup Repair.

1. Select **Repair Your Computer**, the first choice on the **Advanced Boot Options** screen.

2. Choose the **US** keyboard layout in the dialog box that appears, and click on **Next**.

3. Log in to your computer using your Administrator account.

4. Click on **Startup Repair** in the **System Recovery Options** window that appears. The computer will scan itself and fix any problems it finds.

A CLOSER LOOK

Don't see **Repair Your Computer**? Your machine may not have this tool on its hard drive. In that case, grab your Windows 7 installation disc or the system repair disc you made after reading *Prepare for the worst before it happens* in *Windows 7 tools: update, maintain & protect*.

Insert either disc into your machine and restart the computer. You should see a black screen with the words "Press any key to boot from CD or DVD." Act fast and do what it says — press any key on your keyboard.

Snap a picture to solve problems faster

A picture of your screen can help tech support or a tech-savvy friend understand the problem or error message you're struggling with. Try these two ways to "photograph" your screen.

Use your keyboard. Press the **PRTSCN** or **Print Screen** key to make a snapshot of the entire window. Click on **Start > All Programs > Accessories > Paint**. When Paint opens, press **Ctrl + V** to paste the screenshot into a Paint file, and save the file.

Snip a window. Open the Snipping Tool by clicking on **Start > All Programs > Accessories > Snipping Tool**.

When the Snipping Tool palette appears, click on the drop-down arrow next to the **New** button. Choose one of these:

- **Free-form Snip** to snap an oddly-shaped section of screen you outline with your mouse

- **Rectangular Snip** to snip any rectangular section of the screen

- **Window Snip** for a particular window

- **Full-screen Snip** to capture the entire screen

If needed, outline the section of screen for the Free-form Snip or Rectangular Snip or click on the window for a Window Snip.

When the screenshot appears, click on **File > Save As**, name the file, and save it as a PNG, JPG, or GIF image file or as an HTML file. Attach the file to an email, and send it to your tech support person.

Remote help with built-in tool

Your favorite teenager says he can still help with your computer problems even though he's going away to college. In fact, a built-in Windows 7 tool called Windows Remote Assistance (WRA) means you can get help from someone across town or across the country — but your helper can fix your computer almost the same way he would if he were visiting your home. Here's how WRA works.

You contact your helper to make sure he's at his computer. To start WRA, you go to the **Start** menu, type in "assistance," and click on the **Windows Remote Assistance** option. When the WRA dialog box appears, you choose **Invite someone you trust to help you**. Next, you invite your helper to view your screen, receive a password from WRA, and send that password to your helper.

Your helper receives your emailed invitation and clicks on **Help someone who has invited you**. Once your helper types in the WRA password, WRA asks you if you want to allow him to connect to your computer. Click on **Yes**, so your helper can see your screen, and you can show him the problem. You can also click on the **Chat** button to discuss the problem.

To take temporary control of your computer to fix the problem, your helper clicks on the **Request Control** button. But he can't take over until you click on the options to agree to it. Once he has fixed your problem, either of you can click on the **Stop Sharing** button. That disconnects your computer so your helper no longer sees your screen or has control of your computer.

For details on using WRA, visit *support.microsoft.com*, type "remote assistance Windows 7" in the search box, and review the results.

CAUTION

Windows Remote Assistance gives you two safeguards to help protect your computer and your passwords. Clicking on the **Pause** button temporarily turns off your helper's ability to view your screen or control your computer.

Use this when you need to type in a password or other information your helper should not see. This is also useful if you have called a technical support hotline or service.

If a tech support representative begins doing something you find suspicious, you can even end the session with the **Stop Sharing** button.

Top 10 free technical support sites

Have a computer problem? There are lots of places to go for help. Start with these websites and solve your problem fast.

5Star Support. *(www.5starsupport.com)* Go to this site for forums, tutorials, and a large database of searchable information in their Troubleshooting FAQ section.

AskMeHelpDesk. *(www.askmehelpdesk.com/computers-technology)* Browse their easy-to-navigate subcategories from Hardware to Web Development.

Computer Training For You. *(www.computer-training-for-you-through-online-education.com)* Here you'll find topics on Microsoft applications and operating systems, as well as info on viruses, a FAQs page, tips and tricks, latest news and news feeds, a blog, a very informative newsletter, and much more.

Free Desktop Support. *(www.freedesktopsupport.com)* You can get answers 24 hours a day to basic questions by surfing their posts or directly emailing them for those more troubling issues. They also have tons of tutorials on computer hardware and software.

Microsoft Support. *(support.microsoft.com)* Get live help by contacting Microsoft, or you can explore top support issues, access downloads, and ask questions through a community forum.

Protonic. *(www.protonic.com)* This site, manned by volunteers all over the world, offers completely free computer support and computer-related information online and by email.

Suggest A Fix. *(www.suggestafix.com)* Here you'll find support on many topics, from Windows to computer hardware issues. The technologically savvy volunteers who staff the forums here can answer your questions in plain English.

Tech Support Guy. *(www.techguy.org)* This site is run completely by volunteers and paid for completely by donations and sponsors.

TechTutorials. *(www.techtutorials.net)* TechTutorials offers a discussion forum and a directory containing thousands of free tutorials for IT professionals, hobbyists, and home users.

Techie7. *(www.techie7.com)* This is a completely free computer help site that requires a registration to post questions.

Software simplified

helpful hints to make the most of your applications

Software Nuts & Bolts

Discover free software hidden on your computer

Software vendors don't want you to know this, but lots of what they sell is already free inside your computer. You just have to know where to look. Before you spend another dime on expensive software, see if these free Windows programs already offer what you need.

WordPad. This basic word processor now includes formatting like fonts, bullets, highlighting, line breaks, and paragraph styles. You can even insert pictures and save in a format you can open in Microsoft Office. To use WordPad, click on **Start** > **All Programs** > **Accessories** > **WordPad**.

Sound recorder. If your PC has a sound card, speakers, and a microphone, you can use the Sound recorder to record a birthday greeting you can email to a friend, a how-to guide, or anything else you can think of. To begin, click on **Start** > **All Programs** > **Accessories** > **Sound Recorder**.

Paint. Use this to draw or paint pictures, add new pictures or shapes to photos, edit scanned photos, and more. Paint offers options to draw with a pencil, a curve tool, a line tool, or various brushes, or you can add shapes or callouts. To give Paint a whirl, click on **Start** > **All Programs** > **Accessories** > **Paint**.

Games. Enjoy games like Solitaire, FreeCell, Hearts, Minesweeper, and more. Click on **Start** > **All Programs** > **Games**.

Calculator. Previously, this was a simple calculator, but now it can do conversions, such as inches to centimeters or Fahrenheit to Celsius. It can also calculate your mortgage payment, car payment, the number of days between dates; do basic statistics; or double as a scientific calculator. To try it, click on **Start** > **All Programs** > **Accessories** > **Calculator**.

Windows Media Player. Listen to music and other audio files, watch videos, organize media files, synchronize with a music player, and more with this software. Click on **Start** > **All Programs** > **Windows Media Player**.

Internet Explorer. Surf the Web with a full-featured browser. Click on **Start** > **All Programs** > **Internet Explorer**.

Snipping tool. This takes a snapshot of part or all of your screen. When the snapshot appears in a new window, make mark-ups on it with drawing tools; save it as a JPEG, GIF, PNG, or HTML file; or print it. A saved copy can be emailed or pasted into another document to show tech support what's wrong, or sent to a friend or colleague to clear up confusion. This tool may not be available in every version of Windows 7. To check, click on **Start** > **All Programs** > **Accessories** > **Snipping tool**.

A CLOSER LOOK

Windows 7 also includes software like:

- Narrator that reads text on your screen aloud.
- Mouse Keys to help you ditch the mouse, and use the keyboard instead.
- Speech Recognition to help you go mouse-free, and control your computer with voice commands and a microphone.

See the *Easy access: fine tune Windows settings* chapter to learn more.

Although Windows no longer includes software for email, messaging, movie making, parental controls, or photo management, you can still download most of that software for free. To learn how, see *A Closer Look* box in the *Simple setup for a speedy start* chapter.

Add speed by removing old programs

Is your computer slowing down? You may have loaded it up with too many programs. Find out how to safely and easily remove the ones you don't use anymore — or never used at all.

You may have hesitated to remove software because you have heard horror stories of people who have accidentally uninstalled vital parts of Windows. But you can take precautions to avoid that. For example, create a Restore Point before removing the software. For instructions on how to do this, see *Plan 'B' guards against disasters* in the *Windows 7 tools: update, maintain & protect* chapter. In addition, only uninstall software you installed. Follow these steps to remove a program.

- Click on **Start** > **Control Panel** > **Programs and Features**.

- Click on the icon for the program you want to remove. If you can't find the program, scroll down to look further in the list.

- If you are asked to confirm the uninstall, click on **Yes**.

- If you are asked whether you want to run an **Automatic** or **Custom** uninstall, choose **Automatic**.

- Follow the instructions on the screen (if any appear) until you are returned to the **Add or Remove Programs** Window.

Fix a missing program. If the program does not appear in the list of programs to uninstall, close the **Control Panel** window. Click on **Start**, and find the program's icon to see if an uninstall option is included with the program. It may look something like this.

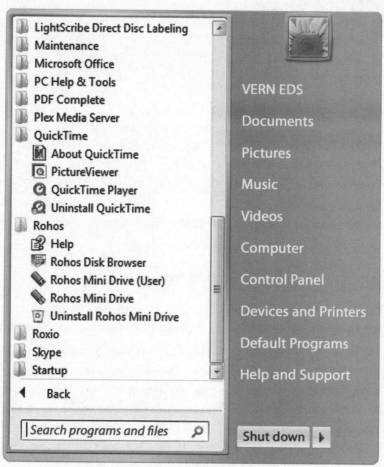

Uninstall options in the Start Menu

If you don't find an uninstall option, open the program. Search through its menus and help files for uninstall instructions.

Handle leftover files. Sometimes the uninstall process doesn't wipe out everything a program installed on your machine. This may be an error. Check the printed materials, PDF manual, or the program's help files to see if any other uninstall information is available. If you don't find anything, visit the website of the software maker. Check the Support section for software or instructions that can help you clear out the remaining files.

MONEY-SAVER

When free software won't do, consider the software discount site *www.bitsdujour.com*. It offers two 20- to 75-percent off deals daily that expire at day's end, but BitsDuJour's free e-mail newsletter previews what deals are coming soon.

If a one-day deal does not offer software for free and you download a free trial version of the program, you must buy the full version before its deal expires to get the discounted price. For both its one-day and longer-lasting discounts, BitsDuJour arranges the deal, but you buy the fully legal and licensed software from the software maker.

6 free programs everyone can use

Some software programs are notorious for sticker shock, but you can also find useful programs like these that won't cost you a penny.

LibreOffice. Don't fret if you can't afford Microsoft Office. LibreOffice is a free, full-featured software package that includes substitutes for Microsoft Word for word processing, Excel for spreadsheets, and PowerPoint for presentations. You also get database software, a drawing program, and software for math and equations. You may be surprised at how many features you find in LibreOffice, but it's still easy to use. What's more, you can work on Microsoft Office documents in Libre Office. Download this software from *www.libreoffice.org*.

Rainlendar Lite. This is a desktop calendar and to-do list. Add one-time or repeating events to this calendar, and even set reminder alarms for them. Dates with appointments are highlighted so you can note your important days with a glance. To download, visit *www.rainlendar.net*.

AceMoney Lite. Manage your money with this budget-tracking program. Excellent help files make AceMoney Lite easy to learn, but it's also rich in features including password protection, the ability to import data from Quicken, and plenty of reports to help analyze and track expenses. This free version is limited to two accounts. To try it, visit *www.mechcad.net*.

Google Earth. This software combines maps, satellite images, and more to help you search for restaurants, hotels, and more — locally or in distant places. You can get driving directions, see terrain and buildings in 3D, view famous or far-flung spots, take virtual tours half a world away, explore the night sky, and much more. Visit *earth.google.com* to download the latest version.

7-Zip. When you need to make a file smaller so you can email it or fit it on a flash drive, 7-Zip can compress or "zip" it. This converts the original file to a significantly smaller file called an archive, but without losing any of the original file's information. 7-Zip supports commonly used archive file formats like TAR and ZIP, as well as many others. The program can also encrypt a compressed file, so no one can view it unless you approve. When you are ready, 7-Zip can decompress and unencrypt the file to bring it back to normal. Visit *www.7-zip.org* to download.

PDF Xchange Viewer. When you don't have the program that created a document, you can still view the file with Acrobat Reader if the sender turns it into a PDF. Unfortunately, Acrobat Reader won't let you do much with the file, but PDF Xchange Viewer can help. It allows you to type comments into a PDF, add mark-ups, add bookmarks, fill out and save forms that are in PDF format, and use OCR (optical character recognition) to turn a page-image PDF into readable and searchable text. To download this small-but-fast software, visit *www.tracker-software.com*.

HIGH-TECH HEALTH

Your monitor's bright, blue-tinted light may contribute to eyestrain, even if you have no blue in your color scheme. To help ease eyestrain, try f.lux, the free software that adjusts monitor brightness and tint with the time of day. F.lux aims to match the look and feel of staring at a printed page under your current lighting or daylight.

At sunset, the monitor shifts to gentler light and nudges its colors toward the less-blue feel of incandescent or fluorescent lighting. At sunrise, the monitor returns to a brightness and tint like daylight. To try f.lux, visit *stereopsis.com*.

Block unwelcome toolbars when installing software

You might be excited about your new software now, but you'll be horrified when you discover all the extra software the program's installer added to your computer. Even worse, software developers often slip toolbars into their installers. These toolbars can slow down your computer or browser, add spyware, leave you open to viruses, or make permanent and unwanted changes to your browser and PC.

Fortunately, you can prevent most of these problems and still install your new software. Here's how.

Each software program comes with an installer that walks you through a series of screens to help install the software. The worst ones may install software without your knowledge, but most installers just find sneaky ways to get your consent to install unexpected software, or make other changes you don't want.

When you install a new program, remember that every screen the installer displays may be rubber-stamping a change or program you would normally turn down. Read each screen thoroughly, and watch for prefilled checkboxes, preselected radio buttons, or other offers. And don't agree to:

- add a toolbar or "quick launch bar" to your browser, especially if the toolbar has no obvious link to the software you are installing.

- install a new program other than the one you expected.

- add unexpected programs to your desktop, Taskbar, or startup routine.

- change your default search engine, default browser, browser home page, or new tabs page.

Not all of these options will be unwanted or unnecessary every time, but reading the installation screens can help make sure nothing is installed or changed without your knowledge.

Choose software that's right for your computer

You found a fabulous new software program, but the download page offers one 32-bit version and one 64-bit version. Which is right for you? To find out, determine whether your version of Windows is 32-bit or 64-bit. Here's how.

- Click on **Start**.

- Right-click **Computer**.

- Click on **Properties** as shown below.

Where to look for System Properties

In the section labeled **System**, look for **System type**. The text directly across from that should be either **32-bit Operating System** or **64-bit Operating System**.

In that same section, look at **Installed memory (RAM)** and make a note of both numbers you find there. For example, you may see **8.00 GB (7.89 GB usable)**.

System

Manufacturer:	Hewlett-Packard Company
Model:	HP Z210 Workstation
Rating:	4.7 Windows Experience Index
Processor:	Intel(R) Core(TM) i5-2500 CPU @ 3.30GHz 3.30 GHz
Installed memory (RAM):	8.00 GB (7.89 GB usable)
System type:	64-bit Operating System
Pen and Touch:	No Pen or Touch Input is available for this Display

System properties

If you have **32-bit Operating System**, any software you buy or download must be the 32-bit version. But if you have a **64-bit Operating System**, both 32-bit software and 64-bit software can run on your version of Windows 7.

As long as you have 4 GB of RAM or more, the 64-bit software will probably run noticeably faster, especially if it is photo-editing or video-editing software, a database, or a program that often seems to run slowly on your computer.

If you aren't asked to choose a version when purchasing or downloading new software, that does not necessarily mean anything is wrong. Some software programs don't have both a 64-bit version and a 32-bit version.

CAUTION

For safety's sake, remember two things when you get new software:

- If you downloaded the software directly from the Internet, scan it with your anti-virus and spyware software. If the file passes, make a backup copy of the file and save it to a DVD, CD, flash drive, or external hard drive, in case the original file ever gets damaged or lost.

- If the software installer asks you whether you want a **Typical** installation or a **Custom** installation, choose **Typical**. Unless you have plenty of expertise with the software, choosing **Typical** will save you both time and potential trouble.

Thaw a frozen program

You know something is wrong when all the menus and tool palettes in your program stop responding. You click on menu commands repeatedly, but nothing happens. Your program is frozen solid. Try these tips to thaw it out.

Take a break. Some programs are notorious memory hogs. They may appear to freeze when they are actually so busy working they delay responding to your commands. Even programs that aren't memory hogs sometimes need a few minutes to complete a particularly demanding command. So take a quick bathroom break, or refill your coffee mug. By the time you return, your frozen program may have thawed itself out.

Check your messages. Press the **Windows Logo (WIN)** key and the **M** key at the same time. This should minimize all open programs so you can see the desktop. You may find a dialog box from the "frozen" program that is requesting some input from you. Answering that request may unfreeze the program.

Try cloning. Some programs allow you to open a second window or second instance of the program. If you know how to do this from the **Start Menu** or another location that is not frozen, try it. This may cause the original program to thaw or may allow you to work in the new window or instance of the program long enough to salvage what you were working on.

Break the ice. Bringing the program back to normal may no longer be possible, but you can still end the freeze with one of these methods.

- If your mouse still works, move the mouse cursor to the **Taskbar**, and right-click the icon for the frozen program. Click on **Close Window** to exit the program.

- If your mouse is frozen, press **Ctrl-Shift-Esc** to immediately bring up the **Windows Task Manager**. If your program's status is **Not Responding**, click on the program name to select it, and then click on **End Task** to force-quit the program.

Nab a repeat offender. If this particular program has frozen repeatedly, consider whether all its freezes have something in common.

- Does the freeze only occur when you work with a particular file? Something may be wrong with the file. Re-create the file or transfer its contents to a new file.

- Do problems crop up when you try to use the program with a peripheral such as your printer or scanner? Make sure your printer or scanner has the latest drivers.

- Could something be wrong with this particular program? Visit the software maker's website to check for any new patches or updates you need to install.

To make sure malware is not causing the problem, update your spyware and anti-virus software, and make certain you have all the latest security updates for Windows 7. Scan your hard disk for viruses and other malware. These changes may thaw your freezes permanently.

MICROSOFT OFFICE 2010 SECRETS

Speed up your work in Microsoft Word

Imagine how quickly you could get things done in Microsoft Word if you didn't have to work your way through several mouse clicks for some commands.

First, you click a tab, then a button, and it just seems to keep going. If clicking through the layers of Word's Ribbon or menus seems too time-consuming, copy your most-used commands or buttons to Word's convenient Quick Access Toolbar.

This tiny toolbar perches at the top left corner of your Word screen, and you won't have to click or type anything to make it appear. It already features the **Undo**, **Redo**, and **Save** buttons.

To quickly add a common command or button, right-click the drop-down arrow at the right side of the **Quick Access Toolbar**.

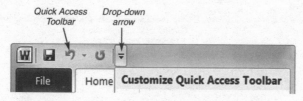

The Quick Access Toolbar drop-down menu

Click on any command to instantly add it to the toolbar. But this short list of commands may not include all the commands you wanted. If you do not see a command you need, click on **More Commands** at the bottom of the drop-down list.

When the **Customize the Quick Access Toolbar** panel appears, find the command you want, and click on it. Click on the **Add** button to add it to the toolbar. Keep adding commands until you have all the ones you need or until you fill up the toolbar's space.

If you still have not been able to find a particular command in the list, you may not be viewing the **All Commands** list. To fix this, check near the top of the **Customize the Quick Access Toolbar** panel for **Choose commands from**. In the drop-down list box just below, click on the drop-down arrow, and choose **All Commands**.

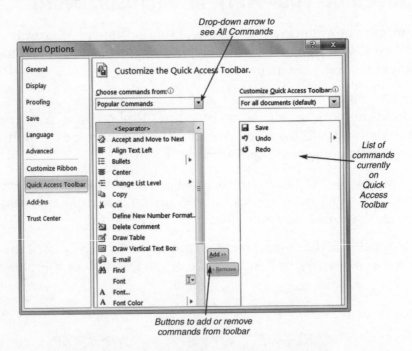

Customize the Quick Access Toolbar panel

Finish finding and adding the commands you want, and click on **OK**. Your newly added commands are now displayed in the **Quick Access Toolbar**, ready for you to use.

A CLOSER LOOK

To remove commands from the **Quick Access Toolbar**, right-click the drop-down arrow at the right end of the toolbar, and click on **More Commands**. When the **Customize the Quick Access Toolbar** panel appears, move your mouse to the command list in the right half of the screen, and click on a command you want to remove.

Click on the **Remove** button between the two lists of commands to take the command off the toolbar. Remove any other commands you no longer want on the **Quick Access Toolbar**. Click on **OK** to close the panel.

Type symbols and accented letters like a pro

Häagen-Dazs, sauté, and jalapeño all contain accented letters you won't find on your keyboard. And what do you do if you need to type ¢, the cents symbol? You ask Microsoft Word to type the symbol or accented letter for you. Just follow these steps.

- To start, click on the spot where you want a symbol or accented letter inserted.

- Click on the **Insert** tab.

- Move your mouse to the far right side of the Ribbon, and click on **Symbol**.

A small group of symbols appears including the cents symbol, math symbols, and more. If one of these is the symbol you need, click on the symbol, and it appears in your document.

But if you don't see the symbol you need, click on **More Symbols** at the bottom of the list. The **Symbol** panel appears. Scroll down the list to find the one you're looking for.

When you spot it, click on it, and click on the **Insert** button in the lower right corner of the panel to place the symbol or accented letter in your document. When you finish inserting, click on **Close**.

> ### BRIGHT IDEA
>
> You accidentally hit the **CAPS LOCK** key, and now your entire sentence is capitalized. Select the text, and press **SHIFT + F3** to convert the sentence to lowercase. Press **SHIFT + F3** again to convert it to sentence case, where only the first letter of the sentence is capitalized.
>
> Pressing **SHIFT + F3** a third time returns the text to all uppercase. Pressing **SHIFT + F3** cycles the text through these three cases no matter what case you are using at the time, and it may be a faster way to change cases than using the Ribbon commands.

Remedy a frequent time-waster

You may try to save all your documents, spreadsheets, and other files in just one place, so they'll be easier to back up quickly. But the folder you choose for your files may not be the same folder Microsoft Word thinks you should use.

So Word automatically defaults to the wrong folder every time you save a new document, and you waste precious seconds navigating to the right folder. If this happens to you regularly, follow these steps to change the default folder Microsoft Word recommends.

- Click on the **File** tab.

- Click on **Options**.

- When the **Options** panel appears, look down the left side of the panel and click on **Save**.

- Find **Default file location** and click on the **Browse** button at the end of the line.

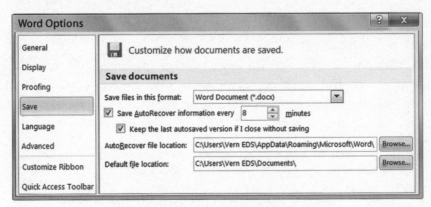

Choose the default file folder location

Navigate to the folder you would prefer to use, and click on it. Then click on **OK**. Now when you save a new document, Microsoft Word will always default to the folder you selected as its preferred location for saving documents.

MONEY-SAVER

Someone has sent you a Microsoft Office document, but you can't open it. This may happen because the sender is using a newer version of Microsoft Office than the one you have. You may also have this problem if the file was created in a Microsoft Office program you did not buy.

But don't worry. Microsoft offers free software for viewing or converting files created in newer versions of Office or files created in a current Office product you don't have.

Visit *office.microsoft.com* and type "viewer" in the search box to find and download your free software.

Protect private files with a password

You can protect a Word document or Excel spreadsheet with a password if it contains sensitive financial or personal information — or if you just want to keep nosy people out of your business.

To set up password protection in an Excel spreadsheet, you follow almost exactly the same steps you use in Word. Here's how you add password protection to a Word document.

- Click on the **File** tab.

- On the left side of the screen, click on **Info**.

- Find the **Protect Document** button, and click on the drop-down arrow in the button's lower right corner.

- Click on **Encrypt with Password**.

When the **Encrypt Document** dialog box appears, type in a password that would be tough for others to figure out, but easy for you to remember. That password can be up to 255 characters long.

Just keep in mind that passwords are also case-sensitive, so you must remember which characters are uppercase and which are lowercase. For more advice on creating a good password, see *Successful tips for setting an ironclad password* in the *Safe & secure surfing* chapter.

Make a note of the password you choose, but keep it in a hidden location that you will remember. Microsoft Office does not offer a way to retrieve forgotten passwords. Click on **OK**.

When the **Confirm Password** dialog box appears, type your password a second time to verify that you typed it correctly. Click on **OK** again.

The text next to the **Protect Document** button now changes to **A password is required to open this document**. Click on **Save** to save your document as a password-protected file. The next time you open the document, you will be asked to enter the password before the document can display.

A CLOSER LOOK

To remove password protection from a document, you follow nearly the same steps you use to set up password protection. Click on **File** > **Info**. Click on the **Protect Document** button's drop-down list, and click on **Encrypt with Password**. When the password dialog box appears, backspace over the characters until the box is blank. Click on **OK**, and then click on **Save**.

Recover files you didn't save

Your new document isn't lost forever just because the power went out or because you clicked on **Close** instead of **Save**. That Word, Excel, or PowerPoint file may be just a few mouse clicks away — as long as you set the right options.

To retrieve a document that has never been saved or named, click on the **File** tab. Near the bottom right corner of the screen, click on the **Recover Unsaved Documents** button.

The **Open** dialog box appears. This is where rescued documents are listed, but finding your document may be tricky because it may not be saved under a name you recognize.

Microsoft Office names unsaved rescued documents based on the first word in the document. So if the first word were "Ginger," you would check for a document name beginning with the word "Ginger," followed by "Unsaved" and a long sequence of numbers.

For example, the name might be "Ginger ((Unsaved-3028722902 40677216))." If you find your document in the listing, click on it, and then click on the **Open** button. When your document displays, this bar will also appear just above it.

⚠ **Recovered Unsaved File**   This is a recovered file that is temporarily stored on your computer.   [Save As]

Recovered Unsaved File bar

Take no chances. Click on the **Save As** button immediately, and save your document. Be careful to choose a name and location that makes the document easy to find and remember.

This handy feature only works if your Autosave options have been set. To check these options, click on **File** > **Options** > **Save**. Make sure the checkbox for **Save AutoRecover information every x minutes** is checked, and that the number of minutes has been set higher than zero. In addition, confirm that the checkbox for **Keep the last autosaved version if I close without saving** is also checked.

CAUTION

Be careful how high you set the minutes on **Save Auto Recover information every x minutes**. For example, if you set that number to 60 minutes, the first backup copy of any new document won't be saved until you have been working on that document for 60 minutes.

If you close the document without saving before your 60 minutes have passed, clicking on **Recover Unsaved Documents** won't display a document for you to recover. Keep that in mind when you decide the number of minutes to set.

Create eye-catching documents in a flash

Using fonts and formatting commands can help make your document easier to read, but using Word's styles feature can quickly turn plain-looking files into spectacular documents that look professional.

Each style is a set of font and formatting settings you can apply to a particular type of text. For example, the **Title** style could be applied to the title of a document, and the **Heading 1** style could be applied to headlines within the document. Applying styles like these can give you a document like the following example.

Fascinating secrets of *The Wizard of Oz*

Interesting tidbits about the book and movie

L. Frank Baum may have written *The Wonderful Wizard of Oz* in 1900, but the story doesn't end there — or even with the famous movie 39 years later. Discover the delightful ways *The Wonderful Wizard of Oz* has become so much more than most people know.

6 times over the rainbow

Dorothy was glad to get back to Kansas, but that didn't keep her from coming back to Oz. L. Frank Baum wrote sequels to his famous book including these books which brought Dorothy back to Oz again and again.

- *The Marvelous Land of Oz*
- *Ozma of Oz*
- *Dorothy and the Wizard in Oz*
- *The Road to Oz*
- *The Emerald City of Oz*

Word 2010 document with styles applied

Using a style saves you time. These formatting changes would take far longer to do by hand. That is why applying styles can give you professional-looking documents in less time. To apply a style, follow these steps.

- Select a block of text to style.

- Click on the **Home** tab.

- Notice how the sections of the Ribbon have labels along their bottom edge. Find the one labeled **Styles** in the right half of the Ribbon. In that **Styles** gallery, find the drop-down arrow to the left of **Change Styles**. Click on the bottom arrow to see all the available styles.

Select a style from the Style gallery

- Hover your mouse over the style you want, and the text you selected temporarily changes to that style. If you like how it looks, click on the style name to make the change permanent.

Repeat this process for each block of text you want to style, including headers, titles, subtitles, quotations, lists, and more. These styles are saved with your document, so the styles still appear even if you copy or move the document to another folder.

If you don't like the look of the current styles, you can choose another group of styles. Here's how:

- Make sure you have applied styles to your document.

- Find the **Change Styles** button next to the **Styles** gallery, and click on its drop-down arrow.

- Hover the mouse pointer over **Style Set**.

- A new menu of style sets appears. Hover your mouse over each style set to see how your document changes. Click on the style set you like best to apply all its styles to your document.

 MONEY-SAVER

> If you are using styles because Word doesn't include a template that suits you, stop right there. Plenty of new, free templates are waiting for you at the Microsoft Office website. You just have to download them.
>
> Visit *office.microsoft.com*, and look for a link to **Templates**. You will not only find templates for Word, but for other Microsoft Office programs, too.

Fix the mystery horizontal line that won't delete

A horizontal line has suddenly appeared on your page, and you can't imagine why. You try every way you know to delete it, but it won't go away. This problem has been plaguing Word users for years.

In fact, any time you type a few dashes or hyphens together after a paragraph, and press **Enter**, Word's AutoCorrect function may automatically turn your hyphens into a bottom border for the previous paragraph. To get rid of this border, follow these instructions.

- Click inside the paragraph located just before the horizontal line.

- Click on the **Home** tab.

- Check the labels along the bottom of the Ribbon to find the **Paragraph** group. In the bottom right corner of that group, find the Borders icon as shown below.

The Borders icon

- Click on its drop-down arrow, the small upside down triangle at the bottom of the button.

- Click on the **No Border** option, and the mystery line will vanish as if it had never been there.

A CLOSER LOOK

To prevent this "undeletable line" problem permanently, try this.

- Click on **File** > **Options**.

- When the **Word Options** panel appears, move your cursor to the list on the left side of the panel, and click on **Proofing**.

- In the **AutoCorrect options** section, click on the **AutoCorrect Options** button.

- In the **AutoCorrect** panel, click on the **AutoFormat As You Type** tab.

- Move your cursor to the **Apply as you type** section, and click on the checkbox for **Border lines** to unselect it.

- Make sure the checkbox is empty, and click on **OK**.

- Click on **OK** again to close the **Word Options** panel.

Customize the Number of Recent Documents list

Open Word or Excel and click on **File** > **Recent**, and you'll probably see a list of the documents or spreadsheets you worked on recently. Click on one, and it opens immediately. Some love this convenience, but others would rather not have a **Recent Documents** list.

After all, you don't want the guest of honor to see the "Surprise Party Invitations" document in the list if you are planning a surprise. Fortunately, you can decide whether the **Recent Documents** list displays as well as how many documents should live there.

To do this in Word:

- Click on **File** > **Options** to make the **Word Options** panel appear.

- On the left side of the panel, click on **Advanced**.

- Scroll down to the **Display** section and find **Show this number of Recent Documents**.

- In the numeric box, click on the up arrow to increase the number of documents displayed in the **Recent Documents** list or click on the down arrow to decrease the number of documents. To make the list disappear, keep clicking on the down arrow until the number is zero.

You can use a similar process to make changes to Excel's version of the Recent Documents list.

BRIGHT IDEA

You can pin documents to the **Recent Documents** list so they always show up even if you haven't used them recently. Just look for the white pushpin icon near a document in the **Recent Documents** list. Click on the icon to pin the document. The icon changes to a blue pushpin viewed from above.

If you later decide you no longer need the document pinned in the **Recent Documents** list, click the blue pushpin to unpin it. When the blue pushpin turns white, the document is no longer pinned.

Fit long text into short spreadsheet cells

Long text entries can be tricky in Excel because they are often wider than the standard column width. As a result, the text is usually cut off by the cell border like this.

Fortunately, you can choose from two ways to fix this. You can either stretch the column or wrap the text.

Stretch the column. If you have enough space, simply widen a column to fit the length of the text.

	A	B	C	D
1	Snowiest Places in the USA			
2	Place	Snowfall ir	Snowfall in feet	
3	Mount Wa	260.6	21.72	
4	Blue Canyᶜ	240.3	20.03	
5	Marquette	144.1	12.01	
6	Syracuse N	118.1	9.84	
7	Sault Ste. I	117.4	9.78	
8	Caribou M	112.3	9.36	
9	Mout Shas	104.9	8.74	
10	Flagstaff A	100.6	8.38	
11	Lander WY	100.1	8.34	
12	Sexton Sur	97.8	8.15	

Column width is narrower than the text

181

To do this:

- Select the column that contains the lengthy text.

- Click on the **Home** tab.

- Notice the section labels along the bottom edge of the Ribbon. Move your mouse to the **Cells** section, find the **Format** button, and click on the drop-down arrow.

- Click on **AutoFit Column Width**.

This widens the column's cells so all the text is visible and can fit on one line.

Use text wrap. Sometimes the text is too long to fit in a single, wide column. Or you need to limit that column's width just to fit all your columns on a printed page. Try these instructions to make the text wrap.

- Select the column of cells that contains lengthy text.

- Click on the **Home** tab.

- Move your mouse to the **Alignment** section and click on the arrow. In the drop-down list, click on the checkbox beside **Wrap text** and then click on **OK**.

The text will wrap to the next line to fit the column width. Even if you change the width of the column, the text wrap simply adjusts to the new width.

Solve Wrap text side effects. If your text doesn't look exactly the way it should after you click on **Wrap text**, correct it by solving one of these problems.

- If words are split between lines instead of remaining whole, shift each split word to the next line by entering a line break. Just double-click inside the cell, click on the spot where you want to add a line break, and press **Alt + Enter**. This moves the entire word down to the next line.

- If only one line of text appears, and you can no longer see all of your text, adjust the row height. Click on the **Home** tab. Click on the **Format** button's drop-down arrow, and then click on **AutoFit Row Height**. If that does not solve the problem, click on the Format button's drop-down arrow again, and click on **Row Height**. Type a new row height in the box, and click on **OK**.

A CLOSER LOOK

Occasionally, when **Wrap text** splits words between lines, widening the column slightly may help — particularly if you only need to accommodate one long word at the beginning of each cell or a couple of long words on two or three lines.

If you have room to widen the column, click on the **Home** tab, and click on the **Format** button's drop-down arrow. Click on **Column Width**, and change the numbers to widen the column just enough to fit the long words properly.

Stretch your worksheet title across columns

Take your worksheet title out of that cramped little corner in the A1 cell, and center it over all the visible columns. You may have tried to do this by widening the cell the title lives in.

But widening the cell also widens the column beneath it, making your other columns disappear off the far side of the page. That is why Excel supplies the **Merge & Center** command to help.

The **Merge & Center** command affects two or more cells you select with your mouse. You can select cells that are side by side or part of a column, or you can select a square or rectangular group of cells. **Merge & Center** turns two or more neighboring cells into a single cell.

But be careful. This command deletes the contents of every merged cell except the one in the upper left corner of your selection. If you need to preserve the contents of other cells, copy those contents to another location before you merge the cells.

To merge the cells, follow these steps.

- Select the cells you want to merge by clicking the column heading to select a column, the row heading to select a row. To select a group of cells, click in the cell at the upper left side of the cells you want to select, hold down your mouse button and move your mouse pointer to the cell at bottom right side of the cells you want to select, and release the mouse button. Make sure the cell containing the text you want to keep is in the upper left corner of your selection.

- Click on the **Home** tab.

- Move your mouse to the **Alignment** section, and click on the **Merge & Center** button.

The borders between the selected cells vanish, and they become one cell with text located in the center. Now your title is a cross-column heading that stretches across several columns without affecting the width of those columns.

You can also use this process for any other heading that needs to span several columns.

BRIGHT IDEA

Excel isn't just for your finances and budget. Excel includes templates like Calendar Creator, Home Contents Inventory List, Grocery List, Weekly Meal Planner, Multifamily Garage Sale Calculator, Holiday Shopping Planner, and Travel Checklist for Plane Trip.

It also includes health and medical templates like Blood Pressure Tracker, Patient's Medical Bill Tracker, Personal Health Record, Medication Log, Exercise Planner, and more. Click on **File** > **New** in Excel to see the many other free templates available. You may be surprised at how many useful items are waiting for you.

Stream, sync, view & share

how to have fun with your digital devices

TV & MOVIES
Cutting-edge ways to watch

Buy a movie once, then watch it anywhere

You buy your favorite movie on a Blu-ray disc to watch on your big-screen TV, but then you decide you want to watch it on your iPad when you go on vacation. But you can't, so you purchase a digital copy of the same movie from iTunes for your tablet.

So far, you've paid twice for the same movie, and if your disc gets damaged, you're out of luck. If only you could pay once and watch the same film on any device — television, PC, iPad, Kindle, or whatever the next great gadget will be.

New services are making it possible to store your movies and TV shows in the Cloud, then download or stream them to watch in any format.

You may have purchased a "combo pack" containing both a disc and a digital file of the same movie, but these sometimes come with playing limits. And, of course, you can purchase digital files from the iTunes store or Amazon Instant Video service, but they won't play on all gadgets.

The leader in this innovation seems to be a service called UltraViolet. This service, developed by a group of Hollywood movie studios, retailers, and gadget manufacturers, aims to help you create a library of movies you can store permanently.

Then you can play the movie on any gadget, any format — even letting you pay a bit more to upgrade old titles to High Definition with Dolby digital plus surround sound (HDX).

You create a free UltraViolet account, then add movie titles to your library by inputting codes that come with UltraViolet-compatible DVDs and Blu-ray discs. You can also add movies to your library through VUDU, WalMart's disc-to-digital service. When you're ready to watch a movie, stream it or download it through an Ultra Violet-approved website like *Flixster.com* or *VUDU.com*.

Unfortunately, not all movies and TV shows are available to add to your UltraViolet account, based on digital licensing. But you can expect more and more titles as time goes on. For more information about how the service can work for you, see the information page at *www.uvvu.com*.

BRIGHT IDEA

If your DVD won't eject from your computer's optical drive, try the paperclip trick. Find the tiny hole on the front of the DVD drive. That's the emergency release mechanism.

First, turn off your computer. Unbend a paperclip, and press the tip into the hole until the drive door opens. If you hear a click but the door doesn't pop open, you might have to help it along by pulling gently with your fingers. If this happens repeatedly, it might be time for a new drive.

Cleaning tips for smooth-playing movies

Sometimes the simplest way to watch a movie on DVD is to pop it into your computer's internal disc drive. No need to connect a separate box or even configure WiFi.

But you can't enjoy the show if the movie keeps skipping, pausing, or freezing. Try these quick fixes to get back to the story line.

Eject the disc and check for scratches. Be sure you always handle discs by the edge or in the center to avoid touching the part where data is stored.

Polish out small scratches using a tiny bit of toothpaste on a cotton ball. Rub gently from the center of the disc toward the outer edge. You can also use metal polish or Brasso.

Look for dirt on the disc. Dirt buildup might also be the problem. You can clean a dirty disc with a soft, lint-free cloth. Wipe gently in the same direction as with polishing, moving from the center of the disc toward the edge.

Clean the disc drive. Open the tray, remove the disc, and blow out dust and debris from the drive using a can of compressed air. This step may be all it takes.

Then do a more thorough cleaning by using a blunt stick, such as a long cotton swab. Take a small square of soft cloth and dampen the center with a couple drops of water or rubbing alcohol.

Cover the end of the blunt stick with the moistened cloth, and insert it into the drive. Move it back and forth gently to clean the lens inside the drive. Let it dry out completely before use.

If the thought of cleaning the disc drive by hand scares you, look for a drive-cleaning kit at your local computer store. They're available for a few dollars, and they usually work just fine.

BRIGHT IDEA

To fast-forward when watching a DVD movie on TV, you use the remote control. But how can you fast-forward a movie on your computer using the Windows Media Player? You actually have two options.

- Press and hold down the left mouse button on the double arrows to the right.

- Press and hold down **Ctrl + Shift + F**.

And there are two ways to rewind the movie:

- Press and hold down the left mouse button on the double arrows to the left.

- Press and hold down **Ctrl + Shift + B**.

Cut the cable and still watch great TV

Go one step farther than watching television shows on your computer. You can also enjoy just about any TV show and movie available — and listen to any kind of music — from the comfort of your living room. You need two things to make this happen — one little box and the right streaming service.

Pick a box. If you've bought a new television set recently, it may already have built in the ability to stream video from the Internet. But you don't need a new TV as long as you have a set-top box with this ability. High-end models of Roku or Apple TV boxes each cost around $100, but you can also find simpler models for much less.

If you're willing to pay around $200 for an upscale model box, you can also get a full Web browser so you can access nearly anything from the Internet. That's helpful if you want to see photos from Snapfish on your TV, for example.

The set-top boxes typically connect to your TV through an HDMI input, although some work with older televisions that don't have this feature. The boxes even come with their own remote control, so you can surf through channels as usual.

You may already have a device that can connect the Internet to your TV. Common gaming systems like the Nintendo Wii and Sony PlayStation, along with some Blu-ray DVD players, can all stream video to your television.

Most likely, your box will be able to connect to the Internet through your WiFi home network, so you probably won't even need to run extra cables.

Select a service. Along with the hardware, you'll also need to sign up for a service to provide your TV shows, movies, and music. Any streaming device will connect using Netflix, but there are lots of other choices out there.

For movies and TV shows, VUDU, Amazon Instant Video, and Apple iTunes get good reviews from users looking for variety and ease of use. But Amazon Prime and Hulu got high marks for best value.

And, of course, you can get music from the same streaming music sources you use to listen to music through your computer, such as Pandora and Spotify. Once you sign up for a free account, you can set up channels that bring you music of a certain genre or tunes from your favorite artists.

Keep reading for more tips on how to pick the right streaming service for your needs.

Save money with the right streaming service

You can spend $60, $70, or much more every month for cable television. That's nuts, since lots of current network and cable TV programs are now available free through the Internet. When that monthly bill gets too much for you to stomach, it may be time to stop paying for cable and still watch your favorite shows.

One option is streaming TV shows on your computer, accessing them directly through network websites or sites like Hulu or Netflix that offer programming from multiple networks and cable stations. And don't think you're tied to your desk chair. A WiFi network can let you view TV on your tablet or laptop while sitting on the back patio or lying in bed.

Consider these features as you look for an online TV service.

Your shows. Obviously, if you want to watch certain shows, you'll need a service that includes those titles. Otherwise you would still be missing out on your favorites.

Each service has its own focus, so you might consider Netflix if you like to watch classic television. For current shows, look to a service like Hulu or one hosted by a network. Or consider a service with content from several networks if you want a variety.

Simplicity. Check out the service's website to see how it's organized. Is it easy to search for a show title? Are the player controls simple to understand?

The cost of commercials. You sat through ads on television in return for the programs, and you'll probably have to do that to watch for free online. But experts say you'll see an average of two minutes of ads during a 30-minute online show, while you would have to watch about eight minutes of ads when viewing the same show on TV.

The alternative might be paying for commercial-free programming. You can pay about $2 per episode to watch recent TV shows from a service like Amazon Instant Video or iTunes.

Quality and features. Some people like to watch in high definition, while others want the option of sending videos to friends. And because problems can arise in even the best-planned service, it's good to pick one with reliable customer service.

MONEY-SAVER

Rabbit ears are back. Roughly 46 million Americans rely on free over-the-air TV programming. Affiliates of the three major networks, along with PBS, FOX, and others, provide programming this way.

With a $13 indoor antenna or a $50 rooftop model, you may be able to enjoy TV the old-fashioned way. Quality is much better than in the past. Picture resolution, color, and clarity all improved with the 2009 switch to digital television.

To see what's available in your area — and how strong the signals are — type in your ZIP code or city at *http://transition. fcc.gov/mb/engineering/maps/.*

Close the gap between your TV and PC

You've already downloaded some great movies to your computer, but you want to watch them on your big-screen TV. It's easy to get these two machines talking to each other if you have a Roku box. Here's how.

• Add the free Plex channel to your Roku account.

- Go to your PC, then download and install the Plex Media Server utility for Windows. You can get this at *www.plexapp.com*.

- Right-click the **Plex Media Server** icon, then select **Media Manager**.

Once a new tab opens in your browser, you can select media to share with your Roku. You'll click on, say, **Photos** or **Movies**, then select **Add** and navigate to the folder containing the title you want to share. When you're done, click on **Add a Section**.

Finally, get settled in by your television, turn on the Roku, and choose the Plex channel. The Roku will be able to locate the Plex Media Server and display the movies you selected — assuming your Roku and PC are on the same network. Enjoy the show.

HIGH-TECH HEALTH

Nowadays, 3D viewing is not just for the movie theater. You can watch 3D movies on your TV with a 3D-ready television. You can even watch 3D movies and play 3D games on a computer. The technology looks great, and it can make you feel like you're inside the action.

But sometimes the sensation is a bit too real, causing visual problems and motion sickness. Many eye doctors say to sit farther back from the screen with a wider viewing angle to avoid the queasiness and blurred vision.

5 slick tricks to smooth out choppy video

Movies, TV shows, how-to videos, even news programs — they're all available to watch on your computer via video streaming from the Internet. But sometimes a streaming video can look choppy, with movement starting and stopping for no apparent reason.

Stop watching herky-jerky videos and enjoy a feed so smooth, you'll forget you're not in a movie theater. Try these easy upgrades.

Pause before you play. Sometimes video looks choppy because the data streaming isn't happening fast enough to keep up with the video player. First, click on the **Play** button, then click on **Pause** and wait for several seconds to a few minutes to allow a buffer of loaded data. Then you should be able to click on **Play** and see a smooth video.

Check Internet speed. See how fast data is being downloaded from the Internet by opening the **Control Panel** and double-clicking **Network and Sharing Center**. Then double-click the icon for your Internet connection, and you'll see the connection speed within the menu that opens up. A speed of at least 28.8 kilobits per second (Kbps) should be fast enough for most videos to stream smoothly.

If your speed is slower, try disconnecting and then reconnecting the Internet connection. Then check the speed again to see if it's any faster.

Get wired. Connecting your computer to the Internet through a Wi-Fi connection is convenient, but it may be the cause of choppy videos. If you watch a lot of videos, consider using a wired high-speed broadband connection instead.

Upgrade your Wi-Fi standard. If you prefer to stick with a wireless connection, be sure you have a Wireless N (802.11n) router for best viewing. Pair it with a Wireless N adapter that connects to your computer in a USB port if your computer doesn't already have it built in.

Consider a power line. It sounds like magic, but you can use your home's electrical wiring to extend a wired network or boost a weak Wi-Fi signal. A power line connection involves two or more small units — adapters that plug into the wall sockets.

Place one in a socket near your router and connect to it with a cable. Place another in the room where you want to watch videos.

Then you can connect to the second adapter through WiFi or a cable. Power line adapters work best if the two outlets are on the same electrical circuit in your home.

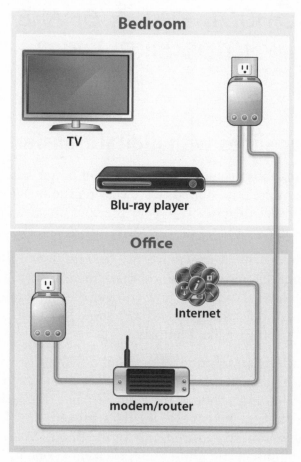

Power line adapters extend your network

SHOOT, EDIT & SHARE PHOTOS LIKE A PRO

Save your slides with digital transfer

Your old Kodachrome slides are not getting better with age. Time, temperature, and humidity are causing the images to fade and mounts to disintegrate. Turn your precious pictures into digital files so you can save the memories for future generations.

Several methods will let you convert slides into digital files on your computer. Choose the method that's in your price range and fits your skill level. No matter how you get the slides into digital form, your final task will be to clean up scratches, dust, and other damage using software like Photoshop.

Spring for a lens attachment. For around $90 or less you can purchase a lens-attached copier. This gadget connects to your camera lens, holding a slide at the right distance to take a digital photo of it. The attachment also includes a macro lens so the slide's image will fill the entire frame of the photo. With this method, you'll insert and photograph each slide, one by one.

Put your scanner to work. Some high-end flatbed scanners come with attachments to hold slides and even film in place, so you can scan the images. The process takes time, but the results are usually very good.

Consider a standalone copier. A freestanding slide and film copier may be the way to go if you have lots of slides to digitize. It does not connect to your computer, so images are saved as digital files on a memory card, which you then transfer to your computer.

Dig out your projector. A cheap and simple method involves projecting slides onto a screen, then using a digital camera to take photos of the images. This method may not produce the cleanest results, but if you are careful with camera placement, you can do a good job.

Locate the camera on a tripod at the same height as the projector, and just off to one side. Keep the camera as close as possible to the projector to reduce the amount of distortion of the image you take. Place both pieces of equipment as far from the screen as you can without causing a dim image. Even with the best placement, some amount of parallax, causing one side of the image to be slightly out of focus, will occur.

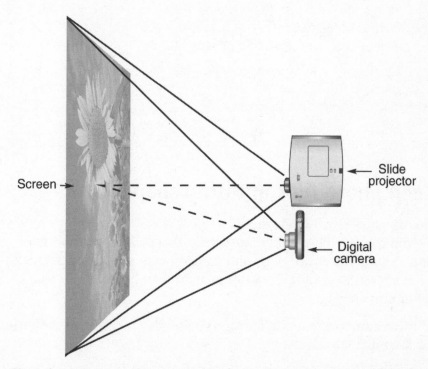

Place the camera as close as possible to the projector when you shoot a photo of a projected slide. This will bring the digital image into sharper focus.

Call in the experts. If you have lots of slides to transfer, or if you just don't want to deal with the hassles of buying equipment and learning a new process, you can send your slides to a company that will digitize the images and return the slides to you. Professional slide scanning services may also include retouching the images.

Expect to pay roughly 30 to 50 cents per slide, which may be cheaper than buying the equipment to do it yourself. Reputable companies include *www.digmypics.com* and *www.peggybank.com*.

MONEY-SAVER

If you're in the market for a new photo printer, check the ink cartridges. You'll find printers that use eight individual ink cartridges rather than a single tricolor or five-color cartridge.

A combination cartridge — with several ink colors in one — means you'll replace the whole cartridge once one color runs dry. But separate cartridges could mean you'll spend more to replace each, say eight colors times $16.

The decision may be a balancing act based on what you print. If you tend to use a lot of a single color, then separate cartridges may cost less in the long run.

Keep photo files in tiptop shape

Taking photos with your digital camera is easy — keeping track of the photos may be another story. But it's a bad habit to fill your camera's memory card with photos and never sort through them. That amounts to digital hoarding, and it can be a never-ending spiral into chaos.

At least once every month, manage your digital treasures by following these simple sorting steps.

Download photos to your computer. Put them directly into photo-organizing software, such as the free Windows Photo Gallery on a PC or iPhoto on a Mac computer.

Delete the duds. Get rid of bad photos as soon as possible. They only make it harder for you to find the gems later on.

Sort into folders. You can organize in many ways, but here's a quick and easy approach:

- Create folders by date, since the photos should already be date stamped by the camera.

- Within the date folders, sort by theme or topic, naming subfolders like "Beach trip" or "Family" or "Landscapes."

- Rename each photo with a tag that makes sense, and place it in the correct folder.

Back up photos. You can choose an external hard drive or store copies in the Cloud. Online photo-storage sites like Shutterfly, Picasa, and Snapfish offer free versions.

Clear your camera. If you don't delete the photos from your camera's memory card, you set yourself up for two potential problems.

- Multiple copies of the same photo on your computer, scattered among various folders.

- A memory card full of old pics, taking space the next time you want to take a photo.

Doing this task regularly makes it easy to find that special shot next time you want to print, share, or scrapbook your memories.

BRIGHT IDEA

Get a new passport photo for free, without even leaving your home.

Grab a friend, have him take a photo of you with a digital camera, then upload it to *www.epassportphoto.com*. Work through the steps to create a passport photo, selecting the 2-by-2-inch option. Then click on **Get My Passport Photos**.

Be sure to complete step 2, **Ensure compliance**, so your photo follows the United States passport rules. When you're asked about shipping options, click on **No thanks**, then select **Download the passport photo sheet image**. Open the file, and you can print your passport photo.

Tag photos now for simple searches later

Sorting photo prints was always a chore, and keeping your digital photo collection in order can be just as tricky. Tags can help.

Tag and store. A tag is not the name of a digital photo file, but it's a keyword or phrase that relates to what's in the photo. A photo can have more than one tag, so you could use tags like "nature" or "2012 vacation" or "Lindsey" all on the same photo.

Later, if you want to put together a slideshow about that trip, simply search for all photos tagged "2012 vacation," and you'll have what you need. To create a photo book of your own nature photography, instead search for photos tagged "nature."

Tagging also lets you sort photos without creating duplicates. If you tried to sort photos simply by placing them in certain folders, say labeled "nature" and "2012 vacation," you may want to put a photo in both places. Then you end up with multiples, taking up space and causing confusion.

Tag faces. Windows Photo Gallery, a free download in the Windows Live Essentials suite, can help you tag people in your photos. When you first open a new photo, the software will place a white frame around a person's face. Then you can add the name.

- Click on **Who is this?** under **Tag someone** on the right side of the screen.

- Type the name into the box, then click on **Add new person**.

- The next time you tag that same person, the name will appear on a drop-down list.

Tag and share. If you post photos to your Google+ account to share with friends, tagging is easy. The service lets you tag your Google+ friends in photos, and these same people will receive notifications that they've been tagged. Then they'll know to check out what you've posted.

Conserve digital space with the right file format

The alphabet soup of file formats — letters on the end of a file name — can be confusing when you're working with digital photography. Use the wrong file format to save or scan a photo, and you can end up with poor-quality pictures or waste too much storage space. The good news is only a few formats are relevant to photos and other graphics.

- JPEG or JPG. The Joint Photographic Experts Group format can reproduce millions of colors, so it works for high-quality photographs. JPEG is a great format to use if you are scanning or downloading a photo from a digital camera, and you may want to print it or post on the Internet.

- TIF or TIFF. Photos and other graphics in Tagged Image File Format tend to be large files, since they're not compressed. If you plan to scan a photo or download photos from your digital camera, then edit it only on your computer, TIF may be a good format to choose.

- GIF. A Graphics Interchange Format file works well for simple line drawings or photos that use only a few colors. GIFs can store only 256 colors, so they tend to be smaller files that can download quickly.

- PNG. Short for Portable Network Graphics format, PNG is a relatively new format that allows photos to be compressed to take up less space without lowering quality. Save photos you plan to post to a Web page as PNG files, and they'll allow the page to load faster.

No-fuss methods to get photos on your computer

You can have fun with digital photos, editing and sharing and creating projects and photo albums. But first you have to get the pictures to your computer, whether they're on your smartphone or your camera. The transfer can work in several ways, depending on where the photos are coming from.

Dig out the cord. Your camera probably came with a cord to connect it to your computer through the USB port. Hook it up, turn on the camera, and your computer should automatically open up software to let you transfer photos.

Find a card reader. Many laptops and PCs have card slots made to fit the memory card from your camera. If yours doesn't, or if you want to move photos to a computer and you don't have a cord, consider getting an external media card reader that connects using a USB connection.

Email photos to yourself. This works if the photos are on your smartphone. Then from your computer, simply download the photos from your email program and save them to your hard drive.

Put Bluetooth to work. A Bluetooth connection is a wireless method of moving files between devices that are near each other, say within a few yards. If your smartphone is Bluetooth enabled and the software is activated, your computer should recognize it.

MONEY-SAVER

You can crop and print digital photos to any size you want using your computer, but your photo-printing software and paper probably work best with standard sizes. If you override these standards, you won't get the most photos on a page of pricey photo paper. That's a waste of money.

So set the cropping grid in your software to your preferred standard size, such as 5 by 7 inches. Then slide the grid around to cover the part of the photo you really want. You'll get a perfectly cropped photo and avoid wasting paper.

5 ways to share large files for free

You may be able to email a photo to a friend if you format it right. But when you have a number of photos to share, or the file size is very large, email may not be the best method. And who wants to use "sneakernet" — that old-style method of sharing that involves walking a CD or flash drive from one computer to another?

Easy access to the Internet means you have many options when it comes to sharing photos with your friends. Some of these methods also work great for other types of large files, such as videos and PowerPoint presentations.

Put them in the Cloud. Use the free Cloud-sharing services that are probably already loaded onto your computer, such as Windows Live SkyDrive. You can share oodles of photos and documents in the 7 gigabytes of storage space included for free.

For more information about SkyDrive and other Cloud options, see relevant stories in the chapter *The Cloud: don't leave home without it*.

Find a sharing service. Similar sharing services let you post large files on their website, then send links to friends who may be interested in seeing them. Free versions of Dropbox and MediaFire have options to let you access your goodies through your Internet browser or directly from a link on your computer desktop.

Get email help. The free service YouSendItLite lets you send files of up to 50 megabytes through your email. You can also choose the YouSendIt Express version, which lets you upload directly from your desktop.

Send a link to your online storage site. Free services like PicasaWeb, Flickr, and Photobucket make it easy to post your photos, then send your friends a link so they can view, download, or buy prints.

Use your favorite social media. Post photos to Facebook, and your friends can see them quickly.

Worry-proof your photo collection

Flood, fire, a swarm of locusts — any number of worst-case scenarios can wipe out your treasured photos. Be ready before the unthinkable happens by taking steps recommended by archiving experts from the Library of Congress.

Share, share, share. Spreading the word is a great method of making sure something lasts, whether it's a good joke or a "secret" recipe.

Duplicate your best photos and distribute them to friends and family, and you'll have multiple sources if you need a copy later on.

It's also a good idea to store copies outside your home, whether a safe deposit box in your bank or an online storage service. The more the merrier.

Start from the top. It's a daunting task, but start with the best or most significant photos first. That way if you lose steam before the project is complete, at least you've handled the most important materials. And if you never get to the duds, maybe that's OK.

Label with details. While you're writing a name and date on the back of prints, also jot down the file name. Some photo-printing services will do this for you.

Go for redundancy. Flash drives, CDs, an external hard drive — all can work to hold oodles of photos. It's a good idea to save your treasures on multiple types of media in case of later changes in technology. If you have old files stored on ZIP disks, you'll understand.

A CLOSER LOOK

Saving copies of digital photos on CDs or DVDs is a good idea, since optical discs generally last a long time. If you store them in a clean, climate-controlled place, good-quality DVDs should last for decades.

If that's not enough, the makers of Millenniata's M-Disc claim it will last for 1,000 years. It's composed of stone-like metals and metalloids, and a focused laser burns pits into the data layer of the disc.

But you need an M-Disc-capable burner to write on these discs, and there's no guarantee future generations will be able to play them.

AUDIO MAGIC
Music to your ears

Arrange your songs to fit your mood

Once you load your favorite songs into the Windows Media Player on your computer, you can listen to them by album, artist, genre, or in a random order called "shuffle."

You can also create one or more custom playlists, letting you listen to certain songs without hearing the rest of your library. Here's how.

- Open the Windows Media Player by navigating to **Start** > **All Programs** > **Windows Media Player**.

- Click on **Create playlist**. A new playlist will appear on the left-hand side of the screen. Type the name of your new playlist into the text box, then click on **Enter**.

- Display the tracks you want to include in the playlist by opening up an album, artist, or genre.

- Drag and drop the track to the playlist name in the **Playlists** section. You can also accomplish this by right-clicking the track, clicking on **Add to**, then clicking on the name of your playlist in the menu that appears.

- Continue dragging and dropping tracks from the album, artist, or genre lists until you've included everything you want in your playlist.

- Click on the playlist's name to be sure it contains the songs you want.

Now you're ready to enjoy your favorite songs as a group. You can make this playlist portable by moving it to your MP3 player the next time you sync it with your computer.

Pick the best headphones for your needs

You can find a variety of headphone options that can work with your MP3 player or your computer. Most styles have models in a range of prices, so consider how and where you will use your speakers before you decide on a style.

Headphone style	How they work	Best when you
earbuds	fit inside your ear to block outside noise	need portable headphones that fit in your pocket and don't look awkward when worn
behind-the-neck	band fits around the back of your neck to keep headphones in place	want to cycle, run, or hike without having headphones slip
clip-on	stay on using a clip that slides over your ear	need to be able to take headphones off and on quickly
on-the-ear	smaller pads fit on outside of ear, letting you hear surrounding noise	want comfort while listening to music, yet still need to hear traffic or other outside noise
over-the-ear	larger pads fit over entire ear, blocking outside noise; some have noise-canceling features and high-quality speakers	want to protect your hearing; will stay at your computer, since they tend to be bulky

HIGH-TECH HEALTH

Be careful with those earbuds. Researchers in England warn that turning up the volume on your music player may lead to temporary deafness. They say sounds from a personal music player can reach levels as high as a jet engine.

Exposure to sounds louder than 110 decibels, easily attained if you turn your music volume to a high level, can damage the myelin sheath of your auditory nerves. That can cause hearing loss and tinnitus, a ringing in the ears.

The damage may be temporary, but you can cut the risk by keeping your music volume down to 70 percent of maximum.

Hush computer sounds for musical enjoyment

Your computer makes a lot of noise. Beeps, clicks, background sound effects — it can all become annoying when you're trying to listen to tunes while you work.

Take a moment to change your computer's settings so these background noises are muted while your music plays through the computer speakers. Here's how.

- Click on the speaker icon on the Taskbar.

- Click on **Mixer**, and a volume window will open up.

- Lower the volume on the **Applications/System Sounds** slider to the bottom.

- Leave the **Device/Speakers** volume slider turned up.

- Close the volume window, and enjoy your music with no distractions.

Load music from CDs onto your computer

If you already have a CD of your favorite album, there's no need to purchase those songs from iTunes or another online music seller.

You can easily load the music from all the CDs in your music collection onto your computer.

The process is called ripping. It takes time if you have lots of CDs, but an autoloading CD drive can speed up the process. Then use the Windows Media Player or the free iTunes software to listen or load music to your MP3 player.

Once you've loaded your songs to the PC, synched your MP3 player so you can listen on the go, and created a backup of your entire music library, you may be tempted to sell those old CDs. After all, a large CD collection can take up storage space, even if it's fewer shelves than the same number of old vinyl albums.

But don't sell your CDs. It's illegal to sell or donate CDs that you've ripped, since that's like making and selling copies of the music without a license.

Instead, destroy the CDs if you're done with them. An easy way to do this is to ship them to the CD Recycling Center of America, where they will be disposed of for free. Navigate to *www.cdrecyclingcenter.org* for more details.

Simple trick to transfer music files

Let's say you ripped your favorite CD of piano solos to your desktop computer, but now you want to listen to a song on your laptop.

Transferring a music file from one computer to another is actually pretty simple. A single MP3 file, used for a music track like a single song, can be moved around like any other data file on your PC. So you can attach it to an email message, just like you would do with a photo file.

If you have two Internet email accounts, such as a Yahoo account and a Google mail account, simply send the file from one account to the other from your PC. Then access your email from the laptop, download the MP3 attachment, and save it to the hard drive. You're ready to listen.

Expand musical options with a docking station

You can charge up the battery in your MP3 player, iPod, or tablet by plugging it into the USB port of your computer or laptop. That's also how you sync your music player with the songs on your computer. It's the simplest way to keep your gadget charged, but it may not be the best method. A docking station made to fit your particular gadget may be a better option. You can buy one for less than $50, and it offers several benefits.

- You can listen to your music with friends. Many docking stations have speakers, so you don't need to resort to earbuds or headphones to listen to your tunes.

- Sound quality is improved. Some docking station speakers have higher-quality woofers and tweeters than the speakers in most computers.

- Add radio. Find a model with an AM/FM tuner, and you can listen to local radio stations when you grow tired of your playlist.

- If your gadget is charging in the docking station, it's not using up one of the USB ports on your computer. Then you can use the ports for other tasks, like uploading photos from a digital camera.

Another good option may be to charge your gadgets using a charger that plugs into the wall outlet. These work faster than charging in a USB 2.0 port, but about the same as in a newer USB 3.0 port.

CAUTION

Don't let your music gadget distract you from driving. Many new cars have built-in systems to connect your MP3 player or iPod, so your music plays through your car speakers. Even in an older car you can still play your favorite tunes while you drive. Adapters and connectors use the cassette player, FM radio, or a Bluetooth connection to play music from your player.

But they may not be safer. Experts say both built-in gadget connections and after-market devices can increase distraction by requiring more steps and time to find a song or switch radio stations.

Lights, camera, action
Have fun with video

Get great video from the get-go

It's tempting to want to shoot lots of video willy-nilly, expecting that you'll edit it down to the good stuff later on. You can do that if you have time. But the best movies are created from great shots, so it's worthwhile to pay close attention to details as you shoot. Try these video-shooting tricks from the experts.

Be still. Avoid that shaky-cam effect by investing in a tripod to hold your camera still.

Zoom wisely. You may get better results by moving in closer when it's time for a close-up shot rather than using the camera's zoom feature.

When you do need to zoom, use your camera lens's optical zoom first, then the digital zoom. The camera may automatically switch to digital mode once you pass the longest optical range. Just remember that while the optical zoom uses a telephoto lens, the digital zoom simply magnifies the image, which lessens the quality.

Go slow. Don't pan or zoom too quickly, and you can further avoid a herky-jerky shot.

Don't forget white balance. This feature lets you set the camera to fit the color and lighting of your surroundings. It's especially important if the video you shoot tends to have a yellowish tint.

Frame it right. Pay attention to how much space your subject takes up in the frame, and don't automatically place it in the center of the shot. Also notice what objects are visible in the background.

And be sure to give yourself options by shooting some B footage — artistic or thematic clips that can add interest to your finished movie.

Train your smartphone to take quality video

When the old camcorder you've been using for years finally dies, don't assume you need to replace it with a newer model. It's possible your smartphone has enough video-shooting power to do what you need. In fact, mobile phones recently edged out cameras as the most-used gadget to shoot video.

Quality improvements in smartphones are a big part of the reason. Newer models of iPhones, HTC's Evo and Sensation, the Kyocera Echo, and others — or perhaps your digital camera — can take great video. Some even take high-definition-quality video. When you use your smartphone as a video camera, there's no need to remember to bring an extra device or keep its battery charged. And that's yet another gadget you don't have to pay for.

But you'll need to pay attention to a few simple guidelines to capture the best video possible with your smartphone.

- Shoot in a bright location, since your smartphone camera probably won't provide great lighting.

- Don't forget to clean the camera glass to remove dirt and fingerprints.

- Keep your smartphone still while shooting to avoid shaky video. You can buy a tripod made just for smartphones, or find a mount that will let you connect your smartphone to a regular camera tripod.

- Load video-capture software on your smartphone. A free app like iMotion HD lets you be ready in a pinch to shoot great video.

A CLOSER LOOK

Ensure the movies you burn to DVD can be played anywhere by picking the right type of disc. Only those marked DVD-R will work on nearly all computers and DVD players, including older models.

You can burn your home movies to discs marked DVD-RW, DVD+R, or DVD+RW, but you can't be sure they'll play on the machines of everyone you share the movies with. Then your whole project may be a waste of time.

Pick the right video-editing software

You need software to help you edit videos into a form people will love to watch. The free Windows Live Movie Maker can do basic tasks, but the version for Windows 7 has fewer features than older versions.

Other free software is available, including the powerful program Lightworks, which you can download at *www.lwks.com*. It's used by professionals, but it might be a bit tricky for a video-editing novice.

So consider purchasing software with the features you need — designed for the home user. When you're ready to take the plunge, keep these qualities in mind.

Look for something simple. If you can't figure out how to use your software, it's a waste of money. Features like the ability to drag and drop video clips for easy editing create a program that's intuitive enough for anyone to master. Look for a free trial version of software so you can give it a test drive before you buy.

Invest in surround-sound capabilities. Be sure your computer also has a good sound card and high-quality multichannel speakers.

Prepare for 3D options. If you're planning to edit video in 3D, you'll need the appropriate 3D glasses and monitor to make it work.

Add bonuses to make life easier. Some packages include templates, stock footage, and images that can spice up your videos. You'll never know how useful these options can be if they're not available.

Enjoy hassle-free uploading. If you plan to post videos to YouTube, Vimeo, or Facebook, look for software that makes the task easy.

And nowadays, you can edit video footage directly on your tablet. Inexpensive apps like Avid Studio for iPad and Movie Studio for the Motorola Xoom let you do the job without moving your video clips to the PC at all. Now that's convenient.

Prepare your PC for high-graphics use

Once you decide to do video editing on your computer, you've moved into the realm of the graphics-intensive users. That means you need the right memory to allow programs to run smoothly, just like people who use AutoCad software or play video games with complicated graphics and animation.

One way to check your graphics memory is to open the software provided by your computer's video chipset manufacturer. Common manufacturers include AMD, Nvidia, and Intel.

Access this information on your computer by clicking on the **Start** button and then on **Control Panel** > **Appearance and Personalization** > **Adjust screen resolution**. Then click on **Advanced settings** and open the **Adapter** tab. Here you'll see details about your computer's video card, including memory. You'll find listed the **Total Available Graphics Memory**.

Check the system requirements label on the box of the software you want to buy, or find this information on the company's website, to know if your computer can handle it. If not, you may want to upgrade to a more powerful graphics card.

Save your tapes with easy conversion

Capturing your video memories on VHS tape was a good start. Back in the day, that was what you used to film the babies and birthdays in your life. But these magnetic tapes don't last forever.

In fact, every time the tape is played, it gets damaged just a little. Stretching, tearing, brittleness — it all adds up to the fact that a VHS tape has a life span of years or at most decades.

It's really not that difficult to convert your old videotapes into DVDs before they break or rot or before there aren't any VCRs left to play them. Along with your computer and the tapes you want to copy, you'll need these four items and a little time.

- A gadget to play the tapes. This could be either your old VCR or a video camera. You will connect it to the capture device using either the color-coded RCA cables or an S-Video connection. If you have a choice, use the S-Video connection to get the best quality.

- Some kind of capture device. For around $50 you can pick up a little box such as Dazzle DVD Recorder Plus from Pinnacle or Honestech's VHS to DVD. These devices typically connect to your computer using a USB connection. They usually come with software, which you should load onto your computer before connecting the USB cable.

- Video-editing software. If you just want to dump the video from VHS to a disc, you can do that. But why not take a little time to create a movie your family will enjoy watching? If your computer is running Windows 7, you can download and use the free Windows Live Movie Maker software. This can let you do basic editing and add transitions and some effects.

- Blank DVDs. Once you have digital copies of your video memories on your computer, you're still not done. Burn the videos to DVDs for storage or to share with friends and relatives. Most software lets you select from various quality settings, which affects how much DVD space your memories will require.

Some capturing devices and software also let you save video in formats that you can load onto an iPad or iPod for easy sharing. If you go that route, there may be no DVD involved. But think about also saving to DVD for posterity.

BRIGHT IDEA

Save time by spending a little money to have professionals convert your videos to DVD. Companies like ScanCafe, DigMyPics.com, and PeggyBank.com will convert old VHS tapes, 8mm film — even photo slides, negatives, and audio recordings — to digital formats.

Most services let you choose what type of media to use for your digital memories, like DVD or CD or flash drive. And some will even store your memories online, then let you access them or share the website with family.

Start by requesting a box to ship your tapes. Check the prices so you're not shocked by a large bill.

Network & Internet know-how

get more out of going online

NETWORK NECESSITIES
How to set up, fix & secure

4 great reasons to have a home network

A home network isn't just for the geek-minded. You may be surprised to find out how useful — and painless to set up — one can be.

First, make sure you understand exactly what a home network is. It allows all the digital devices in your home to "talk" to one another.

If all you have is one computer and one printer connected by a cable, even though they do communicate back and forth, you don't have or need a network.

On the other hand, if you own multiple computers all sharing one printer, you're in need of a network. Here are some important benefits of a home network.

Share the Internet. Most homes use a modem to connect to the Internet through an Internet Service Provider (ISP) — a telephone or cable company, or a satellite service.

You probably have a single Internet account and a single public IP address that identifies you to other computers on the Internet. You need a network of some kind to allow multiple devices to log onto the Internet using that one IP address.

Transfer files. Using a network to move files back and forth between computers and devices is as easy as drag and drop. You can start a document on your PC and finish it up on the couch with your laptop.

Access documents. Turn on file sharing, and you don't even have to move a document to let someone else on your network read and work on it. You'll learn more later in this chapter, but remember sharing through a network also works for applications.

Play games. If you only ever play card games against the computer, you're probably set, but if you enjoy the challenge and fellowship of multi-player games with friends and family in your living room, then a home network is for you.

There are two types of networks, wired and wireless or Wi-Fi — short for wireless fidelity. Wired, of course, means everything is connected with cables. Wireless networks involve a few more steps to set up and can pose unique complications.

Cut the cord — go wireless with all your gadgets

A wireless network lets you connect all sorts of devices in your home — not just computers, but also printers, smartphones, tablet computers, audio components, and even your television.

You'll need a wireless router that physically connects to your cable or DSL modem and a wireless network adapter in each device you wish to connect. They are pretty standard on anything you'd buy today.

If your PC or notebook does not have an internal adapter card, use a desktop wireless adapter. This handy device turns a wired system wireless and lets an older computer stay part of the family without compromising security. Choose between these two formats.

- USB. Plug this into any USB port, let the drivers install, and you've got a wireless signal. It's super convenient, but some experts say there's a downside — it might not deliver as strong a long-range connection as your second option.

- PCI. You must install a PCI adapter onto your system's motherboard, so it isn't as convenient. But this type is known for outstanding wireless power.

Now make all your gadgets part of your wireless network. Here are a few fun and different reasons to connect.

Laptop. Making your laptop part of your wireless network is a no-brainer. But maybe you never thought of transmitting video from it to an HDTV using a connection like Intel's Wireless Display. Makes streaming content brilliant to watch.

Tablet. Take a photo with your tablet and send it wirelessly to your printer. Then save space by offloading it from your tablet to your PC.

E-reader. Install a reader app on your tablet or phone, and keep up with your e-book even when your e-reader is somewhere recharging.

 MONEY-SAVER

Lease or rent a modem from your cable company and you could pay anywhere from $4 to $7 a month. That could top out at $84 a year. Buy one from Amazon or Best Buy, for instance, and you might pay as little as $60.

Even if you go with a more expensive model, you'll get your money back the first year. Just make sure you buy a modem that is compatible with your service.

How to find the perfect wireless router

Most people focus on getting the latest and greatest computer, then think nothing of hooking it up to an old router. But if your router is more than four years old, you're networking with a handicap.

Remember, a router lets you connect multiple devices to the same network. It's how your printer, tablet, and laptop can access the Internet, share files, and do much more. Time and advancing technology, however, can turn your router into a drag on your system.

- Years of heat can damage the delicate inner components causing your router to function more slowly and even experience power blips.

- If your router doesn't support the latest Wi-Fi standards for speed and range, you'll feel it when you try to connect.

- Unless you have dual-band wireless, you're likely to experience interference from other household devices like microwaves, baby monitors, and cordless phones. Dual-band means it operates in both the 2.4 and 5 GHz Wi-Fi frequency bands.

Know your standards. The term "band" refers to the radio frequency used for wireless communications — 2.4 GHz or 5 GHz, for instance. Each device meant to operate wirelessly uses a Wi-Fi standard which, in turn, uses a particular band. For instance, 802.11B and G devices use the 2.4 GHz band. 802.11N can use either 2.4 or 5. So what does that mean to you?

Many experts believe the best way to perk up your wireless network is with a Wireless-N router. It will support numerous PCs, tablets, notebooks, smartphones, game consoles, Blu-ray disc players, and more.

Consider the range. The whole point of having a wireless router is so you don't have to punch holes in your walls and run a tangle of cables throughout your house. And your devices should function equally well whether you're in the far corner of an upstairs bedroom or in a lounge chair on the back deck.

When shopping for a router, you'll see a distance range listed on the box, but that may be a best-case scenario, not accounting for walls and interference. *PC Magazine* says the average wireless range is 180 feet indoors and 1,500 feet in a space without walls or other types of interference. Experts suggest buying a router with considerably more range than you think you need.

Routers with external antennas seem to pump out a stronger signal, but some people complain they aren't as streamlined, don't easily fit into narrow shelving, and tend to break off. Don't automatically reject a router with internal antennas. Some models have increased the number of internal antennas to boost performance.

If signal strength continues to be a problem, consider purchasing a signal amplifier or adding another wireless router to your system.

Sign on for security. You'll read more about securing your wireless network later in this chapter, but keep these things in mind when choosing a wireless router.

- WPA2 (Wi-Fi Protected Access 2) is a form of encryption protecting you from hackers. Make sure this is a security option.

- Built-in firewall protection is a must.

- MAC filtering should be a standard feature on just about any wireless router. It allows you to decide what devices can and cannot access your network.

- If your devices use WEP (Wired Equivalent Privacy), your network is vulnerable. A Wireless-N router brings with it the latest security protocols to keep your sensitive data safe.

Top 5 Wi-Fi power boosts

It's not unusual for a Wi-Fi signal to fizzle or skip out entirely. Since speed and reliability are the cornerstones of computing today, here are a few ways to make sure you can always connect and stay connected to your network.

First, check the basics. Establish that your router is on and functioning. Most have LEDs that stay lit or flash to let you know all is well. Go to your router manual for specifics. Then check all the physical connections between your router and wired devices like your modem. If you're still having problems, move on to these solutions.

Reboot. Shut off your PC, router, and modem. Wait a couple of minutes and restart them in this order — modem, router, then computer. If this doesn't work, try unplugging your router for about 15 seconds then plugging it back in.

Reposition. Now check the physical location of your router. In a perfect world, it would be:

- in a clear open space, not covered or blocked by other objects, especially metal ones.

- in a well-ventilated area with plenty of space for cool air to circulate around it.

- in a central location without walls built of materials that reflect or absorb radio waves, like metal, concrete, or brick — or things like mirrors.

- as close as possible to all receiving devices, with a clear line of sight to each.

- as far as possible from microwaves, wireless landline phones, or active Bluetooth devices, which emit competing radio signals that can create interference.

Of course, you can only do so much. You're restricted by your home's floor plan, the location of cable or telephone jacks, and other non-negotiables.

Restore. There should be a small reset button on the back of your router. Press and hold it for about 10 to 15 seconds — use a pen or paperclip — and you'll restore the router's settings to factory defaults. Since this wipes out all settings, you'll have to reconfigure connections and reset security.

Reinstall. Make sure you have the latest wireless adapter driver or software on your PC. Check the manufacturer's website and follow their instructions to reinstall, then reboot your computer. At the same time, check for the latest firmware update for your router. Firmware is software that's programmed on a hardware device. A new release could fix problems and add features. Go to the router manufacturer's website for the latest drivers, utilities, and firmware.

Repeat. According to tech experts at *PC World*, you can increase your Wi-Fi coverage — as much as 40 percent — with a wireless repeater, Wi-Fi booster, or range extender.

One of these gadgets can cost anywhere from $20 to over $100, but it needs to be compatible with your router and have an easy setup.

Place it at the outer edge of your router's coverage. It will connect to your current wireless network and repeat the signal, bouncing it farther into the rest of your home.

You may take a hit on speed when using a repeater, but at least you should get a signal.

For another method of boosting your home network, read about power line connections in *5 slick tricks to smooth out choppy video* in the *TV & movies: cutting-edge ways to watch* chapter.

Secure your Wi-Fi network

Let's face it — a wireless network means your connection and possibly your information are simply out there floating in the air.

Anyone with the means and motivation can snag onto either one and go for a ride. Therefore, security is priority one.

Enable WPA2. If you've been around the network security block before, you're probably familiar with WEP, Wireless Encryption Protocol. It's a decades-old technology that, while better than nothing, will leave as many holes in your network security as a slice of Swiss cheese.

Routers purchased within the last six years, however, come with a powerful new security technology called Wi-Fi Protected Access 2 (WPA2), which encrypts your information while it is traveling.

Enable WPA2 on your router and set a tricky password for it, sometimes called a passphrase or key. Make it long, possibly random, and with no names or numbers related to your identity.

While turning on your router's WPA2 can be ridiculously easy, in some cases as simple as pressing a button labeled "Wi-Fi Protected Setup" — you can always check your router manual for specific instructions.

You'll want all your other wireless hardware to support WPA2 as well. Then make sure you enable WPA2 when you connect each one to your network, keying in the same password. Now, any device that tries to connect to your network will need to input your WPA2 password.

Turn on MAC address filtering. This security measure is best for a home environment where you have a set number of known devices you want to allow access to your network. Here's how you make it work.

Every device, whether a tablet, smartphone, or computer, has a Wi-Fi adapter inside with a unique identifying number, or a Media Access Control (MAC) address. Go into your router settings and turn on MAC filtering. Then enter the MAC address from each device on your approved list. Any unapproved MAC address that attempts to connect won't be allowed network access.

This is a bit of work, and certainly not foolproof, but it is a smart security step to take.

Secure your SSID. Your Service Set Identifier (SSID) is a unique ID — maximum of 32 characters — for your wireless network. It's used to make sure information gets sent to the right place. Your router comes with a default SSID, which you should change as soon as you set up your network. Then turn off your router's SSID broadcast feature so no one near your home can hack into your network.

Block WAN ping. If you see this setting on your router, turn it on. It essentially tells hackers scanning for a valid network that yours is not responding, and they'll move on.

BRIGHT IDEA

You may have many wireless networks in your area competing for airspace. This interference could slow your network down. Since you can operate your network on any number of channels, changing your network channel to a less-congested one could give you some additional speed.

Use a free utility, like inSSIDer, found at *www.metageek.net*, to analyze the traffic near your home and help you find a wireless channel with the least congestion.

HomeGroup makes home networking a snap

Windows 7 has a great new feature that makes sharing between home computers fast and easy — HomeGroup.

Any computer you have running Windows 7 can use HomeGroup to share printers, movies, songs, documents, and images. It's password-protected so you control what is shared and what stays private. Plus, you can make any file you want read-only, so others can look, but not touch.

When Windows 7 is installed on the first computer in your network, it automatically creates a HomeGroup. Then each new computer joining your network has the option to become part of your Home-Group. Here's how to add a computer to an existing HomeGroup.

1. First, get the password for your HomeGroup that's on your original computer. Do this by clicking on **Start** > **Control Panel**. Then type "homegroup" in the search box and click on **HomeGroup** > **View or print the homegroup password**.

2. On your new computer, click on **Start** > **Control Panel** > **Network and Internet** > **Choose homegroup and sharing options**.

You'll see all the existing HomeGroups on your network. Choose the one you wish to join, the types of files you want to share, and enter your password. Then whenever you click on **Network** on any of your computers, you should be able to see all the computers in your HomeGroup and access their files.

Remember, in order for HomeGroup to work, be sure:

• network sharing and HomeGroup are turned on.

• you're connected to the network.

• your network location is set to **Home**.

• **Network Discovery** is turned on.

3 easy ways to share your files

Your mother taught you to share. Your toys, your snacks, your crayons. But what about your files? It can be a good idea — for certain files, with certain people. Here are different situations where you might want to share files, and how to make it happen.

Share public library files across your network. Remember that Windows 7 has four default libraries — Documents, Music, Pictures, and Videos. Each of these has a Public subfolder. These are not automatically shared, but it is easy to turn Public sharing on so other computers on your network can access them.

1. Navigate to Windows Explorer if you have this on your Taskbar, or click on **Start** > **Computer**.

2. In the left pane of the dialog box that opens, select whatever library you wish to share — **Pictures**, for instance. Double-click it and you'll see a **Public Pictures** subfolder appear below it.

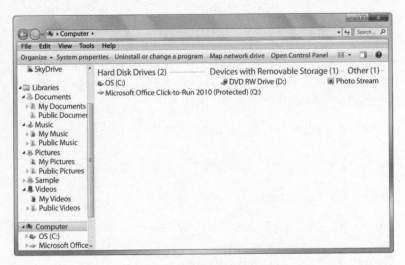

Your Public folders

3. Right-click the subfolder, then click on **Share with** > **Advanced sharing settings**.

4. A dialog box will open and under **Public folder sharing**, select the option **Turn on sharing so anyone with network access can read and write files in the Public folders**.

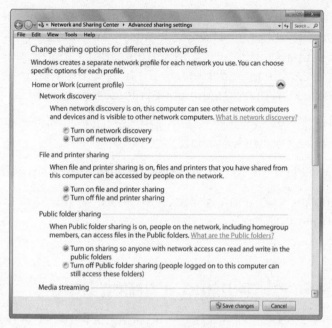

Turn on file sharing

Share specific files with your HomeGroup. In order for someone in your HomeGroup to see files and folders on your machine, you must specifically mark them to share.

1. Click on **Start > Computer** to open the Explorer window, then navigate to the folder you wish to share.

2. Right-click the folder and choose **Share with**.

3. You have several choices including **Homegroup (Read/Write)**, which will allow others to change your files; **Homegroup (Read)**, which allows others to only view your files; or you can choose the **Specific people** entry and type the name of another user in the HomeGroup. You're able to choose a **Permission Level** for each person.

4. Click on the **Share** button to save your changes.

Share files with other users on one computer. If you've set your computer with different User Accounts, then you know each person has his own password, files, and settings. But suppose you want to let another family member see your photos. You might want to allow sharing on that specific photos folder.

1. Navigate as explained before to the folder under your account you wish to share.

2. Right-click the folder and select **Share with** > **Specific people**.

3. Type the user name you wish to share with and select a **Permission Level**.

Give shared printing a green light

One of the advantages of setting up a home network is the ability to use one printer for all the devices in your house. To make sure everyone can actually share your printer, you need to walk through three different sets of steps.

Turn on printer sharing. You must tell your network that you want printer sharing turned on.

1. Click on the **Start** button > **Control Panel** > **Network and Internet** > **Network and Sharing Center** > **Change advanced sharing settings**.

2. Click on **Turn on file and printer sharing**, then **Save changes**.

Share a printer. Now you have to make sure a specific printer has sharing turned on.

1. Click on the **Start** button > **Devices and Printers**.

2. Right-click the desired printer, then select **Printer properties** > **Sharing** (tab) > **Share this printer** (checkbox) > **OK**.

Allow a printer through your firewall. Turning on sharing won't do any good if your Windows Firewall stops others in your network from accessing your printer.

1. Click on the **Start** button > **Control Panel** > **System and Security** > **Windows Firewall**.

2. Click on **Allow a program or feature through Windows Firewall**.

3. In the **Allowed programs and features** list, make sure the **File and Printer Sharing** checkbox is selected. Then click on **OK**.

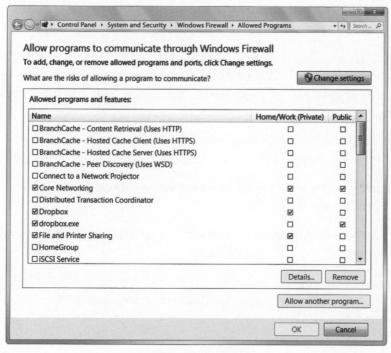

Printer sharing

Troubleshoot Internet speed woes

Does your Internet connection seem slow? It might be you're not getting the bandwidth from your Internet Service Provider (ISP) that you're paying for. You can check your connection with an Internet speed test. Several websites offer these for free, including:

- *Speedtest.net*

- *www.speakeasy.net*

- CNET Bandwidth Meter at *cnet.com/internet-speed-test*

- Consumer Broadband Test at *www.broadband.gov/qualitytest*

If your test results show you are operating at a slower speed than expected, call your ISP. They can check your equipment and connections. If your connection passes the speed test, consider these possible culprits.

Bandwidth hoggers. Is someone on your network transferring big files or spending lots of time online streaming or gaming?

Malicious software. Viruses and spyware can cause an Internet slowdown.

Old hardware. An aging processor or too little memory will affect your speed.

Area users. If you use cable Internet, the number of people sharing your line can impact your connection speed.

Boost your browsing power

Get the most out of your browser

Firefox, Chrome, Safari, Camino, Opera, Internet Explorer. You're probably familiar with some or all of these funny-sounding Web browsers. Chances are you already have a favorite that helps you do all the wonderful things you want to on the Internet.

A browser is a software application that allows you to display and interact with all the text, pictures, video, and other content found on Web pages. You can choose to use one browser on your computer, or several, as each has its different strengths.

Internet Explorer (IE) is the go-to choice for most Windows users, while Safari and Camino work better for Macs. Mozilla's Firefox is considered the best all-around browser, while Opera and Google Chrome are the fastest. No matter which you choose, here are a few basic things to remember.

Keep your browser updated. Make sure you have the most recent version of your browser so you always have the latest features and the most up-to-date security protection. How do you know if you need an update? It's easy to check.

- For Internet Explorer, open the browser, click on the button that looks like a gear in the upper right-hand corner, then click on **About Internet Explorer**. It will tell you if you're using IE8, IE9, or IE10, Microsoft's most recent offering. If you don't have the latest version, you can check for updates by clicking on **Start** > **Control Panel** > **System and Security** > **Windows Update**.

- For Mozilla Firefox, click on **Help** > **About Firefox**, and you'll see the current version, for example **19.0.2**. If this is the most recent version, it will say **Firefox is up to date** below the numbers.

- Google Chrome, Safari, and Opera follow a similar procedure, although not all of them say the browser is up to date. If you can't click on the browser's name, look for an icon to open the information. For example, in Chrome a button with three horizontal lines is located on the right side of the toolbar.

Set your favorite as the default. If you use more than one browser but prefer a particular one, you may want to set it as the default.

To do this in Firefox, for example, select **Tools** > **Options**, and click on the **Advanced** tab. Under **System Defaults**, click on **Make Firefox the default browser**, then click on **OK**.

If you then open another browser like Internet Explorer, it may ask if you want to make that one the default browser. To stop IE from repeatedly asking you, simply uncheck the **Always perform this check when starting Internet Explorer** box. Then click on the **No** button.

You can also make this change in Internet Explorer's **Internet Options** menu. Click on **Tools** > **Internet options** > **Programs** tab.

Under **Default web browser**, make sure the box next to **Tell me if Internet Explorer is not the default web browser** is unchecked.

Boost your browser with special features

Your browser can't provide everything you need, so computer whizzes have come up with the perfect solution — tiny programs that attach to your browser to add extra functions.

These small software codes are called plug-ins, add-ons, or extensions depending on the browser. You may be familiar with some of the more popular ones like Adobe Flash, Adobe PDF, or QuickTime.

If you've ever been shopping on the Web and wished you could compare prices without going to a dozen other websites, guess what — a plug-in can do that for you. Or maybe you'd like to block all those annoying pop-up ads. That's another easy task for a plug-in.

There are millions of these mini programs to choose from, and most of them are free. Don't be afraid to search them out. They can help you customize and personalize your browser, making your Internet experience that much better.

Plus, they're super easy to install. Here's how to do it on some of your favorite browsers.

- Internet Explorer. Select **Tools** > **Manage add-ons** > **Find more toolbars and extensions**. Browse through the plug-ins to see what you might be interested in, then click on **Add To Internet Explorer**.

- Safari calls its plug-ins extensions, and finding them is easy. Click on the gear icon in the upper right of your screen. Choose **Safari Extensions Gallery**. Pick a category or browse around until you see what you want.

- Opera also calls them extensions. To find them, click on **Menu** > **Extensions** > **Get Extensions**.

- Firefox. Look for add-ons for this browser. Select **Tools** > **Add-ons** > **Get Add-ons**. Under **More ways to customize**, choose **Browse all add-ons** if you want to look through their selections. Once you find what you want, click on **Add to Firefox**.

- Chrome has a multitude of plug-ins, themes, and Web apps. To locate them, click on the bar icon in the upper right corner of the screen. Select **Tools** > **Extensions**, and click on **Get more extensions**. Pick a category, or search for the extension you want.

If you decide you no longer want a particular plug-in, it's easy to uninstall. Go to the same place where you found it, for example **Manage add-ons** in Internet Explorer. Find your plug-in, and click on the appropriate uninstall button. It will appear as **Delete**, **Disable**, **Remove**, or something similar.

A CLOSER LOOK

You've taken the plunge and installed a plug-in. So how can you tell it's working? Sometimes it's obvious. You may see a new button or menu choice on your screen or notice more options when you right-click an item. Or the button may appear only when you need it, like when you're shopping online.

If you don't see any visible difference, don't worry. As long as you've successfully installed the plug-in, you can be sure it's working in the background, helping to make your Internet browsing easier and more productive.

Fix the dreaded red X

The Web page you're interested in finally loads, but the all-important picture is not there. All you see is a frustrating red X in the corner. That's common when an application can't find an image or video. If it doesn't appear after a minute or two, here are some things you can try.

Refresh the page. It may be a simple loading error so this should be your first move. The Refresh or Reload button is usually located on or next to the Address bar in most browsers. Look for a circular-shaped arrow.

Right-click the image. Your browser or security software may have blocked the image. By right-clicking, you may bring up an option that will let you view it. Look for something like **Display Image** or **Show Picture**.

Try a different website. Perhaps your site's server is down. Surf the Web and see if you have problems opening pictures on other Web pages. If it seems to be limited to the original page, that site may have broken images. You can either wait and try again later or contact the website Administrator.

Check the browser settings. You may not have your Web pages set to show all pictures. In Internet Explorer, click on **Tools** > **Internet options** > **Advanced** tab.

Under the **Multimedia** category, find **Show pictures**. If it doesn't have a check mark in the box, then check it, and click on **OK**. Refresh the page again to see if the pictures appear.

Clear temporary Internet files. Empty out your browser cache to make sure you're seeing the most up-to-date version of the page. The browser saves a temporary copy and may display that stored version rather than a fresh page.

Be careful to clear only the browser cache and not all temporary files, or you might delete cookies that you need. Most browsers will give you a choice. In Firefox, for example, go to **Tools** > **Clear Recent History**. Click on **Details** and you'll see a list of checked boxes. Uncheck all boxes except **Cache**.

Clearing your Internet browsing cache

Switch browsers. Sometimes the fastest option is to try and open the page with a different browser.

Make life easier with favorites

You've probably visited hundreds of websites to shop, plan vacations, choose recipes, and get health advice. But trying to get back to that one site with the delicious peach cobbler can be a nightmare. That's why browsers have come up with a handy shortcut to save the websites you visit most.

In Internet Explorer you choose Favorites, while in Firefox, Safari, and other browsers you collect Bookmarks. This is one shortcut you'll want to take advantage of, as it will save you time and aggravation. Follow these easy tips to make the most of your Internet Explorer favorites.

Add a preferred website. To save a website, click on the favorites button, which is a star icon in the upper right corner of your screen. Then click on **Add to favorites**. Rename the favorite if you want, choose a folder to save it in, then click on **Add**.

For even quicker access to the site, add the link to your Favorites bar by clicking on the downward arrow next to **Add to favorites**. Then click on **Add to Favorites bar**. If you can't see the Favorites bar at the top of your screen, right-click the star icon, and click on **Favorites bar**.

Fix a broken link. You keep clicking on one of your favorite sites and it refuses to open. Chances are the URL has changed, which has broken the link.

This is one problem you can easily fix. First, you need to search for the new Web address, and copy or write it down. Return to your favorites button, right-click the problem website, and choose **Properties** from the menu.

In the dialog box that appears, click on the **Web Document** tab, type or paste the new address into the URL text box, then click on **OK**. Go back to your favorites and check to make sure the link works.

Save favorite tabs. Wouldn't it be great if you could save all your travel or shopping websites at one time? If you create a tab for each one, you can do just that.

Simply click on the favorites button, click on the downward arrow next to **Add to favorites**, and choose **Add current tabs to favorites**. Type in a name for your folder, and click on **Add**.

Your favorite shopping sites will now occupy a separate folder in your Favorites Center. Click on the right-arrow button next to the folder name to see your group.

Display favorites full-time. If you use your favorites a lot, especially if you've built up a large list, you may find it easier to see them at a glance. You can do that by pinning the list to your home page.

Click on the star icon, then click on the green arrow in the left corner. This is the **Pin the Favorites Center** button. Internet Explorer will open your favorites in its own box on the left side of the page and keep it there for easy access.

BRIGHT IDEA

You have to squint to see the words on your Web page and wish you could make them larger. No problem.

- Press the **Ctrl** key and turn the scroll wheel on your mouse until the text reaches a size you're comfortable with. Pressing **Ctrl +** or **Ctrl -** will also work.

- Change your Zoom setting. Click on **View > Zoom > 100%**, or choose a larger size if you wish. Or click on the gear icon in the upper right, select **Zoom (100%)** and change the percentage.

- Even simpler, click on the Windows logo key and the plus (+) sign. That turns on Windows' **Magnifier** feature in most browsers.

Enjoy old favorites on new PC

Hooray — you've finally upgraded to a new computer. Now don't forget to move all your browser favorites to your fancy new PC. After you've spent years building up your favorites list, you don't want to start over.

The process is easy in Internet Explorer and will be similar in other browsers.

1. Insert a flash drive or disk into the appropriate slot on your old computer.

2. Go to **File** > **Import and export** > **Export to a file**. Click on **Next**, which you'll repeat after each step.

3. Check the box next to **Favorites**.

4. Select a specific folder or the entire **Favorites** folder.

5. Click on **Browse** to look for your flash drive or disk. Select it, then click on **Save** > **Export** > **Finish**.

To transfer your favorites, insert your flash drive or disk into your new computer.

1. Go to **File** > **Import and export** > **Import from a file**.

2. Check **Favorites**, then browse to the saved file containing your favorites on your disk or flash drive. Click on **Open**.

3. Internet Explorer will ask you to select a destination folder. Click on **Favorites** > **Import** > **Finish**.

Trim a URL for easy sharing

If you're a regular on Facebook or Twitter, or simply read a lot online, you've most likely come across shortened URLs that link you to Web pages and articles. The link behaves like any other — all you do is click on it and you're whisked away to the appropriate Web page.

Writers use them to avoid sharing a long, unwieldy Web address. The longer it is, the more likely the link will be broken. Plus, short links are a necessity on websites like Twitter, where characters are limited.

Use a shortening site. If you'd like to create your own tiny URLs, it's as simple as navigating to a website shortening service, pasting your long version in, and receiving a short one in return.

• A popular choice is Bit.ly. Navigate to *http://bitly.com*, and you'll see a field at the top of the page where you can paste your URL. Click on the **Shorten** button, and you'll get a new URL starting with *http://bit.ly*. Click on the **Copy** button, and

241

you're ready to paste it into your email, tweet, or anything else you want to share.

- Google's service at *http://goo.gl* works like Bit.ly and is simple and reliable. Both services let you track your new shortened URL to see how many people click on it. Look for a list of your URLs and a link for more details. You can even find out what countries your viewers are from.

- An easy-to-remember shortening service is Tinyurl. Head to *http://tinyurl.com*, submit your long URL, and click on **Make TinyURL**. Copy and paste it into your document. You can also offer your recipients a preview of the long link so they know which site they're opening.

Find a plug-in. An even easier way to trim a URL is with a plug-in. On Google Chrome, for example, download the extension for Bit.ly, and it will put an icon on your address bar. Click on it when you want to shorten the Web address that's showing, and a convenient sidebar will pop up with a **Shorten** button.

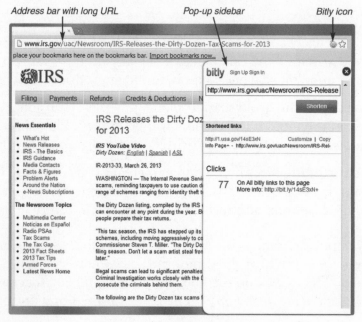

URL shortening plug-in

Check for Bit.ly and other URL shortening plug-ins in Firefox, Internet Explorer, and other browsers as well.

Beware of malware. One problem with a shortened URL is you can't tell where it's taking you. That opens the possibility of linking to a malicious website. Or your click may activate malware that can infect your computer system. Try these tips to protect yourself.

- Check the domain at the end of the link. Recent malicious shortening services have used the .info domain.

- Before you click on a short link, paste it into a filter such as Longurlplease.com to verify its real destination. You can download it as a plug-in or bookmarklet. You can also try Virustotal.com, where the Web link is scanned by six URL analysis engines.

3 great tabbing tips

The tabs option in Internet Explorer (IE) and other browsers lets you flip between multiple websites in a single window. Now you can surf the Web without all those open browser windows cluttering up your desktop.

If you surf often, you know that to open a new website, you click on the small tab button located to the right of the current tab or press **Ctrl + T**. Switching between tabs is as easy as clicking each tab on the toolbar.

But Internet Explorer has come up with other options that make tabbing even easier.

Use the Quick Tabs button. This option is a timesaver if you keep a lot of Web pages open. It will display a series of thumbnail images of your tabbed pages that you can easily view and select.

If you have IE7 or IE8, check for a button to the left of the row of tabs with four small squares on it. It only appears when you have multiple Web pages open. IE9 does not provide a button, so you'll have to use **Ctrl + Q** to open Quick Tabs. You'll also have to set it up before it will work.

1. Click on **Tools** > **Internet options**.

2. Under the **General** tab, find the **Tabs** section and click on **Settings**.

3. In the **Tabbed Browsing Settings** window, check **Enable Tabbed Browsing**, then **Enable Quick Tabs**.

4. Click on **OK**.

5. Restart Internet Explorer to enable the Quick Tabs option.

Open one tabbed window in another. Suppose you have similar recipes open in different tabs. You want to compare ingredients but can't remember them as you flip from one to the other.

Internet Explorer solves that problem by letting you drag one window into the other. Left-click a browser tab, hold the mouse button down, and drag the tab into the window you have open.

You'll now see a smaller version of your selected page on top of the larger window. You can set your recipes side by side and decide which one you like better. To move the page back, left-click the tab and drag it back to the tab bar.

Left-clicking a tab will also allow you to switch tabs around if you'd like to change the order of your Web pages. Simply drag the tab to another spot on the tab bar.

Give tabs their own space. The more tabs you open, the more space they take up. This can be a problem in IE9, where the tabs appear on the same row as the Address bar. To obtain more room to view your Web addresses, give your tabs their own home.

Right-click any tab and select **Show tabs on a separate row**. Your tabs will shift to their own spot beneath the Address bar.

> **BRIGHT IDEA**
>
> You can open any Web link in a new tab — whether you see it in an email, an article, or a Web page — so you can easily read it in a separate page. Just right-click the link and select **Open in new tab**.

Find a search engine to match your needs

The next time you want to know what movies a certain actor starred in, you might be told to "google it." The Google search engine is such a big part of Internet culture that it's now virtually synonymous with searching.

Google is fast and accurate and has a handy preview arrow that lets you view a page before clicking on it. But because of its popularity, it's also a frequent target of malicious attacks that could affect your search results.

Many people swear by this searching powerhouse, but it doesn't hurt to add others to your search bar, so you can pick and choose depending on your needs.

Bing. This is Microsoft's default search engine, so you may be familiar with Bing if you're using the latest versions of Internet Explorer. You can also access it at *www.bing.com*.

Bing takes advantage of Microsoft's giant web of services to help it return relevant links. For example, Bing Travel uses Microsoft's Farecast to help you find the best time to buy your airfare at the lowest price.

Bing maintains a complete history of your searches, which may come in handy if your computer crashes and you have to find all your Web pages again. But if you prefer not to have your searches tracked, look for those that let you turn off search histories and maintain your privacy.

Blekko. This new search engine uses "slashtags" to help people find what they're looking for. After entering your search term, you add a forward slash (/) then another term that acts like a keyword to narrow the search.

For example, you can input headaches/acupuncture or headaches/aromatherapy, and you'll end up with different results tailored to your needs. You can also combine slashtags to refine your results even more.

If you use a backslash (\) before the tag, it will remove all results related to that keyword, so be careful to use the right one. You can learn more about your options by clicking on **Help** at *www.blekko.com*.

Blekko guards your privacy by deleting all IP addresses within 48 hours and refusing to share your information with third parties.

DuckDuckGo. This seach engine shows each website's icon, called a favicon, next to its results, so you immediately see where the information came from. Clicking on it will bring up all the articles or information on that topic the site has to offer.

DuckDuckGo also gives you a handy definition or overview of your topic at the top of the page. Plus, it's another site that doesn't collect or share your personal information or keep track of your searches.

Learn more about this unique search engine with the memorable duck favicon at *www.duckduckgo.com*.

Ixquick. For even stronger security, try the search engine that prides itself on keeping your data out of the wrong hands. It does not record a user's IP address, place cookies for tracking, or share personal data with any third parties.

Check out its policies at *www.ixquick.com*. And for more on safe Internet surfing, see the chapter *Safe & secure surfing*.

CAUTION

One way to protect yourself from clicking on scam businesses or malicious websites is to pay attention to the Web links that come up in your search. The name of the organization or Web page you want should come right before the domain name, such as .com, .org, or .net.

For example, if you see a link to BestBuy.com, you can be sure you're visiting the electronics superstore. But if a site comes up as Bestbuy.computers.com, you may think you're linking to the store — but, in fact, might be rerouted to a less-secure website.

Quick trick for saving images

You're browsing for home ideas, and you see a photo of the perfect table for your kitchen. You try to save it to your ideas folder, but the website won't let you download it. That's probably because the image is part of the Web page itself and not a separate file.

But don't worry. Internet Explorer provides an easy way to solve that problem. Just right-click the picture, and select **Save picture as** from the pop-up box. Then navigate to where you want to save the picture, such as your pictures library or desktop.

You'll also have other options, like printing or emailing the picture, or setting it as your desktop background. Just be aware if it's a small image, it will look fuzzy when enlarged to fit your computer screen. You need to look for a high-resolution image for any picture you plan to print or display.

Safe & secure surfing

5 dangerous security myths you must know

Identity theft in the United States may be declining, but that's not much comfort to the 12 million people who reported identity fraud in 2012. You increase your odds of becoming the latest casualty by hanging on to myths like these.

It won't happen to me. If hackers had to find their targets one at a time, you might stand a chance of escaping their notice, but don't underestimate their level of sophistication. Complex programs run day and night, from all over the world, automatically searching for vulnerable computers and networks.

I installed a security program a few years ago and it's still good. Life in the world of cybercrime moves at the speed of light. And if you aren't updating your security program as well as your operating system on a regular basis, you're going to be left in the dark — alone and vulnerable. New security threats are uncovered all the time, and security software developers work hard to thwart them. You paid for that security program, now get your money's worth by installing their updates.

I don't visit questionable sites so I won't get a virus. In 2012, more than 80 percent of attacks were redirected from legitimate sites that were hacked.

I don't download files so I won't get a virus. There are many ways to get a virus. You could, for instance, be the victim of a drive-by download. This is when a malicious piece of software is downloaded onto your computer when you visit a Web page or HTML-based email that's been compromised. You'll never know it's happened — until it's too late. And in many cases, the administrator of the website doesn't know it's happened either.

I can tell a phony website by the way it looks. This might have been true years ago, but today's website developers, even the criminal-minded ones, have state-of-the-art tools at their disposal. They take great pains to make their sites look and feel legitimate.

This may all sound scary, but don't let your fears keep you from enjoying the wonderful world of the Internet. Yes, it can be a dangerous place, but by using a little common sense and some available security tools, you can safely learn, shop, and just have fun on the Web.

Read on to discover easy ways to browse the Internet securely, avoid online scams and hoaxes, and protect your computer from hackers.

Protect your PC with a double firewall

In the case of firewalls, two is better than one. At least when one operates via your hardware and the other is a software firewall. Together, these make your first line of defense against hackers and malicious software.

Let a router shield your PC. Many experts say you should buy and install a router even if you have only one PC and no plans to set up a wireless home network. That's because most routers come with a built-in hardware firewall.

It will check data flowing to and from your computer, block harmful software, and conceal your computer from prying eyes. Because this firewall is running on a completely different device, it won't conflict with whatever security measures you set up on your computer.

If your router has wireless capabilities, but you don't plan on using it wirelessly, read the manual for instructions on disabling its signal. This will keep your Internet connection from being broadcast throughout your neighborhood.

Keep in mind that the hardware firewall on your router will protect all the computers on your network.

Use the free Windows Firewall. Each computer you own should have its own software firewall installed and enabled. A good basic one comes with Windows 7. Here's how to access it.

Click on the **Start** button > **Control Panel** > **System and Security**. You'll find two options under **Windows Firewall** — **Check firewall status** and **Allow a program through Windows Firewall**.

- **Check firewall status** takes you to a window where you can see if the **Windows Firewall state** is off or on. The left pane of the window has an option to let you change its state. Make sure the firewall is on.

- **Allow a program through Windows Firewall** lets you view a list of programs. Here you can change the setting on a program or feature, or add a new one to the list.

If you choose to install a third-party firewall — one with more control and features, for instance — it will automatically turn off Windows Firewall and disable its setting.

7 signs of a dreaded virus

It's crucial you attack a computer virus early. Just like many human illnesses, the more time it has to take root and spread, the harder it can be to get rid of and the more irreparable the damage.

For instance, some viruses can repeatedly duplicate large programs to the point your computer's memory is full. Then you may not even be able to successfully install an anti-virus program.

Here are seven red flags you've been invaded with rogue software. If you experience any of these symptoms, take immediate action.

- sluggish performance

- repeated error messages

- frequent freezes or crashes

- difficulty saving documents

- frequent pop-up ads, often during computer startup

- unreliable operating system start

- a need to frequently reboot and restart

In addition, you may experience crazy problems like these.

- changed and locked settings

- files and folders that vanish or appear to be locked

- the sudden disappearance of critical programs

- programs launching on their own

- unstable program files that display unusual warnings

- drive trays opening and closing on their own

- unusual sounds that play at random

- problems sending or receiving email

- email attachments that unexpectedly disappear

- new and unfamiliar components on your Web browser

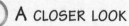

A CLOSER LOOK

Identity theft is the scary monster lurking on the Internet. But you can slay the beast with these security tips. Not only will you safeguard your personal data, but you'll stop ID thieves in their tracks.

- Include a router with a hardware firewall as part of your home network.
- Turn on the built-in Windows 7 firewall.
- Install anti-virus and anti-spyware software.
- Keep your operating system and security software up-to-date.
- Use smart password strategies.
- Enable your Web browser's security features.
- Recognize secure websites, and only provide personal information on them.
- Control how and when others are tracking you online with cookie management.
- React quickly to any security-breach notification you may receive from Windows 7 or a security program.
- Get smart about online scams.
- Never use a public Wi-Fi connection to access your sensitive accounts.

Vaccinate your PC against nasty viruses

The Internet can be a scary place — spyware, viruses, trojans, worms, keyloggers. But fighting back is now fast, free, and easy with Microsoft Security Essentials (MSE).

Download this software bundle at windows.microsoft.com/en-us/ windows/security-essentials-download for immediate and comprehensive protection against malware. It should take only minutes and the payoff is huge.

Get in the know. Here are just some of MSE's key features.

- automatic updates

- an easy color-coded security status notification

- behind-the-scene scans that you can customize to fit your schedule and the number of files you want scanned

- a check for suspicious programs, that includes email and instant messages, multimedia files, and synced files

- protection against rootkits, a nasty type of malware

- a minor drain on your computer's resources with no apparent slowdown of performance

There are some things MSE doesn't do. It does not protect against hackers, spam, phishing attacks, or identity theft. You'll still need to practice smart Internet habits to cover these bases.

Get started. The Microsoft Security Essentials Installation Wizard walks you through all the installation steps, then updates its virus and spyware definitions before doing its first scan. Be aware of a couple of things.

- You may get an error message during MSE install if you have another security program on your computer. You must remove this conflicting program completely.

- MSE turns on the Windows automatic update feature in order to get the latest malware threat information. If you turn Windows Update off, you must update MSE manually or run the risk of missing the newest threats.

- MSE automatically turns on Windows Firewall if you aren't using a different one.

Get acquainted. Become familiar with the MSE dialog box as soon as you install the program. It has four tabs — **Home**, **Update**, **History**, and **Settings**. Each one provides good information and ways to customize this security experience.

CAUTION

Don't undermine your PC's security. You may think twice the anti-virus programs is twice as nice, but in reality, it's double the trouble.

If you have two anti-virus programs constantly monitoring your computer for malware, they are very likely to step on each others' toes. This constant interference can cause freezes, crashes, errors, and false positive messages.

The best security system includes:

- a network router with a built-in hardware firewall.

- a software firewall.

- one anti-virus program.

- one or more anti-spyware programs.

Foil spyware with free defense

Spyware is malicious software installed on your computer without your knowledge or consent. It tracks what you do on the Internet and transmits that information to someone else. There are a number of ways you could become infected with spyware.

- You are vulnerable anytime you connect to the Internet without proper protection — a firewall and anti-spyware.

- It can be hidden in another file — often one you've downloaded from the Internet or gotten through peer-to-peer file swapping.

- You can pick up spyware from a CD, DVD, or other removable media you connect to your computer.

The best-case scenario is that, once you're infected, you receive ads targeted to match websites you visit often. In the worst hands, spyware can capture email addresses, passwords, and credit card information.

Find free prevention at your fingertips. Fortunately, Windows 7 comes with anti-spyware raring to go — a program appropriately named Windows Defender. It runs constantly in the background, checking for suspicious activity, blocking spyware when it tries to install, and alerting you when a program tries to change important Windows settings. All this is called real-time protection.

Search and destroy. You'll usually see signs that your computer is infected with spyware. Many are similar to the general symptoms of a virus — lots of pop-up ads even when you're not browsing the Internet, settings that change and lock unexpectedly, new toolbars on your Web browser, crashes, and slower than normal processing. If you experience any of these, don't waste time. Run a scan.

Windows Defender scans your system for spyware on a set schedule. The default is every day at 2 a.m. But it only runs if your computer is turned on. So you either need to make sure your computer doesn't shut down at night, or change the scan time. In the case of emergencies, though, you can tell Defender to perform a scan at any time.

To access Windows Defender, click on the **Start** button and type "Defend" in the search box. **Windows Defender** should show up in your search results. Click on it. Snoop around in the Windows Defender dialog box, getting familiar with your scan options, alert levels, and more.

Double up on protection. Unlike anti-virus programs, anti-spyware runs happily with a crowd. So even though Windows Defender is powerful, you'll increase your chances of defeating spyware if you have more than one anti-spyware program installed on your computer. Check out these other free options:

- Ad-Aware at *www.lavasoft.com*

- Spybot at *www.safer-networking.org*

- Spyware Terminator at *www.spywareterminator.com*

You can also spend anywhere from $30 to $60 for a highly rated anti-spyware product. Visit the TopTenReviews website at *www.toptenreviews.com* to see how their choices stack up.

Remember, many security suites include anti-spyware scanners, so you don't have to rely on a standalone anti-spyware security product.

> **CAUTION**
>
> Once you have Microsoft Security Essentials installed, Windows Defender becomes redundant and is automatically disabled.

Successful tips for setting an ironclad password

It's easier than you think for someone to crack your passwords. It's also easy to foil a password hacker from the get-go. You just can't be lazy — spend a little time creating and protecting your passwords, and you won't be sorry.

Make them strong. Here are some cardinal rules for setting a tough-to-crack password.

- Use a combination of uppercase and lowercase letters, numbers, symbols, spaces, and underscores.

- Make each password, at the very least, eight characters, realizing that longer is better. According to one source, a lowercase, six-character password takes only 10 minutes to crack. Twelve characters is ideal for most home computers, but try using as many characters as allowed.

- Pick a phrase or sentence to use as a passphrase, such as "MyDogIsSmall&Smart." Notice this one has both upper- and lowercase letters, a symbol, and is 18 characters long.

- A mnemonic is a pattern of letters, numbers, and symbols that help you remember something. For instance, start with a sentence like, "We live in a yellow 2-story house." When you turn it into a mnemonic, it becomes "Wliay#2sh."

- Steer clear of common words, names, or facts from your life that someone might figure out, like your birthdate.

- Start with an idea or an item that is special to you, like a favorite place, movie, food, or song. Then tweak it, using the rules above, so it becomes a complex password you'll easily remember.

- Do the same thing using your profession or a hobby. Math, music, and geography, for instance, have terms and symbols you can use in unique and creative ways to form a super tough password.

Now test just how strong your new password is. Go online to *www.microsoft.com/security* and click on **Create better passwords**, then **Create strong passwords**. Type yours in and see how Microsoft rates it.

Keep them safe. Good passwords do no good if you literally hand them out to every Tom, Dick, and Harry.

- Never use the same password twice. If one account gets hacked, you've opened the door to every other account you have.

- Change them frequently. Some experts suggest creating a new password every 90 days, especially if it guards sensitive information. At the very least, go in and update important accounts every year.

- Don't share. There's no reason to give a password to anyone over the phone, in an email, or on a social networking site.

> ### CAUTION
>
> Some of the most common Internet security blunders involve passwords. To keep your private data secure, don't:
>
> - use any personal data in your password. That includes names and dates.
>
> - simply pick a word from the dictionary and make it your password.
>
> - use the same password for everything.
>
> - keep the same password for more than a year.
>
> - share any password with anyone through email, instant message, or social media.

Never forget a password again

You've worked hard to create strong passwords, you change them often, and you don't share them with your Facebook friends. Then you write them on a scrap of paper by your computer because you keep forgetting them.

Where do you think an unscrupulous person will look first for private account information? The fact is, he won't have to look very hard if you've got confidential passkeys pasted on sticky notes all over your monitor.

There is a solution to this thorny problem — use a password manager.

What you can expect. The beauty of a password manager is its simplicity. You simply have to remember one password. Ever. That password unlocks your chosen password management program and it does the rest.

The program resides on your computer and securely stores, in a protected database and sometimes also in the Cloud, the user name and password to every website and online account you set up. Most password managers will also import any passwords you've previously stored in common Web browsers like Firefox and Chrome.

When you sign in with your master password, then visit a familiar site, you are automatically logged in to that website. When you visit a new site requiring login information, your password manager asks if you want to save the information. That's it.

A few password managers are free. Many are very reasonably priced. Most have a one-time purchase price, although some have a yearly fee.

What you might like. Many features are must-haves. Some are nice-to-have extras. Ask these questions to help determine what's best for you.

- Is your data stored on a strongly encrypted database?

- Does the program include a password generator to help you create complex passwords?

- Does it support all major Web browsers?

- Can it save more than one set of login information for a particular site? If so, you can select a user name from a list and the password manager fills in the rest.

- Are passwords captured for applications as well as websites?

- Will the password manager recognize fraudulent websites and prevent you logging in? This protects you from phishing attacks.

- Can you use the program on your mobile devices? Is it compatible with all of them?

- Does it have the ability to store additional personal information — like your address, phone number, and even credit card numbers? This will save time when filling out online forms.

- Can you use the manager on multiple computers? Will it sync information between them all as it's updated? This is helpful if you and your spouse need to access joint accounts.

- Is there a free trial period?

- Does the manager allow you to export your data to a USB device? If so, you can use it to access password-protected sites on other computers, without having to type sensitive data on the keyboard. This protects you from malicious keylogging software.

You can choose from literally dozens of password manager applications. But before you do, go to a trusted review website like *www.cnet.com* or *www.toptenreviews.com*, search for password managers, and see what they have to say.

CAUTION

Don't put your passwords and user names in your will. It sounds like a good idea at first, but think about it — wills become public documents after your death. That means your private access information could be available to others, maybe even before your heirs have a chance to act. Plus, it will get expensive if you have to revise your will every time you change passwords.

You should leave this information behind so your heirs don't lose valuable assets, but do it right. Create one simple list and include account information, user names, passwords, and PINs. Keep it in your home — perhaps in a lockbox or safe — so you can update it easily. Then let the executor of your estate or a trusted family member know where it is.

Boost Internet privacy with IE features

After securing your network and computer, the next line of defense against thieves and hackers is your Web browser. You can tweak it to more thoroughly cover your surfing tracks and keep private information private.

Your Windows 7 computer probably came loaded with Internet Explorer (IE), Microsoft's flagship browser that has been around since 1995. A recent version, IE9, has some powerful security features you're sure to love. You can access these features in a couple of ways.

- Click on the gear icon in the upper-right corner of an IE window. Choose **Safety** and you'll see a list of the following features.

- Or you can select **Tools** from the top menu bar then view these choices.

InPrivate Browsing. Turn this option on and a separate browser window opens. Nothing you do in this window is stored on your computer — that means no cookies, no history, and no temporary files. Truly private browsing. All toolbars and extensions are also disabled as long as you're in this mode.

You'll know you're browsing privately by the **InPrivate** logo in the Address bar of your new window. When you're through with your private session, simply close the window and return to normal browsing.

InPrivate Browsing

Tracking Protection. When you visit a website, some of the content, images, and ads might be provided by a different website. That content is often used to track and gather information on your surfing habits.

IE9 lets you select and load free Tracking Protection Lists (TPL), which are created and maintained by third parties. Each list contains domains that Internet Explorer will block, preventing them from sending out your information.

Once you select Tracking Protection, you're given the opportunity to download one or more TPL. Any list you download and enable is active for every site you browse, and stays active until you turn it off.

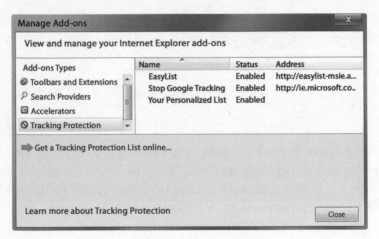

Tracking Protection

SmartScreen Filter. This security feature is designed to target phishing scams. These use emails to lure you to a seemingly legitimate website where you're usually asked to update personal information, like account numbers, passwords, and financial data. The website is, of course, bogus and set up only to steal your information.

SmartScreen Filter lets you check any specific website to make sure it's genuine. The site is checked against a Microsoft database of malicious content. Anything suspicious or previously reported as malicious will trigger an alert. Once you turn on SmartScreen Filter you'll see a new choice under the **Safety** option — **Check this website**.

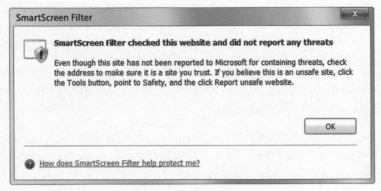

SmartScreen Filter

Application Reputation. This is part of the SmartScreen Filter, and once that's turned on, you'll receive pop-up information about file and software downloads. If they're recognized as malicious you'll get a warning.

ActiveX Filtering. ActiveX is sometimes described as a program that allows other programs to communicate with IE. One example is the software that allows videos to play on your browser.

You've been able to turn ActiveX on and off for some time, but that was an all-or-nothing deal. Now with ActiveX Filtering, you can decide on a site-by-site basis.

ActiveX Filtering is enabled if there is a check mark next to it under the **Safety** option. Then when you navigate to a site, you'll see a blue circle with a slash through it on the Address bar. Click on the circle for more information and options.

Active X Filtering

Be a smart cookie and manage online tracking

Internet cookies are little files with a bad reputation — some undeserved. Over the years, they've evolved from villainous tracking devices into an important and unavoidable part of Web browsing. That means you need to learn how to work with cookies, not against them.

Browse easier with single-session cookies. This type of cookie is fairly straightforward.

- They are enabled by default when you enter a particular website.

- They record information only during that visit to that website.

- They are erased when you leave the site, close your browser, or shut down your computer.

Single-session cookies aren't even all bad. For instance, they allow you to submit a complaint form or complete a survey. They enable the shopping cart feature you need for online shopping. They help you navigate through a site more easily, let you post blogs, and allow you to take advantage of other advanced features.

Be wary of persistent cookies. These cling to your computer like a barnacle to a sea tub — until they expire or you manually delete them. On the plus side, they are the reason you get personalized shopping recommendations and advertisements. Your habits and preferences are stored so a website knows what you like. Cookies can even be a part of safe browsing — helping monitor potentially unsafe sites. The downside is your personal information is often tracked and kept for other purposes.

Learn how to block and remove. You truly don't want to block all cookies indiscriminately. Remember, some have merit. Even the Federal Trade Commission website uses cookies. And there are so many things you can't do without them, you can easily become frustrated.

That said, most browsers offer a fairly sophisticated menu of cookie-blocking options. With a little effort, you can tweak your settings so you get the best of both worlds. The options are usually found under a Privacy or Tools heading.

Most experts agree, however, it's a good idea to clear all cookies periodically. How often you choose to do this depends on your browsing habits and your level of paranoia.

In Internet Explorer (IE) on the Menu bar, click on **Tools** and select **Delete browsing history**. Inside the next window, check the box next to **Cookies**. You can uncheck everything else from the list if you wish to only delete cookies. Click on **Delete** and you've removed all cookies from IE — at least until you start browsing again.

The steps for other browsers — like Google Chrome, Firefox, and Safari — will be different, but usually you're able to delete cookies from the same place you delete your browsing history. If you're still having trouble locating your cookie options, check under a **Settings**, **Tools** or **Privacy** heading.

A CLOSER LOOK

Web browsers like Firefox, Opera, Safari, and Google Chrome also offer good security tools. The terms vary from browser to browser, and you access them in different ways, but all provide ways to browse privately, eliminate tracking, and clear your browsing history. Explore each one to become familiar with its options.

Avoid the Internet's most dangerous people

Stargazing sometimes has nothing to do with astronomy and everything to do with following celebrities online. This seemingly harmless pastime could mean a major breach in your Internet security if you're not careful.

Cybercriminals create websites using the names of popular celebrities to attract people surfing the Web. Then they load the site with malicious software designed to steal personal information. This malware could be hidden in a video or photo you view, or in a file you download.

Every year, McAfee, the world's largest dedicated security technology company, researches popular culture — musicians, actors, athletes, comedians, and more — to see who cybercriminals are targeting. Go online to *www.mcafee.com/us/sitemap.aspx*, and search under Press Releases for their latest list of the "Most Dangerous Celebrities."

To stay protected:

- watch streaming content only from established sites like Netflix, Hulu, NBC, or ABCtv.

- be wary of any free download, and only use familiar and trusted sites.

- keep your computer's security in place and up-to-date.

BRIGHT IDEA

Internet hoaxes may be running rampant, but you don't have to fall victim to them. If you receive any type of warning about a virus or other type of malicious software, make sure it's valid before you act or alert your friends. These sites keep current on the latest scams.

- *www.consumer.ftc.gov/scam-alerts* (Federal Trade Commission)

- *www.us-cert.gov/ncas/current-activity* (United States Computer Emergency Readiness Team)

- *www.dhs.gov/internet-hoaxes* (Department of Homeland Security)

- *www.snopes.com*

- *www.scambusters.org*

Easy tips help ID shady websites

How can you tell when an Internet link is phony? Many bogus websites are practically identical to companies' legitimate sites. But there are always small clues. Here are some things to look for.

- Make sure the domain name has no misspellings or missing letters. It may be subtle — a missing "s," a double letter, or a misplaced capitalization. Unless you're on your toes, you might miss the errors in these domain names — *www.micrsoft.com*, *www.micosoft.com*, *www.mircosoft.com*.

- Check the URL suffix. Is the dot (.) where it's supposed to be? Are there letters after the .com? For instance, the legitimate site is *www.paypal.com*. A bogus site might read *www.pay.pal.com* or *www.paypal.com.com*. And even though there are many valid suffixes beyond .com — .net, .org, and .gov, for example — be wary of any you've never seen before.

- See if you can verify the contact information. The easiest way is to check if the phone number is legitimate.

If you're about to type in personal or financial information, make sure the website uses encryption.

- Look for a URL that begins with https. The "s" stands for secure.

- Check for a closed padlock symbol indicating a digital certificate. Certificates mean SSL (Secure Sockets Layer) encryption is scrambling the data between your PC and the website.

Don't rely on searching for sites or typing in addresses. Instead, whenever possible, use your Web browser's bookmarking tool to navigate to your favorite sites.

You can report phishing — bogus websites set up to obtain your personal information — to the Department of Homeland Security. Just send an email to *phishing-report@us-cert.gov*.

10 steps to stronger hotspot security

One of the great joys of modern technology is computing on the go. There's nothing like relaxing at a coffee shop while you surf the Web. Or taking care of a little business before boarding a plane. But to do all these fun things, you must connect to a public Wi-Fi network.

Unfortunately, many of these are not secure, and scammers have become part of the experience. Dishonest people create their own networks alongside legitimate ones, then just wait for the unsuspecting to log on. Or they hijack your transmissions, hoping to pick up personal information.

But don't let them spoil your fun. Practice all the good security protocols you've already learned — have a good firewall on your mobile device set correctly, install and keep security programs up-to-date, use strong passwords that are not stored on your computer, and enable your Web browser security. Then take these additional steps to enjoy public wireless networking without fear.

Disable sharing. Add another layer of invisibility to your computer by turning off file and printer sharing before you connect to a public wireless network. Read about this in *3 easy ways to share your files* in the *Network necessities: how to set up, fix & secure* chapter.

Go private before you go public. Make sure folders on your computer that contain sensitive data are hidden. Right-click the selected folder then choose **Properties** > **General** tab > **Hidden** > **OK**. Repeat on as many folders as you like. Now you need to tell Windows 7 that you don't want to show these files.

Open Windows Explorer and go to **Tools** > **Folder options** > **View** tab. Under **Files and Folders** select > **Don't show hidden files, folders, or drives**.

Lock your files. If you have Windows 7 Professional edition or higher, you can encrypt any file you plan on using via a public network. The file won't look any different to you, but no one else will be able to access it. Note, encryption doesn't keep your file from being deleted, and the file will become decrypted if you attach it to an email.

To set encryption, right-click your desired file or folder. Then choose **Properties** > **General** tab > **Advanced** > **Encrypt contents to secure data** > **OK**.

Manually select a Wi-Fi network. Don't let your laptop or tablet automatically hook into the first network it finds. This may be a default setting, so change it if necessary.

Click on **Start** > **Control Panel** > **Network and Internet** > **View network status and tasks** > **Manage Wireless Networks** (left pane). Right-click the network you wish to change. Then select **Properties** > **Connection** tab, and uncheck the selection **Connect automatically when this network is in range**.

Look for secure hotspots. The majority of networks are not secure. The most protected ones require you to sign in. WPA and WPA2 are currently the strongest types of encryption. So if you must sign into a hotspot with a WPA password, it is secure and encrypting any information sent on that network. The establishment providing the network should give you the password to connect.

Windows 7 lets you see which networks are secure before you connect. Go to the **Network Notification** icon that is available from your Taskbar. Hover your mouse over each possible connection and you should see its security level. Again, look for WPA or WPA2. Avoid any networks that are listed as unsecured.

Set your location to public. Connecting to a new network prompts Windows 7 to ask for more information. Choose **Public Network** when given the option so certain security steps will be taken automatically.

Look for website encryption. Only log in to or send personal information to websites that you know are fully encrypted. That means it's protecting your data to and from the site. Every page should have https as part of the address.

Turn it off. Don't stay logged in to any online accounts after you've finished your business. And disable your Wi-Fi as soon as you're through using it.

Avoid risky transactions. If possible, don't bank or shop online while you're logged onto a wireless network. It puts your private data in danger.

Install a browser plug-in. Some browsers, like Firefox, offer additional pieces of security you can download from their home website. These can force encryption on sites that don't normally have it.

> **CAUTION**
>
> Scareware is an Internet scam eager to pick your pocket if you're not careful. It poses as a legitimate security utility that pops open a window in your Web browser, appears to scan your computer, then states you have multiple malicious programs or security threats.
>
> It hopes to scare you into buying and installing its own "fix-it" program. What you'll be getting instead is a download of spyware and viruses.
>
> Your best protection is to install and keep up-to-date your own, reliable anti-virus and anti-spyware tools.

THE CLOUD
Don't leave home without it

Reap the benefits of the Cloud

If the word cloud conjures up an image of a white, fluffy puff in the sky, you're behind the times. Today's Cloud is a technological wonderland that's changing the way we store and access information.

Simply speaking, the Cloud refers to a network of servers that stores your data on the Internet rather than on your home computer. Whenever you do any kind of computer work using online data or programs, you're working in the Cloud.

Do you store photos online with Picasa or Shutterfly or use a Web-based email service like Gmail or Hotmail? If so, you're already using the Cloud.

The main advantage of Cloud computing is that you can access your data wherever you go. Whether you use your smartphone, tablet, or a friend's computer, your information is always at your fingertips. You can also share files with other people without having to email them or copy them to a USB flash drive.

Plus, storing your data on a remote server keeps it safe in case of a computer crash or natural disaster. By using the Cloud, you'll never lose a precious document — even from theft, fire or flood.

You can easily find a Cloud service that fits your needs. Most programs offer limited free storage, then charge a monthly or annual fee for additional space in the Cloud.

If you're interested in backing up your data on a regular basis, there are Cloud programs for that as well. It's worth checking a variety of online services to see which works best for you.

SkyDrive — Windows' powerful storage solution

Microsoft SkyDrive is a cloud-storage service that downloads automatically as part of the Windows Live package of free programs. It will give you 7 gigabytes (GB) of free storage — enough for 20,000 documents or 7,000 photos.

Go to *explore.live.com/windows-live-skydrive* to see what SkyDrive has to offer. You'll find tutorials and overviews of its main features.

Set up the program. If you don't have Windows Live, you can download a SkyDrive desktop or mobile application at *https://apps. live.com/skydrive*. You'll need a Windows Live ID to use the program. You may have already created one if you use Hotmail or Xbox Live. If not, click on the option to register for an account. Once you sign up, you can then access the site from the welcome page or by going to *skydrive.live.com*.

Your Skydrive folder will be stored inside your personal User folder. If you would like to put it elsewhere, such as My Documents or on your desktop, click on **Change** in the dialog box that appears while you're registering. In **Browse For Folder**, select the one you want, then click on **OK**.

Upload files. You can easily add files to SkyDrive by dragging them directly into your folder. You can also copy or save files to your SkyDrive folder. Once there, the files will automatically upload to your SkyDrive account in the Cloud. Blue arrows next to the file mean it is synchronizing. Look for the green check mark to show the process is done.

Install SkyDrive on your other computers and mobile devices and you can access your files from any of them. Whenever you make changes in one location, all the others will be updated as well. You can be sure you've got the most recent version of a file no matter which computer you use.

Get organized. Create folders for your SkyDrive files and add them to your Windows Libraries for easier access.

Inside a SkyDrive window, click on the folder you want added. In the toolbar, click on **Include in library**, and select which folder you want from the dropdown menu, like **Documents** or **Pictures**. Your SkyDrive folder will be copied to that folder in your Library.

Take advantage of sharing. You can quickly and easily share photos with your grandchildren or send a recipe to your best friend. All you have to do is create a shared group.

1. Click on the SkyDrive folder you want to share. In the toolbar, click on **Share with > Specific people**.

2. Type in a name or click on the downward arrow to find someone. Click on **Add**.

3. Choose a permission level, then click on **Share**, then **Done**.

Whenever you put a file into that folder, others will be able to see it.

CAUTION

SkyDrive restricts individual uploads to 2GB, so if you have a large file, like a video of your granddaughter's musical, you may not be able to store it. It also prohibits material containing nudity or excessive violence. So if you want to upload a season of your favorite HBO series, you may be out of luck.

Free Office apps at your fingertips

You want to finish a letter to your grandson or add scores to your golf league's spreadsheet, but you're away from home. Not to worry. Just find the nearest computer and log in to your Windows Live SkyDrive account.

SkyDrive offers free Office Web Apps, which are online versions of Microsoft Word, Excel, PowerPoint, and OneNote. Sign into your SkyDrive account online and click on **Create** in the toolbar. Pick the program you want from the dropdown list. You can do everything you're used to — create, view, and edit — whether it's in a document, spreadsheet, or presentation. You won't have all the bells and whistles of the desktop versions, but the programs will have the same familiar look. And whatever changes you make will appear on all your synced devices.

Plus you can share your files online since they're stored in your SkyDrive account. It's easy to collaborate with your friends, even if they don't have Microsoft Office installed on their computers. They can use the free Office Web Apps to view and edit your documents.

Even better, if you and one of your golf partners want to add scores to your spreadsheet, you can both do it at the same time. The Excel Web App will tell you if other people are working in the same document, and both edits will show up in real time.

Maximize your storage protection

SkyDrive is a plus for Windows users since it works seamlessly with all the Microsoft Office programs. But here are some other Cloud storage services you may want to try.

Dropbox. If you want simplicity, go to *www.dropbox.com* and download this program. It will put a folder on your desktop where you can drag documents, photos, videos or any other type of file. These files are uploaded immediately to the Dropbox website so you can be sure they're the latest version no matter when or where you access them. You can also share files by creating a link to a shared folder. You only receive 2GB of storage for the free service, but it provides more if you're willing to pay. And if you get your friends to join, they'll award you bonus space.

Dropbox is also available as an app for your iPhone, Blackberry, or Android products so you can get to your files while you're on the go.

Google Drive. This service keeps all your documents, spreadsheets, presentations, photos, videos, and music safely stored in the Cloud. To download it, go to *drive.google.com/start*.

Google Drive features 5GB of free online storage and the ability to buy more. But one advantage is that any files you create using Google Docs are not counted toward that allowance. Neither are files other people share with you.

File sharing is one of its strengths, and if you need to collaborate with someone on a project, this is a program to try. It seems to work best for those who use Google Docs for word processing, otherwise you may have to convert your document to Google's format.

Sugarsync. Instead of syncing data from one virtual folder on your desktop, Sugarsync allows you to sync data from any folder on your computer. It supports all major mobile devices, which is a plus if you want to use it with your Blackberry or Kindle Fire.

If you upload numerous files from various devices, it will organize them into a single window on your desktop. It comes with 5GB of free storage with larger storage options for a fee. Try it at *www.sugarsync.com*.

CloudStor. Would you like your own personal Cloud? CloudStor combines an external hard drive with the convenience and easy access of Cloud storage. Get 1 terabyte (TB) of storage space for around $100 and 2TB for $200. You won't have any additional fees because your data is stored in the Cloud through your device using PogoPlug as the software interface.

After you set up your account at *www.myCloudStor.com*, you can upload and download files from any Internet-connected PC, Mac, or mobile device.

Apple iCloud. You've probably heard about iCloud even if you're not a Mac user. It's Apple's Cloud service that automatically syncs emails, pictures, music, calendar, and contacts across all your Apple devices. iCloud also gives you 5GB of free storage on secure servers. Learn more at *www.apple.com/icloud*.

HIGH-TECH HEALTH

Unlimited online storage space can have a dark side if you tend to be a hoarder. Amassing thousands of emails, videos, pictures, documents, and other files demands mental energy and can create anxiety, experts warn.

If you identify with any of the following signs, you may want to contact a professional technology organizer for help.

- You break out in a cold sweat at the thought of deleting anything.

- By the time you find a file, you could easily have down-loaded it again.

- You've saved so many movies and TV shows you couldn't possibly watch them all.

- You have to keep upgrading your Cloud storage space at a higher and higher cost.

Make your backups worry-free

Storing your files in the Cloud is a good way to protect them from being lost while giving you easy access no matter where you are. But for even better protection, consider an online backup service.

This is different from a simple Cloud storage service because, once you set it up, your files are uploaded on a regular basis without you lifting a finger. Some of the more popular providers include Carbonite at *www.carbonite.com*, CrashPlan at *www.crashplan.com*, and Backblaze at *www.backblaze.com*.

Here are some things to consider when looking for an online backup service.

How quickly does it upload new or changed files? Speed can be a consideration if you have a lot of files or a slow Internet connection. Your first backup may take several days or even weeks, but after that it should be much faster.

Some programs continually work in the background so any changes you make are updated whenever you connect to the Internet. With other services, you schedule the backups at a time of your choosing.

How easy is it to restore files? The main advantage to offsite backup systems is the ability to recover lost or damaged files, especially if your computer crashes or you're hit by a natural disaster. You may want a service that backs up your operating system and software programs, as well as individual files, so you can recover quickly when disaster strikes. Some services will store your deleted files for up to a month, so you don't have to panic if you accidentally erase that important document you're working on.

Look for an easy process to restore the files you need. For example, in Carbonite, you simply open the software, click on **Restore Files**, and select the ones you want.

Can you access your files remotely? If you travel a lot or rely on your smartphone, you may want a service that's compatible with mobile devices. Look for a provider that has Apple's mobile operating system, Android, and Blackberry platforms.

What type of security is offered? Saving all your files on the Web can be scary. Anyone can get to them if they have your password or somehow breach the site's security. So don't skip this important step. Check into the type of security used, whether your files are encrypted, and where your data is actually stored. Three high-security providers to consider are CrashPlan, SpiderOak at *www.spideroak.com*, and Jungle Disk at *www.jungledisk.com*.

How much does it cost? Cloud backup services vary widely in price so it pays to look around. Many services charge a flat fee for individual users. For around $50 to $150 a year you can protect as much data as a single computer can hold.

If you have more than one computer, you'll want a service like SOS Online Backup at *www.sosonlinebackup.com* or Norton Online Backup at *us.norton.com/online-backup* that will accommo date up to five computers, including both PCs and Macs.

WINDOWS LIVE
Free apps do it all

Pick the perfect program

Windows Live Essentials is a collection of free programs from Microsoft that you download from the Internet. Similar programs used to come automatically with earlier versions of Windows, but now you have the freedom to pick and choose which ones you want — or skip them entirely and go with a third-party program.

Here are the major applications and a general idea what they can do for you.

Mail. Windows Live Mail lets you manage your calendars, contacts, RSS feeds, other email accounts like Hotmail and Gmail, and more — even when you're offline. It has robust security and filtering features, allows you to send lots of photos, organize your conversations, and add events to your calendar straight from your inbox.

Movie Maker. Easily capture video from your digital camera, a camcorder, or even your TV or a VCR, and save everything to your computer. Then edit to your heart's content — rearrange footage; add narration, music, or transitions; and cut those unflattering moments. Preview your movie and, when it's Oscar-worthy, share it on your website or a video site, email it to friends and family, or save it to a DVD.

Photo Gallery. This powerful program makes it a snap to import photos from not only your camera, but from other media like flash drives, the Internet, and scanners. Have fun while you add captions, combine photos into panoramas, tag faces of family and friends, and tweak your photos with common editing tasks. Upload your favorites onto the Internet or burn them to a DVD for sharing.

Family Safety. For greater peace of mind, control how your children and grandchildren experience the Internet. With Family Safety, you get to choose what sites, programs, and games they can access. You can even lock them out of the Internet entirely during certain times of the day. Monitor where they are going online with activity reports you can view right from the Family Safety website.

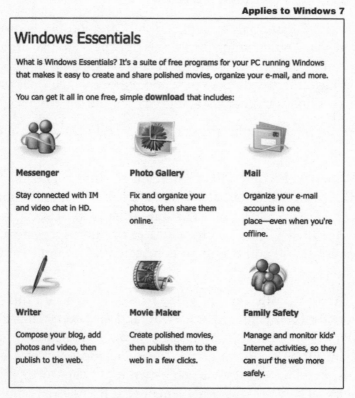

Applies to Windows 7

Windows Essentials

What is Windows Essentials? It's a suite of free programs for your PC running Windows that makes it easy to create and share polished movies, organize your e-mail, and more.

You can get it all in one free, simple **download** that includes:

Messenger

Stay connected with IM and video chat in HD.

Photo Gallery

Fix and organize your photos, then share them online.

Mail

Organize your e-mail accounts in one place—even when you're offline.

Writer

Compose your blog, add photos and video, then publish to the web.

Movie Maker

Create polished movies, then publish them to the web in a few clicks.

Family Safety

Manage and monitor kids' Internet activities, so they can surf the web more safely.

Windows Live Essentials

Writer. This tool is made for the writer in you. Tell your story, share experiences, or just voice an opinion by posting your own blog. Windows Live Writer helps you set it up, create posts, and add photos, videos, or maps. Publish your blog to almost any blog service including Windows Live, WordPress, TypePad, and Blogger.

Toolbar. Add Windows Live Toolbar to Internet Explorer, and you can instantly access other Windows applications like mail, calendar, photos, and more.

Messenger. This instant messaging program — which allowed you to send instant messages to people and groups via Microsoft's chat network — was replaced by Skype in April of 2013. All contacts should transfer from Messenger to Skype.

> **A CLOSER LOOK**
>
> Microsoft Silverlight is one more free tool you'll want to check out if you're into creating applications for the Web or mobile devices. Go online to download the latest version at *www.microsoft.com/silverlight.*

Load Windows Live in a snap

You can download the Windows Live Essential applications onto your computer in two different ways. The first is super simple and gives you all the programs in one fell swoop.

1. Click on the **Start** button.

2. Select **Getting Started**, and you'll see a list of options.

3. Click on **Get Windows Live Essentials**. This will automatically open Internet Explorer and take you to the download page.

4. Click on **Download now** and, when given the option, select **Run**.

Or you can simply start from your Internet browser. Go to the Web address *download.live.com* and download. Here are a few more things to keep in mind.

- You must be logged on to your computer as an administrator to perform this download.

- Even though you don't have to install the complete Windows Live package, you must install Movie Maker and Photo Gallery together because they share several components.

- Windows Live is a hefty download — taking up over 1MB of space. Make sure you have enough room before you start.

- Microsoft SkyDrive is automatically downloaded as part of the Windows Live 2012 package of free programs. You'll read more about this in *The Cloud: don't leave home without it*.

Once you've finished the download, click on the **Start** button, then **All Programs**. In the list that appears you'll see the newly installed programs highlighted. You're ready for the fun to begin.

Change your mind with a quick uninstall

Perhaps one or more of the Windows Live Essential programs isn't making you happy. It's very easy to remove them from your computer.

1. Click on **Start > Control Panel > Programs/Uninstall a program**.

2. Inside the new dialog box, scroll to find **Windows Essentials** and click on it.

3. Once it is highlighted, click on the button **Uninstall/Change** at the top of the box.

4. You'll most likely choose the option **Remove one or more Windows Essentials programs**.

5. Select those you wish to uninstall by checking their boxes, then click on the **Uninstall** button.

Online Shopping
Fast track to super savings

Find tons of free coupons online

Shoppers on a reality television show devoted to saving money with coupons spend hours each week gathering newspapers, clipping and sorting coupons, then scanning store ads to see where they can get the best deals. They save a lot of money, but they spend a lot of time.

Nowadays, you can find great savings with less work by using the Internet to find coupons and other great deals. Get the biggest bang for your surfing by heading straight to the absolute best websites for free coupons and other deals. You'll find three main types of savings.

Coupons to print. Find coupons for just the item you want to buy, like a certain brand of lawnmower, by typing that item and "coupon" into your favorite search engine. You can also type in a store name and "coupon" and get oodles of results. Then print your coupons and take them to the store as usual.

Another method is to navigate directly to coupon websites to do your search. This works well if you're looking for grocery coupons, since you can often get all your coupons in one place. You may need to install a small utility on your computer. If so, scan it for viruses first.

Popular coupon websites include these favorites:

- *www.coupons.com*

- *www.couponcabin.com*

- *www.couponcraze.com*

- *www.couponalbum.com*

Paperless coupons. In some cases, you don't even need to print a coupon. If you have a smartphone, you can load it with mobile coupons and have them scanned at the cash register for savings.

Coupon Sherpa offers a free mobile app at *www.couponsherpa.com* to help you find deals. The site also has free printable coupons — including grocery coupons.

Coupon codes. Many of the same websites you go to for printable coupons and mobile coupons also offer coupon codes. These are so easy to use, it's almost a crime to shop online without looking for one.

Before you make an online purchase, head to a site like RetailMeNot, *www.retailmenot.com*, and search for the name of the store where you're planning to shop, perhaps Target. Limit the list you get to "coupon codes," and you'll get offers for, say, 15 percent off sale items. Copy the code that goes along with this offer, and paste it into the appropriate space when you check out from Target's online store. Easy as pie, you've saved money.

Some savings sites require you to sign up for a free account before you can access certain offers, so read the fine print.

3 slick tricks for online savings

There's more to saving money online than simply comparing prices. Get into the habit of using these computer-savvy shoppers' tricks, and you can rack up some real savings.

Clear out those cookies. Remove these bits of tracking data from your computer before you shop, and you can hide your previous browsing and shopping history. Then you may benefit from special lower prices some retailers use to lure in new online customers. For details on how to remove cookies, see *Be a smart cookie and manage online tracking* in the *Safe & secure surfing* chapter.

It may seem unfair or even creepy that websites track your visits and spending habits, offering different prices based on who you are. You might as well use this trend to your own advantage.

Abandon your shopping cart. If you're not in a hurry to make a purchase, place the items you want in the online shopping cart, then leave the site.

Some retailers make a habit of tracking these unfinished sales, and they'll try to lure you back with email coupons or other offers. They may even send you notifications that the price on an item you wanted has dropped. You must begin the online checkout process, completing enough information so the website has your email address. Then sit back and wait.

Shoppers at *www.amazon.com* can use a built-in option to wait for a deal. Simply place the item you may want to buy in your online shopping cart and click on "save for later." Prices at this retailer change frequently, so check back daily to see if the price has dropped. If it does, it's time to score those savings.

Learn to haggle online. You can do it without even making a phone call. Try negotiating for a better deal, like free shipping or a lower price, through a live chat window before you make an online purchase. It works for some customers, and it doesn't cost a thing.

Making your voice heard can even get you savings after the purchase. If you have problems with an order, from packaging that's hard to open to a slight change in the product, call or email the company to complain. Even if the original problem can't be fixed, you may score coupons for your next order.

Let your smartphone app do the legwork

Comparison shopping just got easier. Forget driving all over town or spending hours leafing through the newspaper looking for deals. Now you can use your smartphone to see if a store's price is really the best.

Free or inexpensive apps let you use your smartphone's camera to scan an item's barcode at the store, then check for prices at competitors. You can read product reviews and decide whether making the purchase now is a good idea. That's a lot more convenient than even researching products and prices using your PC, then heading out to shop.

Before your next shopping trip, download one of these apps to your smartphone.

- ShopSavvy. A free app for Android or iPhone, this option works great for local shopping. It offers online price comparisons, price alerts, and directions to local stores.

- RedLaser. This $1.99 app works on an iPhone and is your best choice for scanning groceries.

- Amazon Price Check. Versions of this free app from Amazon work on your Android or iPhone, letting you compare prices and offerings at the store with what's available through *www.amazon.com*.

Experts say these price-comparison apps work best on newer smartphones with auto-focus cameras.

Best websites for price comparison

A "deal" isn't always a great deal. Some shopping websites misrepresent a product's list price to make their own discount seem greater than it really is. Do your own research on prices so you'll know what you should pay.

But doing a price search using your favorite search engine isn't the best way to go. Experts say the results you get could include fraudulent sites put there by hackers aiming to get your personal information.

So use these trusted price-comparison websites, even if you don't plan to buy online.

- Bizrate.com. You'll find reviews of the product you're shopping for along with reliable price-comparison information.

- PriceGrabber.com. This site lets you compare current prices and see an item's price history over the past six months.

- Dealio.com. At this site, you can compare prices on a specific item and find coupons and deals for your purchase.

- Nextag.com. Along with price comparisons, this site lets you set up alerts so you'll know when the price drops on the item you want to buy.

CAUTION

Some money-saving apps track your every move, sharing that information with friends and acquaintances through social media. Don't get tagged without your permission.

The free app Foursquare, available for iPhone, Android, and BlackBerry, lets you cash in on savings by "checking in" with certain businesses you visit. You can access customized coupons, find out about nearby deals, and save money at stores and restaurants.

But maybe you don't want everyone to know about your activities and movements. Disable Foursquare's social media sharing function, and your online friends won't get updates of your whereabouts while you shop. You still get the savings.

Don't waste money on clothes that don't fit

If the dress fits, wear it. Otherwise, you may have to pay for return shipping and possibly a restocking fee from the online store that sold it to you.

New software lets you type in a few bits of information about yourself, then compare that to the specifications of the item you're considering buying to see if it will fit you.

Find your true fit. Certain department stores, including Macy's and Nordstrom, are teaming up with TrueFit.com to help you determine what size to buy.

Simply enter some basic information about your body and about some favorite items from your closet that fit. TrueFit determines what size you would wear in other brands. Some retailers say the tool has reduced online clothing returns by up to 50 percent, and more stores are joining up.

Buy jeans that fit. FitOfPassion.com gives you a way to shop for jeans online and find a pair that fits.

At this website, you provide information on items of clothing you own, including brands, sizes, and how they fit you. The tool finds other items from a variety of brands that might work for you. It's easy to use, but it only includes information for a limited number of brands, including Gap, Levi's, and American Eagle.

Ask the crowd. If the site you want to buy from doesn't use these tools, you still have the voice of experience to guide you. Check out the customer reviews of a particular item to look for trends, like sleeves that tend to run short or a waistband with no give.

Although you can't trust any review to be 100 percent accurate, read enough of them and you'll get some valuable information.

5 steps for safe online shopping

You can save a ton of money and time by shopping through the Internet. But there are security risks and scammers out there you need to be aware of. In fact, the Internet Crime Complaint Center received more than 300,000 notices of online crime in 2011. Don't be one of those victims.

Remember these five strategies for safe shopping online. The retailers won't tell you these tricks.

Get your software up-to-date. Even before you start shopping online, make sure your computer is running updated firewall protection, anti-virus software, and anti-malware software. Change the software settings so it updates automatically. Also update your browser to the latest version so any available security patches are protecting you.

Confirm seller's security. Always check these two things at a retailer's website before using your credit card to make a purchase.

- Be sure the website's URL begins "https" rather than "http." The extra "s" stands for "secure."

- Look for a lock symbol at the bottom of the page, indicating the site has security software in place.

Avoid the easy click. An unexpected email offering a great deal may be your ticket to getting swindled. Click the link in the message, and you could be taken to a page created to gather your personal information.

Instead of clicking, navigate to the retailer's website and look for the deal there. It's also a good idea to set up an email account specifically for online shopping. That way if a retailer is hacked and your personal information is stolen, the damage can be limited.

Keep it private. Shop online only using a trusted network, like your secured home Wi-Fi network. A public network or Wi-Fi hotspot may be easier for hackers to access.

Go with what you know. Stick with retailers you've heard of or shopped with before. If you need to make a purchase from an unknown vendor, research it by looking for complaints and check the website of the Better Business Bureau *(www.bbb.org)* for warning signs.

Read online reviews with a grain of salt

Word-of-mouth advertising is as old as the first business. Now you can read reviews of hotels, restaurants, and all kinds of vendors online. But some people get paid to write and post online reviews, so you can't always trust what you read.

It's against the law in the United States to hide the fact that you've been paid to endorse a product or service. But a technology research group predicts that within the next few years up to 15 percent of online reviews and social media "likes" of products and businesses will be faked.

The problem is so large, computer science experts are working on ways to spot fraud automatically. They've created a program that looks for fraud in reviews, in part by noting warning signs like these:

- a review that's very different from most others

- extreme adjectives, since real people don't tend to gush

- vague words and phrases rather than specifics

- a user account with a single review

- multiple reviews coming from several accounts on the same computer

Of course, when you see reviews online, you won't have information about the source. But by examining the language of a review, you may be able to spot a phony and avoid getting ripped off.

> **CAUTION**
>
> QR (Quick Response) codes, those square barcodes you can scan with your smartphone to access a retailer's website or special promotion, can help you find deals and win prizes through your favorite store.
>
> But hackers have caught on, and they're using the codes for a new scam. The Better Business Bureau warns that some stickers covering legitimate QR codes actually lead your smartphone to a malware site.
>
> Avoid the scam by examining the square before you scan to be sure it's the original.

Beware of info-sharing credit cards

A credit card you can use without swiping may put you at risk. So-called "contactless" credit cards are adored by thieves. If your card has the curved line radio wave symbol on it, there's a possibility the number could be electronically read by hackers and stolen, even while it's in your wallet.

These cards use a radio frequency identification (RFID) chip to wirelessly send data to a card reader without even swiping, making them convenient. But a clever hacker can purchase a small card reader for around $100, then potentially read information from your card just by getting close.

Radio wave symbol on RFID cards

Experts say the risk is low, since information gathered would be useful for only one fraudulent purchase. A credit card industry group says its cards don't pose a threat, and no consumers have complained about stolen information.

If you're concerned, keep credit cards in a metal RFID-blocking wallet. You can even create your own using duct tape to fashion a wallet, then lining it with aluminum foil. Or ask your bank to disable RFID chips in your cards.

Prep online for supermarket savings

You can buy food online and have it shipped to your home using a grocery-delivery service. Some supermarkets, including Safeway and Harris Teeter, will take your order and deliver it or let you pick it up in the store. But even if you prefer to go to your local supermarket for groceries, the Internet still can help you save money.

And there's more than just money-saving coupons. Check out these top websites to help you plan ahead for big grocery savings.

ZipList. Get help with meal planning so you buy only the food you will use. A free *get.ziplist.com* account lets you access recipes, weekly meal plans, and coupons. The features all work together, so once you pick a recipe you can add the ingredients you need to your shopping list. Load the ZipList app to your smartphone, and you can take it all with you to the store.

Cellfire. If you have a customer loyalty card at your favorite grocer, you're well on your way to savings. Add a free account at *www.cellfire.com*, and you'll gather up even more deals.

This website lets you input your ZIP code and store loyalty card information, then access electronic coupons that can be loaded directly to your card. When you check out at the store, you'll automatically get the special deals. You can also load coupons to your smartphone and save that way.

Cellfire is working to expand to more grocery stores, but currently you can connect and get coupons to use at Kroger, Safeway, ShopRite, Giant Eagle, and Shop 'n Save.

Supermarket websites. Check the website of your favorite store for special deals, then plan your meals around what's cheap. Mainstream grocers are eager to let you know about the weekly specials, and many also offer coupons on their websites. Even specialty markets like Whole Foods Market and bargain stores like Aldi let you plan ahead for savings.

And don't forget to check the Twitter feed of your favorite grocer. You'll get up-to-the-minute information on deals at @genuardis, @safeway, @FoodLion, and more.

BRIGHT IDEA

Narrow your eBay search for local items the easy way. Use eBay's Advanced Search to find items for sale within a limited area around your location. But the website *www.flippity.com* gives you local results in an easy-to-use format.

Simply type in the item you're looking for along with your ZIP code, and the Flippity browsing tool quickly searches through eBay for matching items. The default search radius is 150 miles, but you can expand that range if you need to. Flippity's map even shows you where each of the found items is in relation to you.

Make money as an online seller

Access to the Internet gives you a bigger window for shopping. It also can put you on the other side of the store counter.

Websites like Craigslist and eBay, where you can buy stuff cheap and resell for a profit, make it easy to set up shop. They may be all you need to start a profitable business out of your home.

They're both websites that let you sell items you don't need, like an online garage sale, while also buying what strikes your fancy, as if you're browsing through an antique store. The main difference between the sites is that eBay is an auction site, where people bid on an item offered for sale.

In contrast, Craigslist sellers post an item for sale at a certain price, then wait for buyers. Sellers on eBay also have the option of naming a "Buy it now" price, letting you make an immediate purchase to bypass the auction.

In addition, you can set up an online store on eBay, so potential buyers can see all your inventory in a single place. That's not possible on Craigslist. But also consider the fact that you must pay to place an ad on eBay, while Craigslist ads are free. That's one reason why Craigslist may be the downfall of newspaper classified ads.

To buy and sell online successfully without losing your shirt, follow these basic guidelines.

Write an ad that sells. Skip the gimmicky headlines and include basic information, clearly worded. Don't forget the main six items your customer will be looking for — the what, where, when, who, why, and how of the sale. Without the price, description, location, your availability, even why you are trying to sell, your ad is less inviting.

Steer clear of shysters. Because you are selling to strangers in a faceless environment, it's vital that you take precautions to avoid becoming the victim of a swindle.

- Sidestep the overpayment scam. If your potential customer sends you a check for more than the agreed-upon amount, then claims it's a mistake and asks you to wire him the difference, don't do it. Likely the check will bounce, leaving you in the lurch.

- Stay local. Craigslist started as a website for people in the San Francisco area to exchange stuff for cash. That's still the best way to operate — accepting cash only and meeting with buyers in a public place.

A CLOSER LOOK

You can find free stuff on Craigslist in a place you'd probably never think to look. When people want to get rid of items, but they don't think it's worth the effort to find a buyer, they sometimes offer them for free.

It would make sense to have a section of "free" items, but it's not that simple. Instead, listings for freebies are hidden under the "for sale" banner.

Check in the "free" category, or search for "free" in the search tool. Because folks are always browsing Craigslist for specific items, freebies usually go fast. Keep checking for items you need.

The Internet for fun, health & learning

11 surprising Google services you should be using

Google says its mission is "to organize the world's information and make it universally accessible and useful." With 44 separate tools and counting, Google is well on its way to accomplishing this mission.

But if all you know about Google is its search engine, hang on to your hat. Here's a brief tour of some of its more popular tools and the amazing things it can help you do every day.

Google Earth. This free download, available for your desktop or mobile device, allows you to see the world — and beyond — as you've never seen it before. Explore the oceans or faraway galaxies. Experience 3D imagery as you view cities and landmarks. Travel back in time or learn about famous people and places.

Google Maps. Bring the world down to a more personal level. View your street or your favorite coffee shop. You'll never be lost again with helpful driving, walking, and biking directions. Search, print, share, and more.

Google Translate. What this free translation service does is a lot easier to explain than how. It's enough to know you can get an instant translation of text into any of 64 different languages — from Afrikaans to Yiddish.

Google Play. If it's something you want to read or listen to, you'll find it on Google Play. This service recently merged with Google Music, so now, in addition to books, magazines, movies, and TV shows, you'll also find songs. Rent, buy, stream, or download. Use your mobile device or your computer. In addition, you'll find more than 500,000 games and apps for Android devices. You must have a Google account set up to use Google Play.

Google News. Get all the top headlines from new sources around the world in one place. Create a personalized news page that reflects your interests. Receive alerts on specific topics or condense your updates into an RSS feed. For fun or research, explore their archives, with news dating back over 200 years.

Google Calendar. Create a Google account and then dive into all the handy features this free, time-management Web application has to offer. Share a single calendar with family or co-workers, sync with your mobile device or another calendar application, set up alerts that can be sent straight to your phone, and even work offline.

Google Blog. Like to share your thoughts and ideas? Then blogging may be for you. A blog is a website where you can write pretty much anything you like. Google's Blogger helps you set up your own quickly and easily. A built-in Template Designer gets you off to a fast start, then you can customize with fonts, colors, backgrounds, and more. Access Controls let you decide who can read your blog and if anyone can comment back to you.

Google Finance. Here's an easy way to search for and learn about stocks, mutual funds, public and private companies, market data, and financial news. In addition, you can create, maintain, and track your personal portfolio.

Google Shop. Use Google Shop to search for products offered by online shopping websites and compare prices. Unfortunately, Google Shop only includes merchants who pay to be listed, so you may miss out on some options — including Amazon. Check out the Shortlist feature that lets you save products you're interested in. There's also a Google Shopper app for your phone.

Google Voice. This free service allows you to consolidate all telephone communication through one number. It doesn't matter what kind of phone you have or what carrier you use. You can use one number to ring all your phones, retrieve voicemails online, block and screen callers, and even place conference calls. You can use either an existing number or opt for a new Google Voice number.

Google Offers. Here's how to find amazing deals on the best places to eat, shop, stay, and play in your area. Subscribe to Google Offers, let them know the types of offers you might be interested in, and give them a location. Then purchase a deal directly through their site, and either print your voucher or show it to the merchant on your cellphone.

BRIGHT IDEA

How would you like to have thousands of mouthwatering recipes all gathered together neatly in one spot, with easy access, cross references, and even suggested shopping lists? Welcome to the wonderful world of Internet cooking sites.

Instead of paging through cumbersome cookbooks, you can instantly find recipes from your favorite magazines or TV cooking shows with the quick click of a mouse. Or type in some ingredients from your pantry, and let the Web come up with the perfect meal. You'll save time and money. Here are a few recipe sites to get you started:

- *www.allrecipes.com*
- *www.chow.com*
- *www.foodandwine.com*
- *www.ichef.com*

- *www.epicurious.com*
- *www.cookinglight.com*
- *www.foodnetwork.com*
- *www.simplyrecipes.com*

Can you trust that health website?

The Internet should never act as a substitute for a good conversation with your doctor, but that said, it is chock-full of great health information — some that could save you money and some that could even save your life.

Look for clues. Online research can be reassuring — if you get it from a reputable source. So how do you tell the safe and reliable health websites from the irresponsible ones?

- Check the suffix. If the site's address ends in .gov, .org, or .edu, it's run by the government, a nonprofit organization, or an academic institution.

- Read the **About Us** page linked to the website. Is there a company behind the scenes with an agenda?

- Is there research linked to support their advice? Is it current?

- Look for an advisory board of medical experts connected with the site.

- Make sure the site is not trying to sell anything.

- Don't trust claims that sound too good to be true.

Stick with the pros. Here are some trustworthy websites you should have in your browser's list of favorites, ready for the next time you need to do a little health research.

- U.S. Department of Health and Human Services at *www.hhs.gov*

- National Institutes of Health at *www.nih.gov*

- Centers for Disease Control and Prevention at *www.cdc.gov*

- Mayo Clinic at *www.mayoclinic.com*

- WebMD at *www.webmd.com*

- MedlinePlus at *MedlinePlus.gov*

Save some money. The Internet is certainly the place to go if you want to pinch pennies. Check these websites for help in spending your health dollars wisely.

- For information on the best drug prices: *Consumer Reports Best Buy Drugs* at *www.bestbuydrugs.org*

- A free guide to healthcare pricing: Healthcare Blue Book at *www.healthcarebluebook.com*

- Comparison-shop for your meds: GoodRx at *www.goodrx.com*

- Fight high hospital bills: Medical Billing Advocates of America at *www.billadvocates.com*

- Compare plans and save at the dentist: DentalPlans.com at *www.dentalplans.com*

Exergaming — where fitness and fun meet

It's exercise. It's a game. It's exergaming. And if you're not into it yet, you should be. This fun and practical health craze is turning believers into young and old, alike. And it's even got the researchers in their court.

Start with a video game, throw in some sophisticated body-tracking technology, add a pinch of competition, and you've got something that is getting thousands of people off the couch and breaking a sweat in their living rooms.

Whether you're into dance, hula, golf, tennis, bowling, or boxing, there's a game and a gaming system for you. The main contenders in the exergame field are Kinect for Xbox 360, PlaystationMove, and Nintendo Wii Fit.

And not only can you swing and move against a computer-generated opponent, but many of these allow you to plug into the Internet and play against other people, anywhere in the world.

Current research shows you can burn an amazing number of calories while you're having all this fun. Walk a reasonable three miles per hour for 30 minutes, and you're walking off about 120 calories. Play baseball on a gaming system for the same amount of time, and you've burned 135 calories. Tennis or dancing bump the burn up to 159 calories. What a great way to work out — all without ever leaving your home.

In addition, exergaming can help improve your dexterity, balance, thinking skills, heart health, mood, and more.

> **MONEY-SAVER**
>
> Love music but can't afford the high price of CDs? With your Internet connection you can listen to millions of songs on your PC or mobile device — all for free. Try these music-streaming services to enjoy the sweet sound of your favorite tunes.
>
> - Spotify at *www.spotify.com*
> - Pandora at *www.pandora.com*
> - I Heart Radio at *www.iheart.com*
> - Jango at *www.jango.com*
> - Slacker Radio at *www.slacker.com*

Read unlimited e-books for free

With just a few clicks, you can get free electronic editions of books and read to your heart's content. Here's how to go about it.

Check out your public library. Most have e-books you can download for free for a limited time. The process may vary so check with your local library for details.

Download from an e-bookstore. Thousands of books are now in the public domain, which means you can download them for free. Visit Project Gutenberg at *www.gutenberg.org* to brush up on the classics.

For everything from mysteries to travel, try Free-eBooks.net, which features books by independent fiction and nonfiction writers. The Kindle, Nook, and Sony Reader also offer free books from their e-bookstores. And relax for a bit when you bring your Nook to a Barnes & Noble store — you get an hour's worth of free access to their e-books.

Share with others. E-book Fling will let you share purchased Kindle or Nook books with other people for up to 14 days. Sign up at *www.ebookfling.com*.

Never be put on hold again

Tired of waiting on hold for 10, 20, even 30 minutes when you call a business? How would you like to have them call you instead?

Try these virtual-queuing customer callback services, and you'll never waste your valuable time sitting on hold again.

LucyPhone. Named for the old cradle phone seen on *I Love Lucy*, this technology is a snap to use. Simply log on to *www.lucyphone.com* or download the app for your iPhone or Android smartphone, type in the name or phone number of the company you want to contact, and add the number where you can be reached. LucyPhone sets up the call and automatically calls you back when a live person answers. If you're put on hold during the call, press ** to disconnect and let Lucy pick up from there.

FastCustomer. Take advantage of this technology via the website at *www.fastcustomer.com* or from a free app for your smartphone, and be amazed at how easy it is to bypass phone trees and hold times with a single tap.

Let FastCustomer know the company you wish to contact — the site has more than 3,000 in its database — and when your phone rings, a real person is on the other end.

GetHuman. More than a callback service, GetHuman is a concerted effort to improve customer service in all its forms. Whether you visit the website at *www.gethuman.com* or download an app for your mobile device, GetHuman gives you multiple ways to improve communication with thousands of businesses.

This service provides the best phone numbers for companies based on quality, communication, and wait time; shortcuts to cut down on call holding times; ways to chat instantly with a live person; email addresses; and customer ratings and reviews.

Simply type in the name of the company you want to contact, and browse through its list of options and advice.

Connect with others
email, smartphones, Facebook & more

Supercharge your email & messaging skills

Keep your email safe at home

It's possible to keep track of Web-based email accounts, such as Yahoo or Gmail, from any computer that has Internet access. You might be tempted to see what messages are waiting for you throughout the day, logging on via a public Wi-Fi connection or even using a public terminal in a hotel lobby.

Don't check email when you're away from home — even at work, where you might assume the network is secure. It's possible for someone else on the computer network to use a "man-in-the-middle" attack to spy on you. Then he could steal the credentials to your machine, get access to your email user name and password, and rob you blind.

Instead, check your personal email from your computer at home, and be sure to set up Secure Sockets Layer (SSL) and Transport Layer Security (TLS) protection to create a secure connection between your email provider and your computer. It's the same security you count on when you check your bank account online.

Look through your account settings to activate encryption by default whenever you log in, or check with your email provider to be sure SSL/TLS is supported. When it's turned on, the website address should begin with "https" instead of "http." If you don't see that, type an "s" at the end of "http" and press the **Enter** key for a secure login. Then change your browser settings to activate encryption by default in the future.

> **BRIGHT IDEA**
>
> Help your friends by keeping their addresses secure. Surely you've received a forwarded email that contained the addresses of all the other recipients of the message — and also the addresses from previous forwards. A malicious spammer would love to get his hands on this treasure trove of addresses.
>
> When you forward an email, type your own address in the **To** field, and place the addresses of the people you want to send to in the **Bcc** (blind carbon copy) field. Then delete all the previous addresses that appear at the top of the message.

5 tricks to block spam emails

It's great to open your email account and find lots of messages from your friends and relatives. But what a drag when your Inbox is full of spam — junk mail offers and possibly malicious messages.

Keep your email account free from junk mail overload. You can avoid being a victim of computer spamming by using these strategies to block intrusive emails from getting to you.

Use spam-blocking software. Where there's a computer-related problem, there's bound to be a solution. Spam-blocking programs have filters to keep out junk mail from known spammers.

You can find free or paid services, but do some research to be sure you pick a legitimate vendor. You can also set preferences within your email program to block specific senders, putting those messages directly into the Junk folder in your email program.

Or you can set controls so tight that only emails from senders in your Contacts folder make it into your Inbox.

Don't respond to spam. It may be tempting to click on a link in a spam message promising that you can unsubscribe from the mailing list. But don't do it. Sending any feedback to a spammer simply lets him know your email address is a good one. Then the junk mail barrage will really get rolling. Instead, block that spammer's address.

Create a new email address. You need to have at least two email addresses — one for your friends and family to use, and another to give to retailers or to use in an online discussion group or forum.

Otherwise your main email account will soon be crowded with promotional offers from every store you've shopped at recently, and spammers can grab your address from online posts. You can sign up for Web-based email accounts such as Gmail or Hotmail for free.

BRIGHT IDEA

Here's the simplest way to create a new email account without losing your contacts.

Some email providers, including Yahoo, will import your contacts from the email service you already have. Simply look for an "import contacts" option when you open your new account.

If your new account doesn't have this feature, you have another option. In your old account, use the export tool to copy all your contacts into a Comma Separated Values (CSV) file, then save this to your computer. Open your new account and use the import tool to obtain the contacts from the CSV file on your computer.

Choose a complex email address. Picking a simple email address like JaneDoe@hotmail.com may seem the obvious choice, since it's easy for your friends to remember. It's also easy for a spammer to figure out. Make things a little more difficult by using an email address that includes numbers or punctuation. It's also important to be sure your email password is secure. For more information on choosing a strong password, see the *Safe and secure surfing* chapter.

Change your ISP. Your Internet Service Provider (ISP) should be part of the solution — not part of the problem. Research the policies of your ISP to see how closely it guards customer information and whether it puts up with customers who take part in spamming. Call the company and ask about its anti-spam policies, and keep shopping if you don't like the answers.

A CLOSER LOOK

Users of Hotmail or Microsoft Outlook.com email have an easy way to stop an episode of email hijacking.

If you receive a suspicious spam message from a friend, mark it with the **My friend's been hacked!** label. Then the program will block the unauthorized user if it's a Microsoft account, or it will alert another email provider of a breach. Even if your friend uses Gmail or Yahoo, they'll find out fast there's a problem. That's a good thing, since you may not be able to contact your friend by email for a while.

Don't get caught in a phishing net

They're out there — scammers and spammers who use email to spread computer viruses or lure you in with big promises. Trouble is, these phishing scams are after your cash, one way or another. You don't have to worry about getting hooked by scams and computer viruses over email, as long as you follow some simple rules.

Take the direct route. Rather than clicking on a link in an email, open a new browser window and navigate directly to that company's website. Clicking on a link can lead you to a bogus website, where the scammer can gain access to your online accounts.

You can also investigate a link in an email by letting your cursor hover over the link, watching the status bar at the bottom of the page. When the link's Web address appears, be suspicious if it's unfamiliar or if it ends in something other than .com or .org.

Expect the best. Sometimes scammers try to impersonate major corporations or organizations, like your bank or even a government agency. Be suspicious if the message contains numerous grammar and spelling errors, or if it even misspells the name of the organization itself.

Skip the excess baggage. Be especially careful about opening attachments that you were not expecting. Instead, verify with the sender that the attachment is intended — and is safe.

BRIGHT IDEA

Pick up the phone and call when you want to chat with a friend, or write a newsy email. But when you just need to relay information about an upcoming meeting or change of plans, make it quick. Write emails that don't need to be opened.

If you can say what you need to say in a few words, put the message in the subject line. Then follow it with EOM for "end of message."

Doing this lets your friend get the information without even having to open your email. He will say a silent "thanks" for saving time.

Recover fast from an email hijacking

If your friends and relatives complain that you're sending them spam, you may have been hijacked. That means your email account has been hacked into, and a malicious person is sending junk messages from your account.

Email account hijacking is different from what's called "spoofing," when a hacker changes the return address and other features to make spam appear to be coming from another account. With a hijacking, the culprit actually has gained access to your account.

A Web-based email program, such as Yahoo, Gmail, or AOL, is more likely to be hijacked than one that resides on your computer. It's important to take action fast to limit the damage.

- First, update and run your virus-protection software, along with a malware-removal program such as Spybot Search & Destroy. You can download Spybot free at *www.Safer-Networking.org*.

- Then try to log in to your email account. If you can't, it's probably because the hacker has changed your password. Contact your email provider for help gaining access to the account and shutting out the crook.

- If you are able to log in to your account, change your password immediately to lock out the hacker. Then change the passwords to your other accounts as well, since the crook may be able to use your email account to gain access in other places. Also be sure to disable any forwarding rules the hacker may have set up, which could send copies of all incoming messages to him. Take away this option, and further shut out the hacker.

- Check your folder of sent mail to look for suspicious messages you didn't send. If you see strange spam, that's further evidence your account has been hijacked.

- You may also be able to trace where the spam is coming from. If you use Gmail, scroll to the bottom of the page of your **Inbox** and see the information for **Last account activity**. Click on **Details**, and you can see the IP (Internet Protocol) address for the past 10 times your account was logged into.

- Also remove any recovery account the hacker may have added. If you use Gmail, check the **Settings** option for changes in the

Change password recovery options information. Remove any mystery email addresses in the **Email** section.

- Keep the hacker out for good by changing the security questions needed for account recovery.

- Tell all your email contacts what happened so they can stop any problems before they escalate. They should delete all email messages from you until you let them know your account is back in safe hands.

Find a free replacement for Outlook Express

Microsoft seems to love change, at least when it comes to email programs. Computers loaded with Windows 98 through Windows XP included Outlook Express as the email program. You may have become quite accustomed to checking your email this way.

But if you upgrade to a new computer loaded with the Windows 7 operating system, there's no email program pre-installed. And using Outlook Express is not an option.

You can sign up for any number of free online Web-based email accounts, including Yahoo or Gmail. Microsoft's free online option is Outlook.com, created to replace Hotmail.

If you already have a Hotmail address, your account easily converts to the new Outlook mail program — including bringing in your old list of contacts.

The switch to Outlook.com may seem like just one more hassle of getting a new computer, but the new program has certain benefits. It links with social networks, including Facebook, LinkedIn, and Twitter, allowing you to stay connected directly from your email program.

But if you've been using Outlook Express, try the following steps to bring email files from your old PC's Outlook Express into the email program on your new computer.

1. On your old computer, open Outlook Express and click on **Tools** and then **Options**, then select the Maintenance tab. Click on the **Store folder** button, and you'll see where the email files are located. Select and copy the file path.

2. Go to Start and open a Run command, then paste in the file path and click on **OK**. The folder of Outlook Express files will open.

3. Copy the files with .dbx extensions to a flash drive or onto a CD, then bring the files to your new computer.

4. Use the import feature of your new email program to import the messages.

If you prefer an email program that resides on your computer, you can also choose to download Windows Live Mail. It's part of the free download package Windows Live Essentials, available at *www.windows.microsoft.com*.

A CLOSER LOOK

If you have upgraded your computer's operating system to Windows 7, it's easy to locate your old Outlook Express email files. How you do that depends on the installation type.

- Choosing the Upgrade option during the installation means your email files remain in place. Use the Import Mail troubleshooter to import your accounts into Windows Live Mail.

- Using the Windows Easy Transfer option during installation also lets you use the Import Mail troubleshooter.

- Using an external storage drive to back up data before installation means you'll have to restore your email files by importing them into Windows Live Mail.

Get email without a computer

You can ignore email if you want, but you may be missing out. Nowadays, families communicate with distant members by email, keeping up with what's going on in life, sending electronic greeting cards, and even sharing photos.

An email station is one option for people who don't want to fiddle with email on a computer. You can specify approved senders — say, the email addresses of your family and close friends — to avoid getting spam. Then the folks you love the most can send you a message.

The stations connect through a phone line, and some will print out incoming messages automatically. Some email stations can print both messages and photos, and many have the option of sending outgoing email. You'll need to sign up for a service along with installing the equipment.

You can probably find an email station for less than $100. Shop around for one with the features you need.

- HP Printing Mailbox, along with the HP Presto service.

- Landel MailBug Email appliance, which works with the MailBug service.

Another option is to invest in a smartphone. Then you can set up an email account on your phone and easily keep in touch with your grandchildren.

Turn email into a daily alarm

You'll never miss another appointment when you train your email program to work like a personal assistant. Just sign up for an email reminder service.

When you get an email that's reminding you to do something at a certain time — say, confirming an appointment with your dentist for next Tuesday — simply forward it to, for example, *tuesday@reminderservice.com*. Then you'll get that same email sent back to your inbox on Tuesday. Voila, you have an automatic reminder just when you need it.

You can also set a reminder for a certain time, like this — *6pm@reminderservice.com* or *2hours@reminderservice.com*. Helpful free reminder services include FollowUpThen.com and NudgeMail.com.

BRIGHT IDEA

Turn Gmail into your personal email assistant by turning on the Priority Inbox function.

When you enable Priority Inbox, Gmail sorts your mail into two inboxes — one for the really important messages, and one for everything else. Gmail determines what's important based on several factors:

- whether a message is sent directly to you
- whether you open a message
- which messages you reply to
- your choices in sorting messages

So as you work through incoming messages, marking them as important or unimportant, the system learns from your choices. Then it becomes even more accurate in sorting your email.

Save money and time with IM

Email is old news. Any teenager will tell you she can converse faster and more efficiently through other forms of electronic communications. With little or no trouble or expense, you can send messages in ways you may never have considered:

- from your email program to a smartphone

- from your computer's instant messaging (IM) program to another computer

- from a smartphone to a tablet's IM program

- from a smartphone to an email address

Depending on the program and device you use, you may be sending information via Short Message Service (SMS, also known as texting), Multimedia Messaging Service (MMS, which can include audio or video), IM, or email.

When you receive a message, whether it's in your email's Inbox or on the screen of your smartphone, you may not even know how your friend sent the message.

But if your cellphone carrier charges a fee for each text message (SMS) you send or receive, you'll find out fast that you need to pay attention to how you communicate.

Using an instant messaging (IM) program has benefits that include speed, since messages arrive nearly instantaneously. This communication is also convenient, with many online email programs letting you IM directly from your email account.

Some programs, including Google Talk, let you choose between a text conversation, an audio chat, or a video conference. Importantly, you may also save money, since you can IM between computers or other devices for free.

You may already be using IM and not even know it. Sending messages to friends using Facebook Chat and keeping up with the news via Twitter are both forms of IM.

An easy way to get started with IM may be to check the options in your Yahoo, Gmail, or Hotmail account to see if live chatting with your contacts is available. No matter how you connect, get with it and give IM a try.

For more information on how to connect with a friend through live video, see the *Video chats bring you closer* chapter.

MONEY-SAVER

Instant message your way to a better deal. When shopping on the Internet, you may see the option to open a live chat window at the store's website. Click on this link, and you're instantly connected to a customer service representative through a text conversation.

You can ask questions about the item you want to buy and get quicker feedback than you would get from email or even a phone call. And you'll never be put on hold.

Consumer Reports found haggling via live chat works. Most people in their surveys who requested a better deal got one.

TAP INTO THE POWER
OF TODAY'S CELLPHONES

Program your cell for safety

What's the one number you must have programmed in your cellphone? It's your ICE number, which stands for "In Case of Emergency." Any emergency worker will know this is the number of a close friend or relative who can answer questions about your health if you can't. It could save your life.

But there's more programming to be done. Consider these seven other numbers to always keep in your cellphone for safety.

- Insurance hotlines. You'll need your car insurance emergency or claims number in case of even a minor collision. Also program in your health insurance number so you can find out exactly what your policy covers.

- Your doctor. Input the number of your primary care doctor, and your medical records will be within easy reach.

- Credit card hotlines. The number is probably printed on the back of your card, but that won't help after it's stolen.

- Directory assistance. Pick one of the many free options that let you look up a number. Services like 1-800-FREE-411 gives you free information, although you may have to listen to a brief ad.

- Your home or work. Input a direct line to you, so you can be reached by some nice person trying to return your lost cellphone.

- A local towing service. The side of a highway is not the best place to research a good towing service.

- A trustworthy locksmith. Nobody plans to get locked out of their car or house, but you can be ready by researching a locksmith offering around-the-clock service.

MONEY-SAVER

Don't waste your cellphone minutes calling a friend, then waiting through long-winded greetings and instructions in order to leave a message. Get straight to your friend's voice mail with these shortcuts, depending on what service she uses.

- Sprint — press 1

- Verizon — press *

- AT&T or T-Mobile — press #

If you don't know your friend's carrier, try them all, but in this order: 1, then *, then #. You'll need to pause after each to listen for a beep. If you hear an error message, press the next key.

---

10 things you should never do with your cellphone

Just because you can use your cellphone almost anywhere doesn't mean you should. Some bad cellphone habits are dangerous to your health, while others are just downright rude.

If you value your life, your family, and your friends, don't:

- text while driving. This is so dangerous, it's illegal in 39 states.

- talk while driving. Research shows even a hands-free device won't keep you from being distracted by a cellphone call.

- walk and text. Your mind is distracted, but your feet keep moving. One study found pedestrians who crossed an intersection while texting were almost four times more likely to display risky behavior — failing to look both ways, crossing in the middle of an intersection, and disobeying the lights.

- use your phone during a restaurant meal. It's polite to excuse yourself and step away from a group to have a private conversation.

- leave your phone on during a public performance. Everyone in the venue has paid good money to see the show or concert. Be considerate.

- play games on your phone while others watch. If you're with friends, be polite and give them your full attention.

- behave like an addict. Twenty percent of baby boomers can't go 15 minutes without checking their cellphones.

- talk loudly in public. Nobody wants to hear half of your conversation.

- edit photos right after you take them. Taking the photo was time sensitive, but editing and posting it is not.

- hold a running text conversation. Generally, texts are useful for sending quick messages. If an entire conversation is required, a phone call is probably better.

Crank up your phone's IQ

The flip phone you've been using for the past few years works great for making phone calls, and you've even mastered the art of texting. But it's no smartphone — no Internet access, no fancy apps, and you can't play too many games. On the other hand, your dumbphone is paid for.

With your knowledge of texting and a little ingenuity, you can turn your plain old cellphone into a smartphone and skip paying for an upgrade. Here are just a few tasks you can accomplish.

Find a restaurant. Use Google's treasure trove of information to locate a restaurant or other business nearby. Text the type of food you want and your ZIP code to 466453, and you'll get instant suggestions texted back to you.

Get directions without GPS. Again using Google at 466453, text your start address, "to," then your destination, and you'll get turn-by-turn directions in response. You may get several text messages, depending on how long the directions are.

Check your calendar. If you use Google Calendar, be sure it's linked to your cellphone number. To do this, go to *www.google.com/calendar*, sign in, and click on the gear icon to find **Settings**. Next select **Mobile Setup**. To receive text messages for upcoming events on your calendar, text these messages to 48368 (GVENT):

- next — sends you a text with your next scheduled event

- day — sends today's complete schedule

- nday — sends tomorrow's schedule

Depending on your wireless plan, you may pay a few cents for each text. But if you have an unlimited texting plan, you won't pay a dime extra.

Save money with the right cellphone plan

There used to be just one phone company. Now you have to choose a carrier and a plan when you get a new cellphone. Pick the wrong plan, and you could be wasting money big time — or end up with a shockingly huge bill at the end of the month. Here's an easy guide to help you select the right plan and save a bundle.

Wireless plans come in three major varieties.

Standard contract. People who use their cellphones a lot — to call, text, and browse the Internet through a data plan — can probably control the costs best with a traditional plan.

Look for one that gives you unlimited calling, texting, and data usage. You're probably looking at spending at least $50 to $60 each month.

Also think about where you'll do most of your calling. Will you travel a lot, or do you usually stick close to home? A regional plan can save you money if you don't travel much, while a nationwide plan may give you free long-distance and roaming.

Monthly no-contract option. This choice lets you pay less each month for services similar to those in a contract plan, but you'll probably pay more for the actual cellphone. It may be a good option if you're not dead set on keeping up with the latest model of phone.

Prepaid minutes. This option may be the cheapest way to have a cellphone. It's big in Europe, and it could be right for you, especially if you are a light user of your cellphone and don't need a data plan.

Here's how it works. You pay ahead of time for a bucket of minutes, then use them as you need them. It costs more to talk on a per-minute basis than with a standard contract.

You can find plans for as low as $10 for 30 minutes of service, and those minutes remain valid for 90 days. Spend more for more minutes, and they can remain available for up to a year.

Wireless carriers are realizing how popular prepaid plans have become, offering a greater variety of phones and even smartphones with prepaid minutes.

When it's time to switch plans, use the calculator available at *www.myrateplan.com*. It compares your current plan with others, looking for a deal that may save you money. You can also see coverage maps for the major wireless carriers to be sure you'll get good service at home.

BRIGHT IDEA

Don't add to the 50 million tons of electronic waste disposed of each year. Recycle your old cellphone when it reaches the end of its life, so it won't end up in a landfill, harming the environment.

Exchange it for an Amazon gift card through the Amazon trade-in program at *www.amazon.com*. Click on **Help**, then **Ordering** under **Topics**, and then you'll see **Amazon Trade-In Program**. Search the website for your model to see how much it's worth.

Amazon will pay for the shipping, and you get the credit. Your wireless carrier may even give you cash for your phone.

How to cancel your contract without penalty

It's easy enough to sign up with a cellphone carrier and take your new phone home right away. Trouble comes if you want to switch to a new carrier before your contract time is up.

One survey found nearly half of all cellphone customers would consider switching carriers if they didn't have to pay an early-termination fee. These fees can run to $350 depending on how much time is left in your contract term.

But there are ways to get out of your cellphone contract early, without paying huge fees — although your mobile provider probably won't tell you how.

Have a really good reason. If you're moving out of the country or to a place the carrier doesn't cover, or if you are a soldier being deployed, you may be able to end your contract with no fees.

Ask nicely, and keep asking. When you make your case to your wireless provider, you'll probably talk to a customer service representative over the phone. Don't accept the "no" you'll get from the first call. Instead, call back, ask for an executive in charge, and escalate the issue — whatever it takes to get the attention you need. You can even use social media — Twitter and Facebook, for example — to voice your concerns and try to resolve the issue.

Try for a trade. As much as you dislike your carrier, there's someone else out there eager to join up. You can sell the remainder of your contract to one of those folks through websites like *www.celltradeusa.com* and *www.trademycellular.com*. You'll probably pay a fee of around $20 to $25, but that's much less than an early-termination fee.

Switch to a smaller company. Small carriers and those categorized as mobile virtual network operators (MVNO) may be so eager to get your business, they'll buy out your contract if you sign up for a new plan. MVNOs like Boost Mobile and Virgin Mobile are good services to try.

If you can't get out of your contract, lower your bill by cutting text messaging, switching to the smallest data allowance, and reducing your number of minutes.

> **CAUTION**
>
> Don't take your cellphone into the bathroom while you shower — even if it means you may miss a call. The steamy atmosphere is almost as damaging as dropping your phone into a bucket of water. Moisture from the air can find its way into the cracks of your phone, damaging the metal contacts inside.

15 fun and free apps you need now

Apps — software for your smartphone — can simplify your life. They help you send texts without having to type, let you see in the dark when the lights go out, and do a zillion other handy tasks. Check out these top free apps for busy seniors. Most have versions available for iPhone, Android, Windows, and BlackBerry. Visit *play.google.com* or open your iTunes application and search within the App Store to download these.

App name	How it enhances your life
Flashlight	Turns your screen into a flashlight
Google Maps	Provides maps and directions using GPS
Dragon Dictation*	Lets you send texts and emails without typing
GasBuddy	Finds cheap fuel in your area
Alarm Clock Free	Includes a clock, alarms, and snooze features
FaceTime*	Allows video chats with friends and family
TripIt	Organizes flights, hotel reservations, and more
SitOrSquat	Finds public restrooms when you travel
Laser Level	Helps hang pictures straight
Lose It	Lets you create and follow a diet plan
RedLaser	Compares prices by scanning bar codes while you shop
The Weather Channel	Keeps up with local weather
iPharmacy Drug Guide & Pill ID	Identifies your pills and finds lowest drug prices
MapMyDogWalk	Tracks your route, time, distance, speed, pace, and calories
Tip Calculator Free	Computes your tip and splits the bill among friends

*iPhone only

Top senior-friendly cellphones

Complicated high-priced smartphones aren't for everyone. If you want an easy-to-operate cellphone with big buttons and fewer controls, consider these options.

Jitterbug Plus. Get great reception and call quality, a long-lasting battery, giant buttons, big backlit number keys, a roomy display, a straightforward menu and navigation, and a speaker that is loud and hearing aid compatible. Visit *www.greatcall.com* for more information.

Clarity Pal. This phone offers senior-friendly features like a keypad that says the numbers as you dial, talking caller ID that lets you know who is calling, extra large rubber buttons, amplified sound, backlit numbers, and hearing aid compatibility.

It also includes a panic button that calls your emergency contact when pressed. This phone is sold unlocked, meaning it can be used with carriers like T-Mobile or AT&T. Visit *www.clarityproducts.com* for more details.

Doro PhoneEasy. This flip phone includes big keys, large easy-to-read text in the bright color display, and a one-touch SOS button to contact help during an emergency. Visit *www.consumercellular.com* for more information.

Snapfon EZ. Created for seniors, this phone includes huge easy-to-read, easy-to-use buttons; a large-print screen; a high volume speaker; LED flashlight; FM radio; and a single-press SOS button for calling four emergency phone numbers. The phone keeps calling these numbers until it gets an answer. Visit *www.snapfon.com* for more details.

Just5. Designed for seniors and people with limited hearing or eyesight, this unlocked phone provides a speaking keypad that reads the numbers aloud, big buttons, an FM radio, a flashlight, long battery life, and an emergency button that dials until a connection is made. The button texts and calls up to five numbers including 911. Visit *www.just5.com* for more information.

10 surprising ways to use your phone's camera

A camera on your phone is handier than you might think. Here are some unusual ways to put yours to good use.

- Avoid the can't-find-my-car fiasco in parking garages or large parking lots. Before you leave the car, snap a picture of the row, section, space number, or any distinctive nearby landmarks to help you find your car easily later.

- Turn your smartphone into a portable scanner. CamScanner, a free app for iOS and Android, lets you scan receipts, magazine or newspaper articles, recipes, photos, and more.

- Capture any written information for later. Photograph the whiteboard after a meeting instead of writing everything down. Take a snapshot of a phone number, Web address, or other information from a sign, bulletin board, notice board, or billboard.

- Snap photos of both cars if you're in a fender bender, so you can give the insurance company evidence of the damage done — and not done.

- Take pictures of your home, belongings, and every room in your house. If a disaster should happen, you can give these home inventory pictures to your insurer as proof of ownership.

- Before you unplug the cables to your computer, television, DVD player, or any other complicated assembly, photograph the cable connections. Use that as a guide when you put everything back together.

- If you're in a new town or neighborhood, and don't know your way around, take a picture of the place you are staying, its address number, and the street sign. Also, photograph any subway maps or other maps you can't download on your phone. This can help you figure out how to get back.

- Take pictures of scratches or other imperfections on your rental car before driving it off the lot. Check your phone properties or options to automatically timestamp the pictures to show the date the picture was taken. If your phone doesn't have this feature, download a timestamp app for free. If someone later tries to hold you liable for those damages, you can easily prove your innocence.

- If you need a replacement part, extra can of paint, or some other item that requires specific details, take a picture of the serial number, paint color, part number, or other information on the container or package. Use this to make sure you bring home the right item.

- Create a wish list while shopping. Snap photos of items you'd like to receive and help out that person who hates to shop.

BRIGHT IDEA

What's the first thing you should do if your cellphone gets wet? Turn it off.

Resist the impulse to turn it on to check if it's working. If there's water inside, turning on the phone can short out the circuits.

Instead, take out the battery and SIM card. Then try to remove the moisture from the cellphone using a can of compressed air or a wet-dry vacuum. Finally, submerge your phone in a bowl of uncooked white rice. This will wick away extra moisture. Leave it there for at least 12 hours — if possible, for a few days.

Tethering: share your phone's Internet connection

Your Internet connection is out, and you need to access a website. All is not lost when you know the trick of tethering.

Tethering makes your smartphone's Internet connection available to other devices, like your laptop, desktop, or tablet. You connect your phone to your other device wirelessly, through Wi-Fi or Bluetooth, or use a USB cable — a faster, more secure, and less battery-draining option — and then access your phone's Internet connection and data plan.

Talk to your carrier. Before tethering for the first time, ask your cellphone carrier these questions.

- Does my cellular plan allow tethering? What does it cost?

- Do I have or need a wireless data plan? What are my data usage limits? How close am I to that limit?

- What other requirements and costs are there for tethering service?

Check your systems. Read your smartphone manual to learn whether your phone and your computer's current operating system support USB, Bluetooth, or Wi-Fi tethering. If not, download a third-party tethering app such as PdaNet or EasyTether.

Free versions of these apps may only be free for a limited time or have restricted abilities. Other third-party apps may only be available if your phone has been rooted or jailbroken, processes that remove certain security measures and may void your warranty.

Tethering works on devices running Windows Vista, Windows 7, and Windows 8. Before tethering, make sure your computer won't download large updates during tethering that might push you over your wireless plan's data limits.

Connect to your personal hotspot. The process for tethering varies depending on which carrier and operating system your phone uses. To learn about USB, Bluetooth, or Wi-Fi tethering for your specific phone, check your smartphone's manual, visit your carrier's website, or contact your carrier for help. This example shows how to activate Wi-Fi tethering on an Android phone.

1. Open **Settings**.

2. Select **Wireless & Networks**.

3. Select **Portable Wi-Fi Hotspot** or whatever option your phone has for hotspot or tethering.

4. Next you will configure your phone's hotspot settings with a network or router name (SSID), password, and security level. You may also have the option to manage which users can connect to your network.

5. Turn on Wi-Fi for your PC, tablet, or laptop, and search for wireless networks.

6. Select your phone's network name and enter its password.

 BRIGHT IDEA

Here's an easy way to make your cellphone battery last longer. Simply dim the screen, switching it to a power-saving mode.

Many smartphones let you turn the screen's brightness up or down. Turn it down when you're in normal lighting conditions, then turn it back up when you go outdoors into the sun and need it brighter.

If your phone has a feature to automatically adjust the screen's brightness depending on the light of the room you are in, use it. Then your phone's screen is only as bright as it needs to be.

Don't let your phone spy on you

Your smartphone, just like your computer, can harbor malware that can corrupt your system and steal your personal information. Some hackers even reroute data from your phone, letting them know your whereabouts and follow your Internet activity. With a little attention to security, you can foil the hackers and protect your privacy.

Know your sources. Free or inexpensive apps give your smartphone all kinds of powers. They can also be the source of malware. Download apps only from reliable sources, such as Apple or Google. Stay away from free "unofficial" versions of popular apps, such as the Angry Birds game. And check on the permissions the app requires to be sure they make sense.

Stay up-to-date. Update the security software your cellphone provider offers, and consider a free security app. Again, stick with known vendors like AVG or Norton.

Beware how you connect. Experts say it's usually more secure to connect to the Internet using a 3G network rather than public Wi-Fi. And disconnect from Wi-Fi when you're not using it. If your phone has Bluetooth, keep it in "non-discoverable" mode so hackers can't listen in on your calls.

> **CAUTION**
>
> Every time you make a phone call, your number shows up on the other end. That means the person or business you called now has you in their system. They may call back later, perhaps to try to make a sale.
>
> Keep your phone private without paying a monthly unlisted charge. Simply dial *67 before you place a call, and your number won't show up on the recipient's caller ID screen. Instead, "private," "anonymous," or "restricted" appears.

Print from your phone like magic

Printing from your smartphone or tablet is a snap once you find a printing app or Web service that works with both your printer and wireless device. You may even be able to print to your wired network printer. Here are some options.

Check your device. AirPrint has been part of the iOS operating system used by iPhones and iPads since version 4.2. So if you're running that version or higher, AirPrint is waiting for you on your device.

AirPrint can help print from your iPhone or iPad to any AirPrint-capable printer on the same wireless network. Visit *www.support.apple.com/kb/HT4356* to find a list of printers compatible with Apple's AirPrint software. If yours is not listed, you can still use AirPrint together with helper software as long as you also have a Macintosh or Windows PC on the same wireless network. To make a wireless printer AirPrint-compatible:

- Macintosh users can download handyPrint from *www.netputing.com* for free or an optional donation. The handyPrint app may even connect to wired printers.

- Windows users can visit *www.collobos.com* to download a trial version of a software called Fingerprint. But it will print its watermark on each page until you upgrade to a paid, licensed version.

Search out printer-brand apps. Epson, HP, Lexmark, Canon, and other major printer manufacturers offer free printing apps for their current or older wireless printers. In fact, they offer apps for both iOS devices like iPhones and iPads and for smartphones and tablets running Google's Android operating system.

These apps often provide more printing options than AirPrint. Review your printer's manual, and visit the printer manufacturer's website for more information. You may also need to visit iTunes at *www.itunes.apple.com* for iOS apps or the Google Play store at *www.play.google.com* for Android apps.

Some apps may assign the printer an email address. This means your smartphone or tablet no longer has to be on the same wireless network as the printer. You can send a document to your printer in Nashville even if you're in New Zealand.

Take advantage of the Cloud. Google Cloud Print (GCP) is a Web service that may work where AirPrint or printer brand apps fail. GCP can print from iPhones, iPads, Android smartphones, and Android tablets as long as they can run the Google Chrome browser.

GCP also works with wired printers as long as they're connected to a Windows or Macintosh computer that's turned on and connected to the Web.

To use GCP, you must register for a free Gmail account at *www.google.com* and follow Google's instructions for enabling GCP. Visit Google Cloud Print Help Center at *suppport.google.com* to learn more. If you don't see Google Cloud Print in the listing, click the double arrow symbol below the icons.

CAUTION

Mobile printing technologies are still developing and may not do all you want them to.

- Some printing apps or software may only offer one or two printing options such as "number of copies." Others may only print certain kinds of files properly. Read about software before you download or buy it to be sure it has the options you expect.

- For some devices, Google Cloud Print needs help from an app. If you followed Google's instructions but can't print from your tablet or smartphone, check your device's manual. You can also visit its support pages at the manufacturer's website, or visit Google Cloud Print Help Center at *suppport.google.com*.

VIDEO CHATS BRING YOU CLOSER

Simple tools get you video chatting

The Jetson family had special telephones that allowed them to see the person on the other end of the line. That kind of technology looked pretty amazing when the cartoon first aired in the 1960s. But now anyone with a decent computer can enjoy the same kind of live, face-to-face video conferences with friends far away.

If you bought your computer in the past few years, it probably has all the power you need to set up a video chat in no time. Here's what you'll need to get started.

An Internet connection. Of course, you need to be able to connect to the outside world, since that's where the friends are who you want to video chat with. A broadband connection is your best bet. If you're connecting on a tablet or smartphone, you can use a 3G or 4G connection. But connecting via Wi-Fi will give you a stronger signal.

A webcam. This term refers to a video camera that usually connects to your computer through the USB port, broadcasting video images live through the Internet. It can sit on top of your monitor, or it may have a stand to keep it on your desk at eye level.

A microphone and speakers. Many webcams have a built-in microphone, but you may want to upgrade to a stand microphone or a headset with a microphone. Look for one that lets you mute background noise and eliminate echo and feedback. If your webcam has an internal microphone but you choose to add a headset, be sure to turn off the microphone in the webcam.

If you don't want to bother with a headset, never fear. Your computer probably has speakers installed, so be sure they're in working order.

The right software. Here's the tricky part. For a free video conference, you and the person you want to chat with need to use the same program. So whether you decide to go with Skype or Google Chat or another free program, be sure your friend also downloads and signs up with that service.

If you bought a tablet or laptop recently, you may already have everything you need built in. Check the specifications to see if the tablet has video chat software, such as FaceTime on an Apple device or Google Talk on an Android, and a front-facing camera — one that points in the same direction as the screen.

Look and sound your best on camera

After you set up your webcam and software and get settled in for a video chat, you'll get a preview of yourself on your computer screen. If the image makes you cringe, try these tweaks to improve the way you look and sound to your friends.

First, check out how your face is framed in the shot. Move the camera or yourself so your head and shoulders are visible and centered. You can also play with objects around you, picking a background that sets a certain mood or reflects your personality.

Then consider the lighting. Don't place yourself in front of a window or other source of bright light, since you may appear dark and in the shadows. Instead, try to place a small lamp slightly behind and above your webcam.

If you're using a tablet rather than a PC, it may be simpler to move yourself and the tablet to the light source. If the lamp is too bright, turn it so it reflects off a wall.

Finally, listen for any background noise. If your air conditioner is humming too loudly or there's a television blaring in the next room, your conversation will be difficult to hear. Close doors and mute any background noise.

Once you begin your video chat, ask your friend how you look and sound. You can always adjust things for your next chat.

HIGH-TECH HEALTH

A video chat can connect you to medical help and even save you money. Studies show using video conferencing to link people who have chronic conditions to healthcare providers cuts down on emergency room visits and hospitalizations, and it also works in mental health.

You can book video-conference therapy with a psychiatrist or therapist. Breakthrough, one company organizing such sessions, says people seem to open up more when they "see" a therapist from the comfort of home, and sessions are available at odd hours.

You see a therapist you trust, and insurance or Medicare may even cover the cost of video therapy.

Boost audio quality with auto setting

Tell your computer to quiet down while you talk on the phone or enjoy a video chat through your computer. You can change the sound settings by accessing the Control Panel, but there's an easier way.

Look for the speaker icon on the Taskbar along the bottom of the screen. Right-click the icon, then click on **Sounds**. Switch to the

Communications tab, and see your options for having the computer automatically lower the volume of computer sounds while you are on a call. You can choose to:

- **Mute all other sounds**

- **Reduce the volume of other sounds by 80%**

- **Reduce the volume of other sounds by 50%**

- **Do nothing**

Highlight your choice and click on **Apply**. Then click on **OK**, and the change is made.

Pick a webcam that puts you in your best light

What's the point of setting up a video chat with your distant friends if you end up looking like some shadowy Creature from the Black Lagoon on screen?

As any moviemaker will tell you, the right equipment makes a difference in the quality of a video. You can probably get all the features you want in a good webcam and still keep the price less than $100.

Consider these features when you shop for a standalone webcam.

Video resolution. For the sharpest picture and best color, look for a webcam that supports HD video quality. If you pick one that supports 1080p video quality, you'll enjoy more pixels — and thus more detail in the picture — than one that supports just 720p.

Lens features. An autofocus feature can be useful, but each model is designed to work best in a narrow range of lighting conditions.

And look for a webcam with a lens made of glass rather than plastic. You'll have less trouble with scratches and blurriness with a glass lens.

Faster frame rate. Look for a webcam with at least 30fps (frames per second) capability. Anything less, and your video may look choppy — with moving images leaving a ghostly trail across the screen.

Microphone specs. A good-quality standalone webcam will probably have a built-in microphone, ideal to capture your part of the video chat conversation. Look for features that can reduce background noise, such as your ceiling fan humming or the dishwasher running, by identifying and removing the repetitive sound waves of such noises. A mute button on the microphone lets you turn off your side of the conversation while you're listening.

You might also be interested in features like stereo recording if you plan to use the microphone separate from the webcam's video features.

Software. First, check for compatibility. Whether your computer runs Windows 7 or another operating system, be sure it will work with the webcam. Check specifications on the box.

Next, consider what software utilities come bundled with the webcam. You may want to be able to capture video and still images or add a cartoonish look to yourself on camera, so pick the utilities you need.

Adjustment capabilities. One major draw in buying a standalone webcam as opposed to one that's connected to a laptop or tablet is the ability to move it around.

Look for a webcam that pivots both up and down and right and left, so you won't have to put your body into contortions to get yourself in the middle of the frame.

Also be sure the webcam is built with some kind of gizmo, whether it's a flexible rubber neck or a small tripod, to let you make tiny adjustments.

Get the best sound from Skype

Once you have all the hardware components ready for a video chat, you'll need to pick a software program to use. There are many choices out there, but a service called Skype seems to be winning the popularity contest. It's become so common that people now refer to "skyping" when they may mean holding a video conference on any type of software.

Since Microsoft now owns Skype, if you had an account through Microsoft Messenger, you can easily switch it over to Skype. Just sign in to Skype through your MS Messenger account, and your Messenger contacts will come with you. You can use Skype to video chat on a PC, Mac, iPhone or iPad, Windows or Android smartphone, and even a Kindle Fire or other device.

In addition, using Skype lets you connect with a video chat to your Facebook friends. Just select this option as you work through the software download process at *www.skype.com*.

Can you hear me now? What can you do if you set up Skype and have your system ready to go, but your friend can't hear you? Maybe the Skype software gives you the message that it "can't hear you very well."

Now it's time to troubleshoot the possible causes, starting with the simplest explanation and moving on to more complicated solutions if that doesn't work.

- Be sure the connection is tight between the PC and the microphone — whether the microphone is located on a headset or a standalone webcam.

- If you're using a headset, check to see if you inadvertently muted the input level for volume on the headset's inline controller. Unmute it.

- Look for a problem in the Skype software. Navigate to **Tools** > **Options** > **General** > **Audio Settings**. Then be sure the correct microphone input source is selected.

- In this same window, remove the check mark in the **Automatically Adjust Microphone Settings** option, then set the microphone volume on high.

- Uninstall and reinstall the driver for your audio adapter.

Money-saver

If you don't want to go with big-daddy Skype, you can pick from a number of other free programs to video chat.

- Airtime, which lets you connect with friends through Facebook.

- Oovoo, also available as a smartphone app.

- Google Talk. Download a plug-in, and you can video chat with other Gmail users.

- Yahoo Messenger, also a program for sending instant messages. You can send large files during a chat.

- AOL Instant Messenger, also called AIM, has a feature called Lifestream that lets you follow friends on social networks.

Chat with your entire family for free

Imagine getting together with sons, sisters, cousins, and grandchildren — all of whom live in other states. You may not have the money to travel to a big family reunion, but you can see and talk to them all at once by holding a group live video chat. It's just like having the whole family together in one room.

Numerous video chat services allow you to set up a group chat, but you may not be able to do it for free. You'll pay $10 a month for a Skype subscription that lets you chat with up to 10 people at once.

And most services also require that everyone who joins the conversation be in the same social network. That means everyone on a group chat would need to join Skype, Oovoo, or FaceTime — and you need to remember the different passwords to each network you belong to.

But there's a new service in town, and it's free. Zoom.us lets you hold group video chats with up to 15 people at once, and your friends can be using different types of machines — tablet, PC running Windows, Apple computer, or smartphone.

Even better, the HD-quality video looks great, whether you're using Wi-Fi, a wired network, or even 3G or 4G cellular connections.

You log in to zoom.us through your Gmail or Facebook account, so those contacts are already available for chatting. Just have your friends or family members download the free app from *www.zoom.us* or the Apple iTunes store.

Take your video chat to the street

You don't have to wait until you get home to start a video chat with a friend. With a handy app for your smartphone, now you can connect no matter where you are — as long as you have the right service.

Pick the video chat application you want to use on your device based on two factors — your phone's operating system and the service your friends use. Is your phone Android, Windows, or iPhone? Does it have 3G or 4G data service, or possibly Wi-Fi? And for the most part, you'll need to be connected to the same video chat service your friends use in order to chat with them.

Popular video chat services that work on smartphones include:

- Tango. This service has more than 45 million registered users, so some of your friends are probably available through Tango. It works on Android, Windows, and iPhones, and you can turn off the video in the middle of a call.

- Oovoo. This major rival of Tango has even more users, and you can also connect using a Facebook app. It earns high marks for stability and reliability on Android phones, and it also works on Windows and iOS devices.

- Fring. Connect with up to three friends on BlackBerry, Android, and iPhone devices.

- FaceTime. This popular app works on iPhones and other Apple products.

BRIGHT IDEA

You don't need to miss important events, even if your family lives far away. If your children have smartphones or tablets, they can use them to take you to the baseball games, piano recitals, and spelling bees your grandchildren participate in — live.

Make a date to be available for a video chat at the time of the event, and ask your son or daughter to use the device to broadcast the performance.

Be sure to test the connection and software beforehand. Of course, a Wi-Fi or data connection must be available at the baseball field or auditorium.

THE RISKS & REWARDS OF SOCIAL NETWORKING

Pick the right social network for your needs

The point of becoming involved with a social networking website is to connect with people you want to communicate with. Look for a site where you'll find people with similar interests. These popular social networking websites each fill a niche.

Facebook. By far the most popular social network, Facebook has a billion users worldwide — no exaggeration. That means your own friends and relatives are most likely to join you here.

Twitter. Post updates of 140 characters or less, and your followers can keep track of your actions and moods. Each message is called a "tweet." Also use Twitter to keep up with political causes, public figures, and retailers that interest you.

Instagram. This photo-sharing social network works best as an app for your iPhone or Android smartphone. Sign up for a free account, and you can post photos and related captions, sharing them with friends and family. You can also easily upload photos to Facebook via Instagram.

Google+. Similar to Facebook, this network lets you connect and share photos and text. But Google+ makes it easier to segregate friends into separate groups — say, relatives versus work colleagues versus tennis buddies. That way you can share only what's important to certain people.

Foursquare. This location-based social network lets you "check in" using your smartphone at stores, restaurants, and other businesses. You can link to your Facebook account to share your activities with friends, although you may not want to tell everyone your whereabouts for security reasons. Some businesses offer special deals to customers who check in often.

LinkedIn. Find a new job, gather readers to your blog, or just build a bigger professional network through this business-related social network. You can also answer work-related questions to raise your expertise rating on the site.

YouTube. It's a place to both watch videos and post your own videos. You can also subscribe to follow certain people or topics, like cooking or home improvement, making the site more social.

 A CLOSER LOOK

Social media is not just for trivia. Police departments are using the most popular social media sites to inform people about emergencies and problems in the local community.

In Seattle you can sign up for Twitter alerts related to your neighborhood through the Tweets-by-beat program. Reports are delayed for an hour to avoid citizen interference with a crime in progress.

And police in other cities post mug shots of wanted crooks on Pinterest and Facebook, letting citizens help find the bad guys.

5 ways to get the most out of Facebook

There's more to Facebook than sharing the details of your day. Check out all the other ways this popular website can bring simplicity and fun to your life.

Play games. When you're done catching up with that long-lost niece, challenge her to an online game. Games available through Facebook are created by third-party providers, but most are free and they offer yet another way for you to connect. To see available games, click on the **App Center** at the left of your Facebook Home page.

Share photos. You can swap photos with friends and family for free through an album on your Facebook page.

First, set up a shortcut link on your desktop that takes you directly to Facebook. At the Facebook home page when you're logged in, click on the Facebook icon located at the left end of the address bar. Hold down your mouse button while you drag it onto your desktop and release. If you have Facebook set to remain logged in when you close your browser, you'll go directly to your Facebook page when you double-click this little tool on your computer screen.

You can add photos to a Facebook album by clicking on **Add Photos** at the top of the Photos page. Select one or more photos to upload from your computer, then click on **Open**. You can select who gets to view these photos by changing privacy settings on the album.

Listen and share music. Ever notice the updates about what music your Facebook friends are listening to? They're using one of the many music apps that can link to Facebook. You can use an app like Spotify, Turntable.FM, or iHeartRadio to listen to music you like for free. Browse through the Facebook **App Center** for a service you like, then select your privacy settings during setup to determine whether your friends get updates on what you listen to.

Talk to friends. Use Facebook Chat to send instant messages or even video chat with friends. You'll see a list of friends who are currently logged in to Facebook at the bottom right corner of most Facebook pages. A green dot next to a friend's name shows he's available to chat. It's important to know that these messages, unlike posts you write on a friend's wall, are not visible to other friends — just the person you're sending a message to.

Go shopping. The Facebook Marketplace works like a listing of classified ads from your friends — or from nearby. Just like Craigslist, you can limit the listings you see by location, type of item, or price. In addition, you can limit listings to see only items from your Facebook friends. Also like Craigslist, you deal directly with the seller or buyer, so take precautions like meeting a seller in a public place and checking out an item before you buy.

Access the marketplace at *apps.facebook.com/marketplace*.

HIGH-TECH HEALTH

When close relatives and work colleagues become your Facebook friends, don't be surprised if you start feeling stressed. Research shows the more different social circles you mix with online, the more stressful you may find social media.

The problem is that when people from various parts of your life mingle online, they may see a new and different side of you, perhaps one they don't approve of. It can be stressful trying to avoid offending people in all your different circles.

One solution is to use the **Create list** option under **Friends** and set different privacy settings to control the information each list sees.

Make Facebook a safe space

No doubt you've heard of privacy and security threats that this popular social network can bring into your computer and your home. Some of the dangers relate to social engineering, or a sophisticated method of gathering information about you, then using it to track you and trick you.

Don't be a Facebook fool. Steer clear of these top five risky behaviors.

Forgetting to use privacy tools. Some 13 million Facebook users reported in a recent *Consumer Reports* survey that they had never set up privacy controls on their Facebook accounts. You can set privacy limits when you open an account, but it's never too late to tighten up ship.

Access **Privacy Settings**, then set limits on who can see your friends list, profile information, posts, photos, and so on. It's also possible to block certain people by name by placing them on a restricted list. See your options under **Blocking**.

Being too friendly. The more acquaintances you have as Facebook friends, the more risks you take. That's especially true if any of your information is shared with "friends of friends." You can limit your exposure by only allowing friends you know and trust.

Research has also shown that people can accurately determine traits like political leanings and sexual orientation based on who your Facebook friends are. You may want to be careful whom you friend if that's a concern for you.

Liking more than you should. You can click on the **Like** button on a wall post from your friend, encouraging her about her recent weight loss. You can also **Like** a company or product. That might net you coupons or special offers, but it can also set you up to see targeted online ads you may not want.

But there's a creepy part. When you remain logged in to Facebook, then navigate to a website that has a Facebook logo button, Facebook can collect data about your browsing habits — even if you don't click on the button. To reduce the information gathered, log out of Facebook when you're done on the site.

Losing a game of tag. Facial-recognition software helps you tag your face or your friend's face in photos you post to Facebook using the Tag Suggest tool. It's a handy tool if you like to share photos widely, letting friends — and possibly their friends — know what you're up to.

Problems can arise from the tagging feature, which can let your friends tag you in photos they upload. You may not approve of having the world see that photo of you in an unflattering situation, but you may not know it's happening.

You can force Facebook to ask your permission for tagging. Access **Privacy Settings**, then click on **Timeline and Tagging** and enable the Tag Review feature.

Trusting the timeline. Facebook's new Timeline feature makes it easy to search back through friends' old posts, possibly uncovering embarrassing comments or photos they would just as soon forget. Keep your past private by looking through your timeline, hovering over a post and clicking on the pencil icon, then selecting **Hide from Timeline**.

Limit sharing to thwart identity thieves

Keeping in touch with friends and family by way of social media can be fun — as long as you're aware of what you share. Sometimes it's the simplest facts that can come back to haunt you.

Think twice before you reveal certain bits of information on Facebook. These are the top five things thieves look for on social networks:

- Your birthday. With a correct date of birth and a name, a thief has all he needs to open up a line of credit, credit card, or get a loan, points out one crime-prevention officer. That's why you may want to skip posting your birthday, or at least leave out the year. If you decide to fudge the date, be ready to receive birthday greetings from Facebook friends on your fake birthday. They might not remember the real day.

- Home address. A casual comment about commuting here, a post about social plans there — soon thieves know when the house at your address is empty and easy prey.

- Your mother's maiden name. This piece of information is valuable since it's often used by websites during the security process to access a lost password.

- Travel plans. It seems obvious, but why let strangers know when your house will be vacant?

- A child's date of birth. Posting "Happy fifth birthday to my grandson Johnny" gives identity thieves useful information — John Doe was born five years ago today. Now little Johnny's identity could be a target for credit thieves.

So be smart and don't reveal this personal information openly on Facebook. You can improve your security by changing your Facebook privacy settings to restrict access to these details on your profile.

 A CLOSER LOOK

Behave properly on social media and keep your friends.

- Give credit to any person or website you quote from. And don't break copyright laws.

- If you disagree with a friend's comments on a social media site, focus your remarks on the point being made rather than the person.

- Don't advertise unless the site specifically allows it.

- When a Facebook friend becomes annoying, simply unfriend her rather than getting into a battle. She won't know it's happened, and you can read posts in peace.

Find great ideas in a flash

You know how to use a search engine like Google or Yahoo to find what you need on the Internet. And you can bookmark your favorite websites, so it's easy to find them again. Now you can steal ideas from your friends through social bookmarking sites. They let other people do the work for you.

A social bookmarking site is like a list of favorite websites or images, but it's compiled by lots of people. It's shared online, so you can see what other people have found. The first one started as del.icio.us in 2003, and it's since morphed into *https://delicious.com*. In spite of the name, it's not all about food. Instead, it's a place to store, organize, and share ideas.

Other popular social bookmarking sites include *www.stumbleupon.com* and *www.reddit.com*. You can select areas of interest you want to follow, such as fitness or humor or crafts.

But some of these sites show you only words. Then you click on a link to see the website being recommended. Go to a site like *www.pinterest.com*, however, and you see why they say a picture is worth a thousand words.

Pinterest is organized visually, with photos and graphics taking center stage. Search for what you're interested in, and you'll get pages of images. Save those ideas by "pinning" them to an electronic "board" you create and share. Just think of all the uses:

- Shop for the perfect black boots. You can even compare prices, since some images link to retailer websites.

- Figure out how to rearrange your living room for best use of natural light.

- Find the perfect recipe for tortilla soup — complete with photo.

- Design table decorations for an upcoming party.

- Get a pattern for that sweater you want to knit for your husband.

Some people think social bookmarking sites are for young people, but a solid group of Pinterest users are 54 years and older.

4 fun uses for Twitter

You may not care to follow celebrities on Twitter, getting updates every time your favorite musician or actor tries a new restaurant or weeds his garden. But there's much more you can do than simply people-watch. Sign up for a free account, and try these other fun ideas.

- Keep in touch with Facebook friends. If you log in to Facebook and install the Selective Tweets app from the **App Center**, you'll have the option to cross-post your tweets to your Facebook wall.

- Send a private message. Regular tweets go to everyone following you, but you can also send a private message to a follower through his or her Profile page.

- Share photos. You can upload photos from certain affiliated websites like Flickr and Etsy. Look for a post-to-Twitter option in the site's upload page. Twitter will display your image when followers click on **View photo** in your post.

- Go behind the headline. Sometimes you want to learn more than can fit into 140 characters. Search for #longreads and you'll find posts that link to longer articles. Add a keyword related to the topic you're interested in, and you'll get enough related reading to keep you busy for a while.

A CLOSER LOOK

Whether you're communicating by text message, email, or Facebook post, sometimes you have a limited number of words to make your point. These abbreviations get it across quickly.

AFAIK	as far as I know
AFK	away from keyboard
BFF	best friends forever
BRB	be right back
GF	girlfriend
GJ	good job
G2G	got to go
IDK	I don't know
IMHO	in my humble opinion
JK	just kidding
K	OK
LOL	laugh out loud
MSG	message
NBD	no big deal
NVM	never mind — ignore last comment
PLZ	please
ROFL	rolling on the floor laughing
SFSG	so far, so good
SRY	sorry
SUP	what's up?
TBH	to be honest
TMB	text me back
TOY	thinking of you
TTYL	talk to you later
TYVM	thank you very much
U2	you too
WBS	write back soon
WFM	works for me
YOLO	you only live once

Glossary

3G (Third Generation)   third generation of mobile phone standards and technology, allowing faster transmission and more advanced network features than the previous 2G mobile phone technology.

4G (Fourth Generation)   fourth generation of mobile phone standards and technology, requiring peak transfer rates of 100 Mbps. 4G cellular networks' transfer rates exceed 3G and may even surpass transfer rates of modem and DSL connections.

Active window   the one window that is currently selected. In Windows 7, a new window automatically becomes the active window. Make a window active by clicking inside it with your mouse.

Address bar   a text area in a window telling you the window's location either in your computer or on the Internet — like a street address tells you the location of a building.

Adware   free software that is supported by advertisements, such as free toolbars that work with your Web browser or free RSS news reader software.

All-in-One (AIO)   a space-saving hardware design eliminating the computer's tower by building the entire PC inside the monitor.

Application software or App   a software program for computer hardware or mobile devices, like smartphones and tablets, that helps you complete specialized tasks.

Arrow keys   the four keys on your keyboard with directional arrows — up, down, left, and right.

Attachment   a file or picture linked to an email message. Also called an enclosure.

Autosave   a feature of some programs that automatically saves files every few minutes. You can set how often your program autosaves.

Back button   in Windows Explorer, it's the button with the left-pointing arrow in the upper left corner of a window. Clicking on it returns you to your previous position. Click on the right-facing arrow to leap forward. These arrows work just like the forward and back buttons in Web browsers. The same keyboard shortcuts work, too — Alt + < to go back, and Alt + > to move forward.

Bandwidth   a measurement of how much information can be transmitted at a time, usually via telephone lines, radio signals, etc. The higher the bandwidth, the faster you can receive information. Bandwidth can be measured in bits per second, bytes per second, or cycles per second — also called hertz (Hz).

Bit   the smallest unit of computer information, consisting of a 0 or 1. Short for binary digit.

Blue Screen of Death (BSOD) a Windows operating system stop error appropriately named because the computer locks up and the screen turns blue. The computer stops responding when this error occurs, preventing damage to hardware or data. The cause is usually related to hardware, drivers, or updates.

Bluetooth radio technology that allows communication between devices or the Internet, with a transmittal range limited to about 30 feet. Smartphones, wireless keyboards, digital cameras, and computers are a few of the devices that may use Bluetooth technology.

Bookmark to mark a Web page so you can return to it quickly. Bookmarking creates a link to that site in a Web browser menu.

Bookmarklet a tiny JavaScript program stored as the URL of a bookmark in a Web browser or a hyperlink on a Web page. The bookmarklet performs helpful tasks when surfing and searching the Web.

Boot to start or switch on your computer. Also boot up.

Broadband a type of high-speed Internet connection using coaxial cable or fiber optic cable. Short for broad bandwidth.

Bug a problem or error in a software program that causes it to run imperfectly or to crash.

Bulletin board an electronic message center existing on the Internet, where you can post and read notices or online conversations. Also called a forum or discussion group.

Byte a measure of computer memory, equal to one character, such as a letter or number. Also equal to eight bits. Short for binary term.

C drive the main storage area on your computer, containing your operating system and programs. Also called hard drive or hard disk drive.

Cable modem a modem that operates over cable TV lines.

Cache computer memory of recently stored information that the system can access extremely quickly. A Web browser uses cache memory to store Web pages, URLs, and images of recent websites you have visited.

Card reader an input device for electronic equipment like computers and printers that reads flash memory cards. The reader may be built-in to the device or connected via USB. Memory cards are frequently used to store original image files from digital cameras.

Cascading menu a secondary menu that appears while you are holding the cursor over an item on the primary menu. In Windows, one of a series of menus that open on top of and slightly to the right of each other as you make selections within each one.

Case sensitive the ability of a program to recognize the difference between lowercase (small) and uppercase (capital) letters.

CD-ROM (Compact Disc-Read Only Memory) a hard, round plastic disc that holds a large amount of computer data. You can access the information on this type of CD, but you can't erase or put new information on it.

CD-ROM drive a special disc drive on your computer that can read CDs.

CD-RW (Compact Disc-Rewritable) a compact disc you can put information on, erase, and reuse.

Cell a single box in a spreadsheet, found at the intersection of any row and column. You can store numbers, formulas, or text in a cell.

Clip art drawings or other images designed to be used in computer programs, like word processing and desktop publishing.

Clipboard a special memory area used to store data temporarily. Information that you cut or copy from one location automatically goes onto the behind-the-scenes clipboard until you paste it to another location.

Cloud computing the use of a network of remote servers hosted on the Internet to store, manage, and process data, rather than a local server or home computer. The Cloud allows computer users to access their files wherever they are as long as they have Internet access. Cloud users can also store a backup of their computer files for future use if their hard disk becomes infected or develops problems.

Command button one of the rectangular buttons in a dialog box that you click on to carry out an action. Examples are: OK, CANCEL, and APPLY.

Compression formatting a file so it needs less space for storage but doesn't lose any information.

Control Panel a feature of the Windows operating system that allows the user to modify system settings and controls.

Cookie a tiny piece of text that Web servers place on your hard drive to track information about your computer and your surfing preferences.

CPU (Central Processing Unit) the part of your computer that processes all instructions and information.

Cramming slipping unauthorized third-party charges onto your telephone bill.

Crash a serious computer hardware or software malfunction. Usually when a program crashes it simply closes down without warning.

Credential Manager in Windows 7, if you check the Remember My Credentials check box when entering a network user name and password, Credential Manager stores the confidential information in a special location called the Windows Vault.

Cursor a symbol that indicates the place on your screen where your next mouse click or keystroke will occur.

Cut and paste a set of commands performed to move a section of text or an object from one place to another.

Cyberspace a term for the imaginary place containing the Internet and World Wide Web. Also called virtual space.

Default an automatic setting on computer hardware or software. You can manually change defaults, if you choose.

Defragment to reorganize the information on your hard drive so that all the pieces of each file are stored together. This makes your system run more quickly and efficiently. Most operating systems, including Windows 7, come with a Disk Defragmenter program. This process is also known as defragging.

Demoware software, usually made by major companies, that you can examine and try for a period of time before you must pay for it. When the payment deadline arrives, the software may stop functioning. Some demoware lacks the software's full range of abilities, but you can get the full-featured package once you pay for it.

Desktop a metaphor for the background on your computer screen that appears to "hold" your icons and windows.

Desktop computer a computer that is designed to stay in one location and cannot be powered by an internal battery, like a laptop can. The desktop computer may have a tower or be an All-in-One design, like an Apple iMac.

Desktop publishing using specialized software on a personal computer to produce high-quality, printable documents — like books, newsletters, or brochures — that may contain both text and graphics.

Device Manager in Windows 7, Device Manager manages the hardware installed on your system, such as hard disk drives, drivers, keyboards, USB devices, sounds cards, etc. You use Device Manager to change hardware configurations, set special options, identify hardware problems, and more.

Dial-up a specific kind of Internet connection that uses a modem to dial a telephone number to gain access to the Internet.

Dialog box a window or box that appears on your computer screen asking for information. It usually disappears after you have typed input.

Document a file created by a word processor that usually contains text, charts, pictures, or other graphics.

Dot-com a slang term for the Internet or to describe Web-based companies. Refers to the last four characters (.com) in most commercial Web addresses.

Download to move data from the Internet or another computer to your computer. When you request a document from the Internet and then copy it to your computer's hard drive, you have downloaded a file.

Drag and drop to select an object on your computer screen (usually by clicking on it with your mouse), move it to another location on your screen (by holding down your mouse button and moving your mouse), and place the object in its new location (by releasing the mouse button).

Drive the part of your computer that reads programs and data off a disc. Many drives can also put data onto a disc. Examples are DVD drive, CD-ROM drive, and C drive.

Driver a driver is a small software program that works with your operating system to communicate with a piece of hardware, like a printer or scanner.

Driver rollback in Windows 7, an easy way to uninstall an unsuccessful install of a new driver and reinstall a previous version of a driver.

Drop-down menu a type of menu that reveals more options after you click on its title. The options appear below the title like a window shade. Also called a pull-down menu.

DSL (Digital Subscriber Line) high-speed technology that allows you to talk on your phone and access the Internet through your phone line at the same time.

Dumbphone a cellphone without the advanced features of a smartphone, such as a large, bright touch screen or Internet browsing.

DVD (Digital Video/Versatile Disc) a disc similar to a CD, but capable of storing up to 25 times more information. DVDs are usually used to view movies.

E-reader or E-book reader a portable hardware device used to read digital publications. Amazon's Kindle is one of the most popular brands. There are many different manufacturers of e-book readers, supporting a wide range of e-book formats. While tablet computers like the iPad can perform the same function as an e-book reader, they are not designed primarily as digital readers and have many other capabilities.

Ease of Access Center a group of special settings in Windows 7 that can make the computer easier and more comfortable to use.

Email (Electronic Mail) typed messages sent from one computer to another. Both sender and receiver must have an email address and a connection to the Internet.

Emoticons   short for "emotion icons," these keystroke combinations create images in your email or chat room messages that indicate mood or appearance.

Encryption   coding information for electronic data so it cannot be read without special software.

Ergonomics   designing and placing equipment or furniture so that people stay healthy and comfortable while using it.

Error message   a notice from your computer that something has gone wrong with a program or your system.

Ethernet   a way of accessing a Local Area Network (LAN). Your computer must have an Ethernet port or Ethernet card to connect to the Internet using a Digital Subscriber Line (DSL) or a cable modem.

Expansion card   a circuit board you can buy separately and plug into an expansion slot on your computer. It can provide more memory, improve graphics and sound, or add other capabilities. Also called expansion boards, add-ins, and add-ons.

Expansion slot   an outlet or opening in your computer to plug in expansion cards.

Export   to send data to another program in a format it can read and use.

Extension   the letters or numbers following a period (dot) in a file name. These tell you what kind of information is in that file or what type of program created it.

Favorites   Internet Explorer's name for its Web browser bookmarks.

Favorites folder   in Windows 7, a special folder used to store both favorite Web pages and favorite files. Other programs also have Favorites folders to provide quick access to frequently used items.

Field   an area on your screen (in a program or on a Web page) for entering and/or storing specific information. Some fields require data and some are optional.

Firewall   technology that protects computers and networks from unauthorized access.

Flame   a mean, hostile email or post in newsgroups or social media usually expressing a difference of opinion over a controversial topic. If two people flame each other back and forth, it's called a flame war.

Flash drive   also known as jump drive, thumb drive, pen drive, and USB keychain drive. This pocket-sized data storage device uses flash memory to store your data and has a built-in USB connection.

Fragmentation   the condition of your hard disk after saving, changing, and deleting many files and thereby creating scattered chunks of free memory, rather than long continuous blocks. This means a new file can't be stored all in one space and must be split, or fragmented. Fragmentation slows down your computer while it looks for the pieces of each file.

Frames   separate sections or boxes within a Web page. Each frame acts like an independent browser window.

Freeware   free software you can use but can't sell.

Freeze   when suddenly nothing will move on your computer or respond to input from your mouse or keyboard. To get out of a freeze, you usually must reboot.

Function keys   the set of keys on a computer keyboard (labeled F1, F2, etc.) that give special instructions to whatever program is currently running.

GIF (Graphics Interchange Format)   a common type of image file, often used on Web pages.

Gigabyte (GB)   a measurement of computer memory, equal to 1 billion bytes.

Gigahertz (GHz)   a measure of the speed of a computer processor or RAM. One gigahertz is equal to 1,000 megahertz or 1,000,000,000 Hertz (Hz).

Global Positioning System (GPS)   a satellite navigation system, developed by the U.S. military, that can determine a device's location, speed, and direction. A GPS can be installed in cars, mobile phones, and other mobile technology. Some GPS devices include an LCD map and are capable of voice instructions for travel directions.

Hacker   slang term for a person who "breaks into" computer networks without permission.

Hard drive   the storage area of your computer that contains the operating system and programs. Also called hard disk drive, HDD, or C drive.

Hardware   the physical parts of your computer, such as the monitor, keyboard, and printer.

Hashtag   a hashtag is a number symbol (#) used to label keywords in a Tweet. The social media website Twitter then turns these keywords into links in a constantly updating data feed.

Help system   on-screen assistance or instructions for operating systems and other programs. Usually accessed by a HELP button.

Hibernate   in Windows 7, selecting hibernate as a power option saves the current state of the system from the computer's RAM on the hard disk and then shuts down the system. When the computer is restarted, it doesn't go through the typical boot sequence but loads the saved state.

Highlight   to double-click on or click and drag over a word, section of text, or group of cells with your mouse. This tells the computer you are about to do something with the selection, like move it, reformat it, etc. Highlighted text is often blocked in gray or another color.

Hot spot   a location that provides access to public wireless broadband network services to mobile visitors through a wireless local-area network (WLAN).

Hover   to leave the pointer sitting on an object on your computer screen for a moment. Sometimes, hovering over an object displays a brief description of the object in a small box next to the pointer.

HTML   a code that tells a browser how to display text and images on the World Wide Web.

Http (HyperText Transfer Protocol)   the standard method of exchanging data between servers and browsers via the World Wide Web.

Https (HyperText Transfer Protocol Secure)   a Web server that automatically encrypts data and can handle secure transactions. You usually need a password, user name, or ID to access the secured area on a website administered by this type of server.

Hyperlink   the text or graphic providing an instantaneous connection between Web pages. Access a hyperlink by clicking on it with your mouse. Also called a link.

Icon   a small picture that represents a program, folder, drive, or file on your computer.

IM (Instant Messaging or "IMing")   a computer communications service that allows you to send and receive typed messages in real time. All parties must use the same IM software and be online at the same time.

Image map   a single picture on a Web page that is split into sections so each section is a clickable link. For example, a U.S. map might have 50 links, one for each state shown.

IMAP (Internet Message Access Protocol)   a method for retrieving email messages without downloading them to your hard drive. If you use the mail service provided by your Internet Service Provider (ISP), you need to know if their mail server uses POP3 or IMAP so you can correctly set up your device's email program. The wrong setting will prevent your email program from working.

Import   to bring in unique file data produced by a program into another program.

Index   Windows 7 gathers information about your hard drive's files and stores it in an index. The operating system uses the index to perform very fast searches of the most common files on your computer.

Inkjet printer   a type of printer that shoots tiny, electronically controlled drops of ink onto paper to form text and images.

Internet   a worldwide network of computers that can communicate with each other.

Internet Explorer   Microsoft's popular Web browser, which competes with other browser software like Mozilla's Firefox, Google's Chrome, and Apple's Safari.

Intranet   a private website, usually within a company or organization, used only by employees, members, or other authorized personnel.

ISP (Internet Service Provider)   a company that provides a connection to the Internet. Popular ISPs include AT&T, U-verse, and Comcast.

Jailbreaking   a process of removing security limitations, usually on an Apple device running the iOS operating system. Jailbreaking allows the user access to the core or root of the device's software. As a result, the user has more privileges and can download applications and change settings and features not intended by the manufacturer or developer. Jailbreaking your Apple device will void its warranty and possibly leave you more susceptible to malware attacks.

JPEG or JPG (Joint Photographic Experts Group)   a common type of electronic image, used especially for photographs.

Jump List   new in Windows 7, Jump Lists are more than shortcuts to frequently used documents, pictures, songs, or websites. Depending on the software program, a Jump List can display information about your Favorites, and you can pin additional selections to your Favorites. To open a Jump List, right-click a program button on the Windows 7 Taskbar or click on the arrow next to the program name on the Start menu.

Keylogger   a spyware program that records your keystrokes on a computer, saves the information to a file, and communicates that data over a network or the Internet. A keylogger is installed by a hacker to obtain information like your user names and passwords for accounts. Prevent an unintentional install of a keylogger program by installing anti-virus software on your computer.

Kilobyte (K or KB)   a measure of computer memory approximately equal to 1,000 bytes.

Laptop   a small, portable personal computer, usually capable of being powered by a battery or connection to a wall outlet. Also called a notebook or notebook computer.

Laser printer   a type of high-quality printer that uses a laser, toner, and heat to print text and images on paper.

Libraries   a new feature in Windows 7 that makes it easier to organize and find files scattered across your computer. Although the real files continue to live elsewhere on your computer, Libraries give you a way to view them all in one place.

Mail bombing   when someone, usually as part of a flame war, overloads someone else's mailbox with so much junk mail it causes the email program to crash.

Mailbox   where your computer stores your email messages, either on your hard drive or on a network server.

Malware   short for "malicious software," malware is unwanted software, often downloaded from the Internet, that damages or performs unwanted actions on your computer or other electronic device. Spyware, viruses, Trojan horses, and worms are all forms of malware.

Maximize   to enlarge a window until it fills the entire screen, usually by clicking on the Maximize button in the upper-right corner of that window.

Megabyte (MB)   a measure of computer memory equal to 1 million bytes.

Menu   a list of available commands on your computer screen. Choose one of the options by highlighting it and clicking on it with your mouse.

Menu bar   a toolbar on your computer screen that displays a list of menu items or options. Usually, each item has its own drop-down menu giving more choices.

Microprocessor   a microchip or central processing unit (CPU) chip that resides in a computer or other electronic device that handles input and produces an appropriate output.

Microsoft FixIt Utility   an online troubleshooting website, hosted by Microsoft at *support.microsoft.com/fixit*, that can help solve many of your Windows 7 problems. You can download the utility and save it on your hard drive or USB drive for easy access.

Microsoft Security Essentials   a free software download from Microsoft that you can install for Windows 7, XP, or Vista operating systems. Installation of the program helps guard against viruses, spyware, and other software threats to your computer.

Minimize   to reduce the size of a window or change it into an icon, usually by clicking on the Minimize button.

Modem   a device that allows computers to communicate over telephone lines. Short for modulator-demodulator.

Motherboard   the main circuit board of a computer, containing the central processing unit (CPU) or microprocessor.

Mouse Keys   a Windows 7 tool that virtually eliminates the need for a mouse. You use the numeric keypad on your keyboard to move the pointer on the screen.

MP3 short for MPEG-1 Audio Layer-3, MP3 is a popular, compressed audio file format because of the file format's small size and good sound quality. MP3 files are used to store music files on both computers and portable devices like the iPod and other MP3 players.

MP4 or MPEG-4 (Moving Pictures Experts Group) a file format for movies or video clips that uses MPEG-4 compression for video tracks and AAC for audio tracks. It is a popular format for sharing video files on the Internet. MP4 files are supported by many devices capable of playing video, like Microsoft's Zune media player and Apple's iPod.

Native resolution sometimes called recommended resolution, it is the resolution the monitor was built to use.

Navigation pane found along the left edge of every folder, it presents the user with common actions and destinations.

Netiquette a set of rules for polite behavior on the Internet or in email.

Network two or more computers linked together and able to communicate and exchange information.

Newsgroup an area on the Internet where people can post messages and exchange ideas, usually on a specific subject.

Numeric keypad a set of keyboard keys containing the numbers 0 through 9 and often a decimal point and operation symbols like + and -.

Operating system (OS) a software program that coordinates all the parts of your computer, helping the software and hardware work together. Microsoft Windows, Apple OS X, and Linux are examples of operating systems.

Option button an element within a dialog box. Click on one of these round buttons to turn a particular option on or off. You can only select one option within a group.

PC (Personal Computer) technically, a computer used by one person at a time for word processing, games, financial management, or data analysis. The term is sometimes used to differentiate between a computer running the Windows operating system and an Apple computer, called a Mac, running the OS X operating system.

Peripheral any external device that hooks up to your computer. Common peripherals include your printer, mouse, and keyboard.

Phishing malicious emails sent to you by scammers or con artists attempting to obtain your personal information. The false email usually appears to come from a legitimate source like your bank or a trusted vendor, but the URL in the address field will reveal whether it is a valid source. Never respond to or visit any link or URL address associated with the phishing email. Entering your user name and password on the bogus website is enough information for the scammer to steal your identity.

Pin a program   in Windows 7, a way to link a program to the Taskbar so you can quickly open it rather than finding it by using the Start Menu.

Piracy   copying software without permission from the writer or publisher with the intention of distributing or selling it.

Pixels   small dots that make up images on a monitor screen. The screen's image is divided into a matrix of thousands or millions of pixels. At a low resolution, like 640 x 480, you may be able to see the individual pixels, and the image would be described as "pixelated."

Plug-in   a small software program you can add to your Internet browser to give it extra abilities. Plug-ins allow you to view movies or play audio samples, for instance.

Pointing device   a computer peripheral that lets you move your cursor and select objects on your screen without using the arrow keys. Common pointing devices are a mouse, touchpad, trackball, or stylus.

POP3 (Post Office Protocol)   often called just "POP," it's a standardized method of handling email messages. A POP3 email server receives emails and relays them to user folders, downloading them when a user connects to the mail server. POP3 and IMAP are the most common types of email servers.

Port   an external socket on your computer to hook up peripherals.

Power plan   a power plan is a group of hardware and system settings that manages your computer's power use. Your use of power plans can reduce the amount of power your computer uses, increase performance, or balance the two.

Power surge   a sudden rush of voltage lasting up to several seconds. Power surges — also called spikes — can damage computers and other electronic equipment.

Program   a set of coded instructions to your computer. Also called software, application, or app.

Prompt   a symbol on your computer screen that indicates the system is waiting for you to enter something.

Purge   to remove old and unnecessary data from your computer, often via an automatic command.

QR code (Quick Response Code)   a type of bar code that carries information in both the horizontal and vertical direction. A QR code can be read by a QR bar code reader or by a mobile phone with a camera and QR reader software. When scanned, the QR Code can be coded to display, text, open a URL, provide marketing or contact data, and more.

Quick Access Toolbar (QAT)   a customizable toolbar in Microsoft Office 2010 that can contain a set of commands or a set of buttons that represent commands. The QAT is separate from the currently displayed ribbon and provides a quick way to access your favorite commands.

RAM (Random Access Memory)   the "working" memory of the computer where programs and information are kept while the computer is using them.

Reboot   to shut down your computer and then restart it.

Recover   to retrieve a deleted or damaged file or disk.

Recycle bin   in Windows, an icon that looks like a trash can and represents the place where you temporarily store deleted files. Deleted files can be recovered from the recycle bin before you empty it.

Refresh   to update a Web page so it shows the latest information. A button on a Web browser called the refresh button allows you to reload and update the current page.

Reset button   a button that restarts the computer without completely turning it off first.

Resolution   describes how sharp and clear an image is. The higher the resolution, the better the image. Resolution can refer to computer monitors, printers, or pictures.

ROM (Read-Only Memory)   permanent data storage on a disk or chip that cannot be changed. This built-in computer memory contains necessary system programs.

Rooting   a process that allows high-level or root access to the Android operating system. Similar to jailbreaking for the iOS operating system, Android rooting allows a user to change settings and even the operating system on an Android device. Rooting your Android phone will void its warranty and possibly leave you more susceptible to malware attacks.

RSS (RDF Site Summary)   sometimes referred to as Really Simple Syndication, RSS is a method for sharing news stories or other information in a format that can be read by RSS-enabled Web browsers or other software capable of retrieving news stories.

Safe mode   booting your Windows computer in safe mode allows you to run with the minimum number of system files necessary. It is used after an unexpected crash or when your computer seems to have operating system problems. After booting in safe mode, you can run a disk utility program to correct corrupted files and directories.

Save as   a command, usually under the File menu for your program, that lets you change the name, format, or location of a file before you save it.

Scanner   a device that converts a printed image into an electronic image.

Scareware a software scam that often starts as a browser pop-up window that resembles a legitimate security utility. Clicking on the pop-up allows the scareware software to install viruses or spyware, alter the security settings of your PC, or do both.

Scroll bar a vertical bar on the right or a horizontal bar on the bottom of your screen or window. A Scroll bar appears when the viewing area is too small to show all the window's contents. Click on one of the scroll arrows at the ends of the bar or drag the scroll box located inside the bar to see information outside the viewable area.

Search engine a tool, like Google, that helps find information on the Internet. You activate this program by typing in keywords. The search engine then locates documents or Web sites that match your query.

Searches folder in Windows 7, a shortcut is added to the Favorites section of the Navigation Pane when you save a search, but the actual search is saved to the Searches folder, located in your personal folder under Computer.

Secure server a Web server that codes and decodes messages to protect them against third-party tampering.

Secure Socket Layer (SSL) a format for securely transmitting private files over the Internet for websites, email systems, and newsgroups. If a Web address starts with "https," the "s" after the "http" indicates the website is secure and is probably using SSL certificates.

Select to make an icon, window, menu option, or other object active. This tells the computer you are about to do something with the selected object, like move it, rename it, open it, etc. Sometimes pointing at an object on the screen selects it, but generally you must click on an object to select it.

Server a computer that is host to a website on the Internet or any computer that provides data to other computers.

Shareware software available for a free trial, usually by download from the Internet. It may work for a limited time before requiring payment.

Shortcut a quick way to access a file, folder, or program. An icon that represents a shortcut can be placed on your desktop or in a folder.

Shortcut key a key or combination of keys that performs common commands in a program.

Shortcut menu a list of options that appears when you right-click an object.

Shouting typing in all capital letters in emails or chat rooms, which gives the impression you are SHOUTING at the reader.

Site map an optional Web page that lists all the pages on a website. Some site maps look like an index or table of contents. Check for a link to the site map on the site's main page.

Social media websites and other electronic communication used by large groups of people to share information, ideas, personal messages, images, and video. Facebook, Pinterest, YouTube, and Twitter are popular examples.

Solid State Drive (SSD) similar to a hard disk drive (HDD), the SSD is a mass storage device for data.Internal SSDs connect to a computer like a hard drive but do not have any moving parts and use flash memory for storage. SSDs can access data faster than an HDD.

Splash page a website's preliminary or introductory page that usually features graphics, animation, or important information. Not all websites have splash pages.

Spreadsheet a computer accounting program that can perform calculations and produce documents that resemble a financial worksheet — with rows and columns. You can input text, numbers, and formulas into the spreadsheet.

Spyware a program that secretly monitors your computer activities or can steal confidential information from your computer.

Start button in Windows, the small, square graphic you can click on to open the Start Menu and gain instant access to many of the programs and files in your computer. In Windows 7, the Start button has been replaced with a blue Windows "orb" logo.

Start page the first page you see when you connect to your Internet Service Provider.

Status bar the area at the bottom of a window that displays basic information about the objects in the window.

System Restore a procedure that returns the computer or electronic device to a previous state. It may be returned to a previous system backup or to the original default settings.

Tablet a portable computer that uses a touch screen as an input device. While there are different sizes of tablets, most are smaller than a laptop. Apple's iPad and Microsoft's Surface are two examples of tablet computers.

Tags descriptive terms or keywords you assign to a file. Tags can be used by Windows 7 and other programs to sort and retrieve files.

Taskbar in Windows 7, a bar that runs along one edge of the desktop and acts as a dock for your frequently used programs. You can pin programs directly to the Taskbar for quick access. Icons for programs currently open will show in the Taskbar area in a faint gray box.

TCP/IP (Transmission Control Protocol/Internet Protocol) the one common language that allows all computers on the Internet to communicate with each other. TCP/IP software is a part of all major operating systems.

Template a pre-designed document layout for an application — like a word processing or spreadsheet program — that is already formatted. Use a template as a starting point to create your own documents.

Terabyte   a term often used to measure the data-storage capacity of devices or the data transferred in a specific amount of time. A terabyte is 1,000 gigabytes, 1 trillion bytes, or twice the size of a 500-gigabyte drive.

Theme   a collection of colors, images, and styles that create an overall look in Windows 7.

Title bar   the strip along the top of a window that shows the program or document name.

Toolbar   a strip of icons, each representing a different command in a software program. When you click on a toolbar icon, it activates its command.

Touchpad   a type of pointing device with a flat surface that you touch or tap with your finger. A touchpad is an alternative to a mouse.

Touch screen   a computer display that also acts as an input device. The most recent touch screens can interpret multi-touch gestures, such as pinching two fingers together to zoom in.

Tower   sometimes called the "chassis" or "system unit," the desktop computer's tower is the hardware and case that houses the CPU, RAM, disk drives, slots for peripherals, etc.

Trackball   a pointing device that controls your cursor with a movable ball you rotate with your fingers, thumb, or palm. This is an alternative to a mouse.

Trojan horse   malicious software hidden in a game or other harmless software. These programs often undo security measures and leave computers open to viruses or potentially damaging attacks.

Tweet   a tweet is a short online posting created by a Twitter user. Twitter is a social media website.

Undo   a command, icon, or button that allows you to reverse your last action.

Upgrade   to install new components on your computer to improve performance. Also, to install a more current version of a software program you are already using.

Upload   to move information from your computer to the Internet or another computer.

URL (Uniform Resource Locator)   a unique Internet address that points you to a specific Web page. Example: *http://www.fca.com*

USB (Universal Serial Bus)   the most common type of port found on electronic components. USB is used to connect devices, such as computers, keyboards, digital cameras, game controllers, and external drives. The newest USB 3.0 transmits data at 4.8 Gbps (gigabits per second), while USB 2.0 transmits at 480 Mbps (megabits per second).

USB hub a device that converts a single USB port into several, so there are more ports available to connect additional electronic equipment to the main system or computer.

User friendly used to describe computer software or hardware that is easy for beginners to learn and use, thanks to helpful pictures and simple instructions.

User name the name you type in to identify yourself and gain access to certain programs, devices, networks, or websites. A user name must be unique to that system and is usually paired with a password. It is used to prevent access to a system by unknown individuals.

Video conference where two or more people chat online using both video and audio.

Virus a software program or script downloaded to your computer without your knowledge, often by opening an infected email attachment. These malicious programs can destroy or steal data, slow down or crash your hard drive, or even take control of your computer. Anti-virus software is the best protection against viral attacks.

VPN (Virtual Private Network) a network that does not have to be in one physical location like a Local Area Network (LAN) but can be secured and accessed from multiple locations. The information transmitted through the VPN is scrambled and, therefore, virtually private.

Wallpaper the background pattern or picture on your computer screen. Most operating systems come with several wallpapers to choose from, or you can download or create your own.

Web browser a software program, such as Microsoft Internet Explorer or Mozilla Firefox, that allows your computer to view websites on the Internet.

Web page an electronic document on the World Wide Web containing text, graphics, audio, or video.

Web slice a Microsoft technology used in recent versions of the Web browser Internet Explorer. It allows certain portions of a Web page to be viewed in a fly-out preview window.

Webcam a video camera that usually connects to your computer through the USB port, broadcasting video images live through the Internet. It can sit on top of your monitor, or on a stand to keep it at eye level.

Webmaster the person in charge of managing a website.

Website an area on the Internet that contains one or more electronic documents, called Web pages. Each website is owned and managed by a company, organization, or individual.

Whisper to send a chat room message to just one person without others seeing it.

Wi-Fi (Wireless Fidelity) a technology that allows you to access the Internet or other wireless devices without a physical connection.

Window an enclosed area on your computer screen — usually rectangular — that displays information.

Windows the Microsoft operating system that relies heavily on windows to manage your computer.

Windows Defender a Windows 7 program that protects your hard drive from spyware.

Windows Explorer a file manager application in the Windows operating system that provides an easy way to access the file systems and move files.

Windows Live Essentials a group of Windows applications including Mail, Writer, SkyDrive, Photo Gallery, and Movie Maker. The programs are available as one download from the Microsoft website.

Windows Orb in Windows 7, the Start button in the lower-left corner of the Taskbar has been replaced with the Orb icon. Many people still refer to it as the Start button.

Windows Remote Assistance a Windows 7 feature you can use to invite others to view your computer and chat remotely by sharing your screen. This can be helpful for remote troubleshooting by people you trust to view the settings and contents of your computer.

Wizard a computer help file that gives you step-by-step instructions to complete a process.

Word processing a software program that lets you write, edit, store, and print text.

World Wide Web (WWW) or "the Web" a subset of the Internet, the Web is composed of pages that can be accessed using a Web browser.

Worm a harmful computer program that makes copies of itself and causes computer problems, sometimes by overwhelming the computer to force it to shut down. Worms are often built to spread to as many computers as possible.

Zip file a single file that contains the compressed data from several files. It usually has the file extension .zip. You need special software to decompress or "unzip" these files.

Zoom to change the view of an image on your computer screen — to be more distant (zoom out) or close up (zoom in).

INDEX